SARA JAPHET   ROBERT B. SALTERS

THE COMMENTARY OF R. SAMUEL BEN MEIR
RASHBAM
ON QOHELETH

*Publications of The Perry Foundation for Biblical Research
in the Hebrew University of Jerusalem*

THE COMMENTARY OF R. SAMUEL BEN MEIR *RASHBAM* ON QOHELETH

Edited and Translated
by

SARA JAPHET

Professor of Bible
The Hebrew University of Jerusalem

ROBERT B. SALTERS :

Lecturer in Bible and Old Testament
University of St. Andrews

JERUSALEM-LEIDEN
THE MAGNES PRESS, THE HEBREW UNIVERSITY
E.J. BRILL

Distributed by
E.J. Brill, Leiden, Holland

©
By The Magnes Press
The Hebrew University
Jerusalem 1985

ISBN 965–223–517–2

Printed in Israel
at the Ahva Cooperative Press, Jerusalem

CONTENTS

A COMMENTARY OF R. SAMUEL

PREFACE

The collaboration which underlies this publication began as a result of the good offices of Professor J.F.A. Sawyer of the University of Newcastle, who became aware in 1973 that we were both currently working on the text of this commentary and put us in touch with each other. In 1975 we decided to publish jointly the work which follows.

A joint work, such as this volume is, necessitated a certain division of labour. The Introduction is by Prof. Sara Japhet, while both are responsible for the editing of the Text, the Translation and the Notes.

The joining of forces proved to be enjoyable and fruitful. The physical problem of bridging the gap between Scotland and Israel was not without its difficulties and necessitated a number of journeys between St Andrews and Jerusalem. In this regard we are glad to have the opportunity to thank bodies whose generous funding made this possible: The Research Fund of the British Academy, and the Hayter and Parry Fund of the University of St Andrews.

We wish to thank the Librarian of the Staats- und Universitätsbibliothek Hamburg for permission to examine and study the manuscript which lies behind this work, viz. Codex hebr. 32. (pp. 87–95), and for permission to publish the text. We further acknowledge with gratitude the facilities offered to us by the Institute of Microfilmed Hebrew Manuscripts in the

Preface

National and University Library in Jerusalem, and by the Oxford Centre
for Postgraduate Hebrew Studies.

We are indebted to the Peri Foundation for Biblical Research in the
Hebrew University who have given financial backing to the publication,
and we are most grateful to the director and the Staff of the Magnes Press,
Jerusalem (in co-operation with E.J. Brill, Leiden), for their efforts in
producing this volume.

Finally, we are grateful to Professor Moshe Greenberg for reading the
Introduction and the Hebrew Text and making some valuable suggestions,
and to Mrs. Lea Mazor for preparing the indexes.

S. Japhet   R.B. Salters
Jerusalem   *St.Andrews*

INTRODUCTION

CHAPTER ONE

RASHBAM — HIS LIFE AND WORKS

a. Life

R. Samuel ben Meir (Rashbam) was one of the most outstanding figures of medieval Jewry in northern France. He was celebrated both for his biblical exegesis and for his Talmudic scholarship and regarded as a supreme authority in both fields. However, in spite of his renown and well-established position in Jewish learning, very little is known of his life. Only scant biographic details are found in his writings, supplemented by occasional remarks in contemporary and later books, which, however, are often neither clear nor reliable. Even the exact dates of his birth and death are determined by means of indirect information.

The best known fact about Rashbam is that he was the grandson of Rashi, the greatest scholar of French Jewry in the Middle Ages (1040-1105)[1]. He was most probably the eldest of four sons born to Rashi's

1   A. Grossman, Rashi, *EJ*, 13, 1558ff.; M. Liber, *Rashi,* Philadelphia 1906, reprinted
    New York 1970.

11

daughter Yochebed and her husband, Meir ben Samuel[2]. In his commentary on the Pentateuch, Rashbam mentions that he studied and engaged in discussion with his grandfather (on Gen. 37:2); in several places in Halachic literature it is mentioned that "he decided on various issues before his grandfather"[3]. These statements suggest that he had already become a scholar in his own right during his grandfather's lifetime, and was probably about twenty or twenty-five years of age at Rashi's death. In the light of this consideration, the date of his birth is set between 1080 and 1085 of our era. As regards his death, here too only indirect data are available. In 1158 the Jewish-Spanish scholar Abraham ibn Ezra wrote his "Letter of the Sabbath"[4], a polemic against "books and commentaries on the Pentateuch", which call for the desecration of the Sabbath. These unspecified "commentaries" are usually taken to be Rashbam's[5]. Ibn Ezra's statement that he intends to be no respecter of persons seems to indicate that Rashbam was at that time still among the living. His death, then, must be dated later than 1158[6].

The general provenance of Rashbam's life and activity is northern France. He was born either in his father's home town of Ramerupt (or

---

2 The name of his mother is found only once, cf. below. It has been debated whether he was his father's first or second son (cf. Rosin p. 4 and Urbach p. 45), and whether they were altogether three or four sons (Rosin, ibid. Urbach p. 58-59; D. Kaufmann, "Aus den Vatikanischen Handschrift von Abraham ben Azriel Machzor-Commentar," *MWJ* XIII, 1886, pp. 152-160). The most detailed biographical note is found in Ms. De Rossi 181, in the commentary of Rashi to Job 40:27: "From here onwards it was interpreted by his daughter's son, our Rabbi Samuel the elder, the brother of our Rabbi Jacob, the brother of our Rabbi Isaac, the brother of the Rabbi Solomon, the father of the grammarians, the sons of our Rabbi Meir the elder the son of the colleague our Rabbi Samuel, blessed be the memory of the righteous. And their mother is Yochebed the pious, the daughter of our Rabbi Solomon, blessed be the memory of the righteous." This note was published by Berliner in *MWJ* II 1875, p. 45.

3 See the references in Urbach, p. 45 notes 3-4, p. 22, note 25.

4 M. Friedlaender, "Ibn Ezra in England" *Transactions of the Jewish Historical Society of England,* II, London 1894/5, pp. 61-75.

5 A suggestion made by H. Graetz, *Geschichte der Juden VI,* Leipzig 1894, pp. 177, 377-378 and followed by many. Cf. Simon, Ibn Ezra, pp. 130-138.

6 Golb suggests that he died only a few years before the death of his brother R. Jacob Tam in 1171. Cf. Golb p. 62, and also Rosin, p. 9 note 6.

Rameru), in Troyes, or in Worms[7]. It was in Troyes that he was educated by his grandfather. Where did he stay later? Did he succeed his grandfather in Troyes[8]? Did he go back to Rameru[9], or did he settle elsewhere? In his commentary on the Pentateuch he mentions being in Paris and Loudon, but these seem to have been only visits[10]. There are also references to his stay in Caen[11] and probably in Reims[12]. Recently, Golb has offered a new suggestion, which he develops in considerable detail. He connects Rashbam with a place designated in various Jewish sources as Radom or Darom, which he regards as the Hebrew form of Rothomagus — Ruen, the capital of Normandy[13]. His position is that Rashbam was a Rabbi and the head of the school in Ruen from 1150-1160 at least, perhaps even earlier[14]. It seems, then, that Rashbam "wandered" between several towns of northern France, among which we can number, with more or less certainty, Troyes, Rameru, Paris, Caen, Loudon, Reims and Ruen.

Of Rashbam's own family only a daughter is known, called Marrone (Hebrew: מרונא)[15]; there is a rather late mention of a son, Joseph, whose existence is contested by many[16]. Rashbam made his living probably from sheep-raising, in conformity with the custom of the Rabbis of northern France to have an independent source of income[17].

7 Gross, p. 645; Golb p. 36 note 95; Urbach, p. 41.
8 Rosin p. 8 note 1.
9 Gross p. 637; Urbach pp. 35-36, 46, 115.
10 To Num. 11:35; 30:2. His visit to Paris is mentioned also in one of the Responsa, cf. Urbach p. 46 note 9.
11 R. Jacob Tam, *Sefer Hayashar*, ed. Sh. Rosenthal, Berlin 1898, p. 71 (Hebrew).
12 One of the texts mentions the city חמש, which is universally regarded as a scribal error and taken by many to mean Rameru (cf. Urbach p. 46). Golb, basing himself on scribal practices and orthographic probabilities, suggests that it is רומש or רימש, i.e., Reims. Cf. Golb p. 36 note 95.
13 Golb pp. 23-31, 36-40, 45-66.
14 Ibid. p. 36 note 95.
15 Urbach p. 46 note 13 for the reference. *MWJ* VII, 1880, p. 183.
16 Rosin, Pentateuch, p. X; Gross p. 543; Urbach pp. 114-115.
17 H.H. Ben-Sasson, *A History of the Jewish People* (English translation by G. Weidenfeld and Nicholson) Harvard 1976, p. 458-459.

Rashbam's familiarity with Christian exegesis and the way in which he presents it in his commentary on the Pentateuch show that he most probably participated in the Jewish-Christian disputations of his time[18]. It seems that he was also known to the Christian scholarly world of that period, as traces of his influence are found in the writings of Hugh of St. Victor[19]. However, the whole subject of the relationship between the two worlds of medieval biblical scholarship, Jewish and Christian, is still largely unexplored.

b. Works

For Rashbam's achievements as a Talmudic scholar the reader should consult other authorities[20]; we will restrict ourselves to his contribution to biblical exegesis and scholarship.

We know from various indications that Rashbam wrote commentaries on almost all the books of the Bible[21], but the greater part of this great work has been lost. His existing works, preserved in one form or another, are as follows:

1. The most important and best-known is the commentary on the Pentateuch, which found its way into some editions of the Rabbinic Bible[22], was the subject of an 18th century commentary[23], and was published in an

---

18 Cf. his commentary on Ex. 20:13: "This is a refutation of the sectarians (i.e. Christians) and they admitted to me (the correctness of my interpretation). Although what is found in their books is the Latin expression of . . . they were not precise." On Lev. 19:19 "And to the sectarians I said . . . and they admitted to me." Cf. also on Gen. 49:10; Ex. 3:22 etc., Rosin pp. 9; 84-86; idem, Pentateuch, p. XI.

19 B. Smalley, *The Study of the Bible in the Middle Ages,* Oxford 1952, p. 104 "The idea of conversation at St. Victor between the Christian Mystic and the grandson of Rashi has in it an element of the fabulous, though it differs from many famous "meetings" in being historically possible." Further, pp. 105, 155.

20 Especially Urbach, pp. 45-57.

21 Cf. Rosin, p. 13ff. and below, pp. 16-17.

22 The first was the edition of Berlin, 1705. Cf. Rosin, p. 37ff.

23 שלמה זלמן מפוזן, ספר קרן שמואל על פירוש רשב״ם, פרנקפורט, 1727 cf. Rosin, p. 42ff.

excellent critical edition by D. Rosin in 1881[24]. Rosin had at his disposal
only two manuscripts — one from the library of the Jewish Theological
Seminary in Breslau which contained the major part of Rashbam's
commentary on the Pentateuch (and has been lost since), and Ms.
München 5, which contained *inter alia* one leaf with the commentary on
Gen. 1:1-31.

2. A commentary on Qoheleth, the subject of the present publication,
which will be discussed in detail below.

3. A commentary on Job. Ms. Lutzki 778 of the library of the Jewish
Theological Seminary in New York contains *inter alia* several
commentaries on Job, one of which was identified by Lutzki as
Rashbam's[25]. Investigation of the commentary has just begun, but it is
already clear that it is not free from late additions and glosses. Collation of
the commentary with that of R. Joseph Kara reveals many similarities
between the two and even identical passages. Its authenticity has
consequently been questioned[26]. Our position is that the commentary is
authentic, with some additions by later hands. However, in the absence of a
thorough study, the question should for the time being be left open[27].

4. A commentary on the Song of Songs (?). From Ms. Hamburg Heb.
32, Jellinek published a commentary on the Song of Songs which he
attributed to Rashbam[28]. In spite of specific interpretations as well as some

24 D. Rosin, *Commentarium Quem in Pentateuchum Composuit Samuel ben Meir,*
Vratislaviae, 1881. The Hebrew title is: דוד ראזין, פירוש התורה אשר כתב רשב"ם הוא רבנו
שמואל בן ר' מאיר, ברעסלויא, תרמ"ב.

25 Lutzki's notes and short description of the commentary are found in the library of the
Jewish Theological Seminary. Cf. also: Alexander Marx, *Bibliographical Studies and
Notes,* edited by M.H. Schmelzer, New York, 1977, p. 186.

26 Cf. A. Grossman, *Tarbiz* XLV (1976), p. 339-340 (Hebrew with English summary),
and especially Ahrend. Ahrend's position is very unequivocal: ". . . the commentary on
Job in Ms. Lutzki is not the commentary of Rashbam . . . it is nothing but a compilation
of interpretations, namely the work of a compilator who incorporated in his collection
interpretations from many sources, among them also from the interpretations of
Rashbam." Rashbam, p. 43.

27 Cf. also below, p. 28ff.

28 *Commentar zu Kohelet und dem Hohen Liede von R. Samuel ben Meir,* herausgegeben
von A. Jellinek, Leipzig 1855. On the attribution of the commentary to Rashbam, ibid.,
p. X-XI.

linguistic and stylistic features which can be identified as "Rashbamic", the authenticity of the commentary as a whole was categorically denied by Rosin, who has since been followed by others[29]. Here again, we must await a study of the commentary before we can accept or deny its authenticity.

5. A commentary on Esther. A. Geiger published several commentaries by Joseph Kara including one on Esther, which was later identified by A. Berliner as a commentary by Rashbam[30]. However, the question whether it is a unified commentary, or just a collection of isolated interpretations, is still open[31].

6. Short excerpts from Rashbam's commentaries or even isolated interpretations are found in two kinds of literature:

a. Medieval compilatory commentaries. This genre of medieval exegesis was probably intended to provide what the compilator presumably regarded as a "complete" and "correct" commentary. Their method was to extract segments from the works of the great exegetes and to place them in juxtaposition as a continuous interpretation to the text — with or without specifying their origin. At times the compilator would also add his own words, at times not. The most important in our case are the compilatory commentaries to Esther, Ruth and Lamentations which were published by Jellinek in 1855[32]. Rashbam's interpretations are more abundant in the commentary on Esther than in the other two, but it seems certain that the compilator had at his disposal Rashbam's full commentaries to these books.

b. Later exegetical works. Quotations from Rashbam's interpretations are found in later exegetical works, mainly on the Pentateuch. However, the most important work in this group is a composition outside the field of biblical exegesis, dating from the 13th century. This is "Arugat Habosem"

---

29 Rosin p. 18-19; Poznanski, pp. LXXXVII-LXXXIX; A. Grossman, *Samuel ben Meir*, *EJ* XIV, Jerusalem 1971, p. 810.

30 *Nite-Naamanim*, pp. 9-10b; A. Berliner, *Pletath Soferim*, Breslau 1872, p. 21.

31 Rosin, for example, accepts Berliner's identification but views the work as "a collection of interpretations" rather than a commentary, idem p. 20-21.

32 *Commentarien zu Esther, Ruth und den Klageliedern*, herausgegeben von A. Jellinek, Leipzig 1855. Cf. Poznanski p. LXXXIX.

by R. Abraham ben Azriel, a commentary on the prayers. One of the author's favourite authorities is Rashbam, and he cites his interpretations to more than forty verses from many books of the Prophets and the Hagiographa[33]. Other quotations, with or without a reference to Rashbam, are found in most of the later French commentators, and elsewhere[34].

7. Still within the realm of biblical scholarship we should mention Rashbam's grammar, the "Sefer Daikuth". Its publication by L. Stein in an obscure corner went practically unnoticed[35] and although its authenticity has not been questioned it has hardly attracted any attention since[36]. The book is composed of two parts: the first is a treatise on grammatical issues, opening with the following words: "Open your eyes to see and give your heart and ear to hear, to observe and to understand the history of the Holy Language and all its rules"[37]. The second part is the beginning of a grammatical commentary on all the books of the Bible, opening with the following words: "And now I am going to explain systematically all the phrases and their grammar ... from Genesis through all the twenty four books"[38]. The commentary, however, goes only as far as Gen. 7:5, at which point the scribe declares, "I did not find any more"[39]. Nevertheless,

33 The cited comments are on: I Sam. 13:12; I Kg. 1:21; 8:8; II Kg. 16:7; 18:17; Is. 1:29; 4:4; 26:16; 29:1; 32:5, 7, 10; 34:3; 40:14, 20; 57:15; 63:3; Jer. 2:21; Ez. 1:14; 27:6; Hos. 10:14; 13:3; 14:7, 9; Joel 4:3; Amos 5:3; 6:8; Mich. 2:7; Nah. 3:19; Zech. 3:1; 9:7; 14:7, 12; Ps. 15:4; 45:18; 89:8; Job 10:15; 18:3; 20:10; 37:13; 40:16; Est. 9:6.

34 No systematic collection has been undertaken, which is quite understandable in view of the effort involved. Rosin cites several quotations, especially in reconstructing the missing parts of the commentary on the Pentateuch (Cf. Rosin, *Pentateuch* pp. 9-13, 193 *et al.*). Ahrend has recently collected all the known quotations on Job, cf. idem, Rashbam, pp. 25–40.

35 L. Stein, "Grammatischen Commentar von R. Samuel", A Grammar by R. Samuel ben Meir (Rashbam) and his Grammatical Commentary on the Pentateuch, ed. L. Stein, *Jahrbuch des Traditionstreuen Rabbinerverbandes im des Slovakei*, Trnava 1923.

36 Only H. Yalon has dealt with it to some extent. Cf. H. Yalon, *Bulletin of Hebrew Language Studies*, second printing, Jerusalem 1963, Bulletin to 1942, pp. 28-29. It is worth noting that in the important article on Hebrew Linguistic Literature in *EJ* XVI, the book is not even mentioned. (cf. the list of authors, ibid. p. 1385).

37 Ibid (note 35), p. 35.

38 Ibid, p. 59.

39 Ibid. p. 67.

even the little that is extant provides a welcome supplement to Rashbam's commentary on the Pentateuch, where Gen. 2-17 are missing.

The importance of this grammatical composition has many facets. It exemplifies superbly the close connection between the science of language and the "literal" methods of interpretation; it provides an insight into the state and scope of linguistic knowledge in the sphere of Ashkenazi Judaism in northern France, and affords a better understanding of the development of its linguistic knowledge, and it is a most important contribution to the overall evaluation and appreciation of Rashbam's work. Unfortunately it has not yet been afforded the thorough study it deserves.

CHAPTER TWO

THE COMMENTARY ON QOHELETH

a. The Problem of Authenticity

Rashbam's commentary on Qoheleth was published in 1855 by A. Jellinek in a small book, together with a commentary on the Song of Songs[1]. The Ms. from which the commentaries were taken, Hamburg Cod. Heb. 32[2], contains, *inter alia,* commentaries on the Five Scrolls. These can be clearly classified into two groups: the commentaries on Qoheleth and the Song of Songs are coherent exegetical compositions, while the commentaries on Esther, Ruth and Lamentations are compilatory compositions, whose eclectic character is obvious. Jellinek acknowledged this difference by publishing the commentaries in two separate books[3].

At the head of the commentary on Qoheleth there is a short note in the Ms.: "פירוש של ר' שמואל" = A commentary by R. Samuel. As the script of this heading is identical with that of the commentary, it should be attributed to the scribe himself, and dated in the second half of the 13th century[4]. Jellinek identified the R. Samuel of the heading as the well-known R. Samuel ben Meir, (Rashbam), Rashi's grandson[5].

---

1 Above, ch. one note 28.
2 Catalogue no. 37. A short description of the Ms. is given by L. Dukes in *Zion II,* ed. by M. Creizenach and J.M. Jost, 1841/2 p. 100 and by M. Steinschneider in the catalogue of the Library of Hamburg. The Ms. probably dates from the second half of the 13th century, the date being determined by the method of pricking the pages for ruling (cf. Beit-Arié, pp. 70-71) and by the script (verbally from Mr. Benjamin Richner of the Department of Hebrew Mss. Hebrew University, Jerusalem).
3 Cf. one notes 28, 32.
4 Cf. note 2.
5 He was preceded by Dukes (above, note 2), p. 104, note. No similar heading is found in the commentary on the Song of Songs. On the question of its attribution to Rashbam, cf. Jellinek, pp. x-xi and above pp. 15-16.

The edition itself is rather unsatisfactory[6] but the commentary on Qoheleth was warmly accepted by C.D. Ginsburg as early as 1861[7].

In 1880 D. Rosin published his great work on Rashbam[8] and in a survey of Rashbam's exegetical undertakings he touches upon the commentaries which were published previously by Jellinek. Taking as his point of departure the question of authenticity, Rosin reaches different conclusions for each of these commentaries. Regarding the commentary on Qoheleth his attitude oscillates: on the one hand he states that the commentary "should be viewed as originally the work of this man (Rashbam)"[9]; on the other he seems to detect certain deviations from what he regards as Rashbam's style and exegesis, which lead him to assume the presence of some sort of later reworking. He proposes two possible solutions: either the commentary should be regarded as Rashbam's work in spite of the presumed reworking, or it should be considered to be the work of a follower, immediate or later[10]. Rosin leaves the question open and makes extensive use of the commentary, consciously and systematically including the relevant material in his discussions of the exegetical work of Rashbam[11].

It is of interest to the general dynamics of research to observe how Rosin's cautious attitudes were later handled. Poznanski, in his general introduction on medieval Jewish exegetes (1913), discusses the authenticity of the commentary on Qoheleth and cites the arguments and reservations raised previously by Rosin. However, on the basis of these same arguments he expresses a more rigid and decisive opinion. He explicitly denies the authenticity of the commentary, and regards it as the work of a later author, whom he evaluates as inferior to Rashbam[12]. Thus, the same

6 Cf. below pp. 69-72.
7 Ginsburg, pp. 42-43.
8 D. Rosin, *Samuel ben Meir (רשב"ם) als Schrifterklaerer*, Breslau, 1880.
9 Rosin, p. 19.
10 Rosin, pp. 19-20.
11 The commentary on Qoheleth is referred to about fifty times, *inter alia* in p. 86 notes 3, 7; p. 87 notes 2, 6; p. 90, note 5; p. 97 notes 43-50; p. 108, p. 130 notes 6, 8; p. 132 notes 4, 5, 6, 12, 15, 17 etc., etc.
12 Poznanski pp. LXXXVII-LXXXVIII.

grounds which gave rise to hesitations about the authenticity of certain details, subsequently led to an appraisal ending in an outright denunciation of the commentary.

This attitude towards the commentary was, no doubt, one of the factors which caused the neglect of the commentary and its near relegation to oblivion. Even Jewish scholars, who were not hampered by the handicap of language, failed to make use of it[13]. An exception to the rule is H.L. Ginsberg, who did mention Rashbam's work and made some use of it in his own commentary on Qoheleth[14].

In 1974 a systematic examination of the commentary was undertaken, and one of the questions dealt with was that of authenticity[15]. The conclusion of that study was unequivocal: the commentary is indeed the authentic work of Rashbam and an important addition to what we already possess of his great exegetical undertaking. This conclusion was followed by an animated discussion, initiated by A. Grossman, who — adhering to the views of Poznanski — insisted that the commentary comes from a later author who "adapted the original commentary of Rashbam, altered its manner of presentation and appended his own interpretations as well as those of other commentators, to the main body of his work"[16] A full and detailed repetition of that discussion is of course out of place here, but it would seem in order to summarize and bring it up to date.

---

13 E.g. R. Gordis, in his commentary; M. Zer-Kavod, "Studies in Koheleth" *Beit-Mikra* 18 (1973) pp. 183-191 (Hebrew) and his commentary. All these works make rather extensive use of other medieval Jewish exegetes.

14 Ginsberg, pp. 13ff. cf. below, p. 47, note 118.

15 Japhet, *Tarbiz* XLIV pp. 84-94.

16 Grossman, *Tarbiz* XLV p. VIII. This is Grossman's view as expressed in the English summary of his article. In the article itself his approach to the matter seems less clear and unambiguous. In one place he hints that "R. Samuel" could have been another scholar by the same name who was active at the same time (ibid. p. 336 note 1); later he implies that the commentary should be attributed to R. Shelomo, Rashbam's younger brother (ibid. pp. 336-337; cf. Japhet, *Tarbiz* XLVII pp. 245-246); his final statement in the article is that a later author "took Rashbam's commentary and added to it of his own" (*Tarbiz* XLV p. 340). The transition from these statements to the conclusion expressed above is not clarified. The controversy went on with Japhet, *Tarbiz* XLVII pp. 243-246; Ben-Hayyim, ibid., pp. 247-248 and Grossman, *Tarbiz* XLVIII p. 172.

Two main arguments were raised against the authenticity of the commentary on Qoheleth: (1) Contradictions between Rashbam's commentary on the Pentateuch and our commentary on Qoheleth. (2) Supposed differences in style and discrepancies in terminology between Rashbam's commentary on the Pentateuch and the commentary on Qoheleth.

1. Rosin mentions two instances which he regards as contradictory, without going into detail: 12:2 as against Gen. 22:13 and 7:7 as against Ex. 5:17[17]. Poznanski mentions this argument too but does not demonstrate it[18], and Grossman adds another case to those brought by Rosin, 1:3-11 as against Deut. 20:5-9, and deals with all three in detail[19].

A careful examination of the respective interpretations does not bear out the argument; rather the opposite: it reveals the interrelationship of the interpretations, the specific emphases of their respective contexts, and their interdependence. The most striking example is Grossman's discussion of 12:2 as against Gen. 22:13. The point which Rashbam is making in Gen. 22:13, and which is unique to him, is that the word אחר may be used to mean 'afterwards', the same as אחרי כן. In the course of elaborating this point he cites several examples of that use, among them 12:2. In the interpretation of 12:2 the understanding of אחר as אחרי כן is clearly taken for granted and serves as the basis for explaining the entire passage. Grossman's argument there is hard to follow: although he regards this as an example of a supposed contradiction, he holds that אחר has the same meaning and function in both passages. His exposition thus supports rather than undermines the argument for ties between the two commentaries.

We dealt in detail with the relationship between Deut. 20:5-9 and 1:3-11 in both of which Rashbam's approach is idiosyncratic; the subsequent discussion of Grossman, although intended to refute our conclusion, in effect strengthens it[20]. Only through the commentary on 1:3-9 with its specific structure and ideas, does the comment on Deut. 20:5-9 become fully comprehensible.

17 Rosin, p. 19 note 6; p. 23 note 3b.
18 Poznanski, p. LXXXVIII.
19 *Tarbiz* XLV pp. 337-338.
20 Japhet, *Tarbiz* XLIV pp. 89-90; Grossman, *Tarbiz* XLV, pp. 337-338.

The same conclusion is to be drawn from the last example, 7:7 as against Ex. 5:17. The assumed contradiction was dealt with in detail by Ben-Hayyim. After a careful linguistic examination he not only sees no contradiction between the interpretations of the two verses, but rather concludes the opposite: the interpretation of Ex. 5:17 receives its full meaning from the explicit words of 7:7[21].

Thus, a detailed discussion of these specific interpretations brings to light the close ties between the two commentaries. In two of the three cases the commentary on the Pentateuch is based on interpretations elaborated in the commentary on Qoheleth. It would be too hasty to use this fact as a basis for a chronological sequence regarding the relative date of composition of the two commentaries, but it is clear that they are the fruits of one creative mind finding expression in even the smallest exegetical details.

2. The argument from supposed differences in style and terminology is presented in much detail by Rosin, Poznanski and Grossman. It should be stated at the outset, however, that the basic assumption on which this argument is based is somewhat misleading. Rashbam does not use a clear-cut, systematic and consistent terminology, as a superficial glance at Rosin's book should immediately reveal. The opposite is the case: his stylistic inclination, even in the realm of terminology, is towards variety of expression and a plethora of synonyms[22]. However, one may still argue that certain expressions are completely foreign to his language and even incompatible with it. The specific expressions that have been alleged to be so must therefore be examined.

Rosin mentions the description of "stairway parallelism", found in 1:2, as an example of non-Rashbamic language[23], and he is followed by Poznanski who exclaims: "How far these words are from Rashbam's style"[24]. Both scholars do not specify in what way the description is so

---

21 Ben-Hayyim, p. 247.
22 Even where strict terminology seems indispensable, namely in the realm of grammar, cf. Rosin pp. 128ff. cf. below pp. 83-84.
23 Rosin p. 19 note 9, with reference to Gen. 49:22 and Ex. 15:6.
24 Poznanski p. LXXXVIII.

incompatible with Rashbam's style and therefore no specific reply to their
claim can be made. One should mention, however, that the recognition of
"stairway parallelism" as one of the forms of biblical poetry, its clear and
accurate description and its understanding in terms of "form" alone, rank
among Rashbam's well-attested achievements[25]. That Rashbam included
1:2 as an example is attested to in his comment on Gen. 49:22. Since the
description of "stairway parallelism" in 1:2 conforms in every respect to
Rashbam's understanding of this phenomenon as presented in his
commentary on the Pentateuch, and since none of its specific details are
foreign to Rashbam's language, there is no reason to doubt its authenticity.

The following phrases were also regarded by Rosin as non-Rashbamic:
(on 1:3); בעניין זה מוסבת המלה בשיטתה
(on 2:9); וכל[26] לשון צח של פרשה כי גם אותן שלשה דברים . . .
(on 7:19); עשרה הללו אינן באין לדקדוק המלה לומר לא פחות ולא יותר
(on 8:12). ולא אחז בלשונו מאת לדקדק מלתו
Rosin does not specify what makes these expressions incompatible with the
language of Rashbam, but in regards to the last two phrases he refers the
reader to similar, yet somewhat different explanations found in the
commentary on the Pentateuch[27].

The use of the verb דקדק and the noun דקדוק with the meaning "express
literally", is found in Rashbam's commentary on the Pentateuch and is
taken by Rosin himself as a characteristic feature of his language[28]. So are
the words or terms מוסבת, עניין, פרשה, לשון and שטה found in the above
sentences[29]. It seems, therefore, that what appeared to Rosin as
incompatible with Rashbam's language is just one word, מלה. This is
confirmed by his main example, the phrase כפל מלה, found in the
commentary on Qoheleth, as against כפל לשון, found in Rashbam's
commentary on the Pentateuch[30]. Rosin claims that מלה is a synonym of

25 Cf. below, pp. 51-52.
26 Rosin reads וכל, following Jellinek's edition. Ms. — וכן.
27 Rosin p. 19 note 9.
28 Ibid. p. 21 note 2; p. 87 note 7; p. 156.
29 Ibid. pp. 156-158; p. 58 note 1-2; p. 87 note 1, and Rashbam on Ex. 6:3; Lev. 1:1;
     Deut. 33:1.
30 Rosin p. 19 note 8; p. 16 note 1.

תיבה, meaning "word" and only the latter is used by Rashbam[31]. Moreover, Rosin claims that מלה כפולה, כפל מלה and כופל מילתו, are characteristic of R. Joseph Kara and others but are foreign to Rashbam[32]. Grossman, following Rosin, emphasizes even more the significance of the use of כפל מלה in the commentary on Qoheleth. According to him it "is not mentioned even once in the commentary on the Pentateuch and in other fragmentary remains of Rashbam's commentaries to the Bible"[32] and this fact alone is sufficient proof of a later reworking[33].

These claims are not borne out by the facts. In none of the above phrases does מלה mean "word", nor is it a synonym of תיבה. Its meaning is "expression, phrase, statement, etc." and it is therefore a synonym of certain meanings of לשון[34]. Although it is not found in Rashbam's commentary on the Pentateuch, it is used regularly in his cultural milieu[35], and there is no justification for excluding it from his vocabulary. Moreover, one might gather from this argument that כפל לשון is the exclusive term for parallelism in Rashbam's commentary on the Pentateuch, but this is not the case. As in many other instances, Rashbam uses a variety of expressions, such as כפל, כפילו של, כפילו את דבריהם, דרך המקראות לכפל את דבריהם, and others[36].

The claim that כפל מלה and similar expressions are absent from all Rashbam's commentaries, is invalid as well. All of Rashbam's extant commentaries, except the one on the Pentateuch, make use of the

31 Rosin p. 19 note 8.
32 Ibid. p. 16, note 1.
32a Grossman, *Tarbiz* XLV p. VIII.
33 Ibid., p. 339.
34 It seems that the distinction between these two words and their respective meanings can be fully explained by reference to the influence of Old French. תיבה is probably the equivalent of *"mot"*, meaning mainly "word" in its strict sense, while מלה is a semantic calque of *"parole"*, initially meaning "word" but then used in a variety of expanded meanings. Cf. Tobler-Lommatzsch, vol. 6 p. 339ff, vol. 7 p. 327ff. On the question of the influence of Old French, cf. below pp. 78-80.
35 It is very popular in Machberet Menahem ibn Saruq, cf. p. (1) and onwards, and it is used also by Rashi, cf. Avineri, vol. 1², p. 777.
36 Rosin mentions some of them in p. 16 note 1 and p. 144. A fuller list is found in Japhet, *Tarbiz* XLIV p. 87 and notes 86-96.

expressions כפל מלה or מלה כפולה as well as כפל לשון, especially when referring to parallelism.

a. These phrases occur in passages explicitly attributed to Rashbam:

1. In Nit'e Na'amanim Geiger published a compilatory collection of interpretations on Job, taken from a Ms. dated 1489[37]. Some of the interpretations, attributed explicitly to Rashbam, were collected by Ahrend and republished[38]. In one of these, on Job 4:2, the term כפל מלה appears, as well as אין המקרא נכפל[39].

2. In the limited incidental collection of Rashbam's interpretations found in Arugat Habosem, the phrase מלה כפולה appears once[40].

b. These phrases occur in passages where attribution to Rashbam is very likely:

1-2. In the compilatory commentary on Ruth, Esther and Lamentations[41], which contains excerpts from Rashbam's interpretations, and paradoxically serves Grossman as a criterion of authenticity, we find כפל מלה on Est. 1:4 and מלה כפולה on Lamentations 1:1. The phrases לשון כפול and תיבה כפולה, found respectively on Est. 3:13 and 4:14, relate to other phenomena. כפל מלה is found in the interpretation of the same verse, Est. 1:4 also in the commentary published by Geiger in Nit'e Na'amanim[42].

37 Nit'e Na'amanim pp. 11-16.
38 Ahrend, Rashbam, No. 3, 4, 5, 7, 10, 14, 17, 19, 32.
39 Ahrend, ibid. No. 4, p. 29. The term כפל מלה appears in this collection twice more, on Job 29:18, 23, but the interpretations are not explicitly identified. They are both found in Kara's commentary on Job as well as in Lutzki 778, where כפל מלה is replaced respectively by וכופל המקרא and מלה כפולה. Cf. further below pp. 28-32.
40 On Job 37:13, Arugat Habosem II, p. 191.
41 Cf. above, p. 16.
42 Grossman's attitude regarding these three references should be discussed in some more detail. At first he completely overlooked these references and attributed the phrase כפל מלה in the commentary on Qoheleth to a "later reworking" (*Tarbiz* XLV, pp. 339-340). Later, he claimed that the interpretation of Est. 1:4 in the compilatory commentary should be attributed to R. Joseph Kara, while the interpretation on Lamentations 1:1 is anonymous — a conclusion reached at by separating the last part of a composite comment, expressly attributed to Rashbam, from its preceding part, in which מלה כפולה occurs (*Tarbiz* XLVIII, p. 172). Even at this stage he ignores (or overlooks) the occurrence of כפל מלה in the interpretation of Est. 1:4 in Nit'e Na'amanim, and therefore cannot use it for checking its attribution in the compilatory commentary to R. Joseph Kara. It

3. The commentary on Job 40:25ff attributed to Rashi in the regular editions of the Rabbinic Bible is clearly not his. It is attributed to Rashbam in several Mss.[43], an attribution accepted by some scholars and denied by others[44]. The commentary has not been systematically studied[45] but there can be no doubt that many of the interpretations are indeed Rashbam's. Here, too, we find the similar expressions: כופל מלתו ;כופל לשונו; לא דקדק ;המקרא במלתו; כפל מלה; כפל לשון; מלה כפולה[46].

4. Rashbam's commentary on Job, found in Ms. Lutzki 778[47], has not been published as yet, neither has it been thoroughly studied. Nevertheless, the controversy over its authenticity has already begun. The fact that it includes numerous interpretations by Rashbam is agreed upon even by its strongest detractors[48]. The commentary, which uses these expressions throughout[49], will be referred to in more detail below[50].

Grossman's treatment of all this material begs the question: since he has decided that Rashbam never used מלה, he regards all these occurrences as unauthentic, adulterated, a result of reworking, etc.[51] He does not explain however how independent editors, in different Mss. from different periods, in interpretations of verses from diverse books, could agree on the same

---

should be mentioned, however, that his position on the collection of interpretations of Esther in Niṭʿe Naʿamanim is that they are not authentic. Grossman claims that this was proven by Rosin, but I could not find Rosin's words to that effect; on the contrary, Rosin welcomes this collection as an important addition to our knowledge of Rashbam's work (pp. 20-21).

43 Ms. Münich 5, and De-Rossi 181. Cf. Ahrend, Rashbam. p. 41.

44 The attribution was accepted by Geiger, Kerem Hemed 8, pp. 46-47 and others. It was denied by Rosin, pp. 15-17, followed by Ahrend, Rashbam. pp. 41-42 and Grossman, *Tarbiz* XLV p. 339.

45 Their examination should be combined with the more general question of Rashbam's commentary on Job and its relationship to that of Kara. Cf. also §3 and below pp. 29-32.

46 On Job 40:27; 40:31; 41:9; 41:15; 41:16; 41:22; 41:26; 42:2; 42:10.

47 Cf. above, p. 15.

48 Cf. Ahrend, Rashbam. p. 45; idem Job pp. 68, 76; idem Rashi, p. 187 note 27; Grossman, *Tarbiz* XLV p. 340.

49 Cf. inter al. 1:11; 3:1, 4, 6, 11, 17, 20, 25; 4:5; 5:15 etc.

50 Cf. below, pp. 29-32.

51 *Tarbiz* XLV pp. 339-340; *Tarbiz* XLVIII p. 172.

line of reworking. What motive could they have had for altering so many of Rashbam's supposed כפל לשון which came their way to the unauthentic מלה כפולה and כפל מלה?

The whole matter becomes simple and self-evident when the facts are allowed to speak for themselves. No mysterious, anonymous "later hands" are responsible for the use of this word in Rashbam's interpretations, but Rashbam himself is responsible for it. It is an integral component of his vocabulary and is used wherever parallelism, or other phenomena, are referred to. This explanation alone could account for the uniformity of style and terminology.

As mentioned above, one of Rosin's assertions has been that the phrases מלה כפולה, כפל מלה and כופל מלתו are characteristic of R. Joseph Kara, and some scholars accept his view[52]. The problem deserves a separate discussion, and we will restrict ourselves here to some remarks which are relevant to our issues.

Some important preliminary work in this direction has already been done by Ahrend in his most recent study of the commentary of Kara on Job[53], but it seems that he has not drawn all of the conclusions from his investigation. The starting point of the discussion are the commentaries on Job — of Kara and Rashbam (in Ms. Lutzki 778). As a preliminary remark it should be stated that — as shown already by Ahrend — Kara's commentary on Job abounds in interpretations which can be clearly identified as Rashbam's — both in subject matter and in method[54]. Moreover, according to Ahrend, it contains over a hundred interpretations

---

52 Rosin, p. 16 note 1; Poznanski p. LXXXVII; Ahrend, Rashbam pp. 29, 37, 40, 43; Grossman, *Tarbiz* XLVIII p. 172.

53 Ahrend, Job. The second part of the work, a critical edition of the commentary, has not yet been published and the reader should avail himself of the first edition, published in *MGWJ* V, (1856) pp. 224-229; 268-278; 342-351; 469-475; VI (1857) pp. 71-73; 182-183; 270-274; 350-357; 463-470; VII (1858) pp. 255-263; 345-358, or in H.Y.I. Gad, *Sepher Hamishah Me'oroth Hagedolim,* Johannesburg 1952, pp. 101-156. The following citations from the commentary are taken from a copy of Ahrend's dissertation, which he very kindly put at our disposal. A review of Ahrend's work by E. Touitou has appeared recently in *Tarbiz* LI (1982) pp. 522-526.

54 Ahrend, Rashbam, p. 46; idem. Job, p. 76; idem, Rashi, p. 189, and note 50.

which are identical — verbatim or with slight changes — to interpretations found in Rashbam's commentary on Job[55] (henceforth: Lutzki 778).

In order to probe Rosin's assertion that the expressions מלה כפל מלה, כפל מלתו and כופל מלתו are characteristic of R. Joseph Kara, we thoroughly surveyed the two commentaries, Kara on Job and Lutzki 778, and listed all the expressions containing one of the two components of this phrase[56]. The results were revealing. In Kara's lengthy commentary on Job these various expressions occur thirty-six times, twenty-four (two-thirds) in passages recurring verbatim, or almost so, in Lutzki 778[57]. Of the remaining twelve that have no parallel in Lutzki 778, nine are found in verses uninterpreted there[58]. The lack of parallel passages can be accounted for at least in part by the bad condition of Rashbam's commentary and the many lacunae in the Ms. This taken into consideration, only in three instances do we have כפל מלה in Kara's commentary without a parallel in Rashbam, but even if this is not the case, only twelve instances of such expressions in Kara's commentary are without parallel in Lutzki 778.

---

55 Ahrend, Job, p. 65. The citations from Lutzki 778 are taken from the Ms., which was kindly put at my disposal by the library of the Jewish Theological Seminary in New York in summer 1978/9. I wish to express my thanks to the JTS for their assistance.

56 Expressions which are not relevant to our context were not included, such as the explanation of the word פרחח (Job 30:12) as having a doubled חי״ת (חי״ת כפולה), found in the two commentaries; the definition of צלצל (Job 40:31) as one of the duplicated words (מתיבות הכפולות) in Lutzki 778, and the explanation of the word פימה (Job 15:27) by Kara as meaning: double. Also the many instances were מלין, so common in Job, appears in the commentary as an echo to the biblical text, were not included.

57 There are minor differences between the two commentaries, i.e., when the one has כופל and the other כפל, or when the one has כפל מלה and the other כופל מלתו etc. Since the alterations are stylistic and appear in the two commentaries alike without any guiding rules, they are not recorded. The following list is based on the use of Kara. כינוי מלה (1:11) כפל מלתו or כפל מלה (three times, 3:6, 11; 4:5); כפל מלה (six times, 3:25; 5:22; 20:18; 39:8; 12: 40:16); המקרא כפול (three times, 5:23; 15:6; 30:18); וכופל המקרא (29:19); מלה כפולה (three times, 20:8; 29:23; 41:26); כפל לשון (twice, 27:7; 41:9); לשון הולך סדור המלה (6:19); אחז מלתו (twice, 5:19; 15:10); דקדוק מלה (מלתו) (28:8) כפול (41:26).

58 As follows: כפל מלה (four times, 4:9; 12:17; 16:21; 30:14); כפל מלתו (twice, 5:1; 9:11); פתרון המלה (31:26); חיבור המלה (6:14); תיקון מלה (6:7). The other three are כפל מלתו (4:18); כפל מלה (29:21) and the interpretation of 37:5 which explains the structure of the verse with גומר מלתו... סיים מלתו... בתחלת המלה.

On the other hand, the short, lapidaric and incomplete commentary in Lutzki· 778, contains over a hundred and twenty(!) instances of these phrases, including the twenty-four which are common to both commentaries. In many of these instances the interpretation of a colon comprises merely the observation that it is מלה כפולה, כפל מלה or the like. There is no point in listing all the references, but their distribution is of interest. The most common are מלה כפולה (36 times)[59]; כפל מלה (15 times)[60]; כופל מלתו (17 times)[61]; כפל לשון (12 times)[62]; מקרא כפול (10 times)[63]; כופל לשונו (6 times)[65]; לשון כפול (7 times)[64]; תיקון מלה (4 times)[66]; דקדוק מלה (5 times)[67], and various others[68].

The frequency, consistency, and specific distribution of these phrases[69] indicate that more is involved here than mere technical terms. They are,

59 Par ex. Job 3:4; 6:2, 17; 7:5 etc.
60 Par ex. Job 5:9; 10:22; 15:13, 16; etc.
61 Par ex. Job 5:15; 6:8; 8:9, 15; etc.
62 Par ex. Job 21:8; 27:11; 28:7; 29:17; etc.
63 With slight variations, cf. Job 20:13; 20:16; 33:25; etc.
64 Par ex. Job 26:7; 28:2; 29:20; 32:9; etc.
65 Par ex. Job 38:16, 21; 39:5; etc.
66 Job 9:24; 19:6, 23; and 15:3.
67 With slight variations, Job 16:3; 26:7; 42:10; and 5:19; 15:10.
68 Such as: כופל (Job 13:2); קוצר מלה (3:3); חוזר למלתו (3:17); מלה אחרת (3:22); כפול (18:17) and others.
69 Most of the expressions refer to parallelism and are more common in certain chapters than in others, being most frequent in chapters 15, 20, 28, 38 and 40. This is probably due in part to the incompleteness of the text, but is also occasioned by the nature of the various chapters. Some expressions such as דקדוק מלה and תיקון מלה do not refer to parallelism but to other phenomena. For the sake of brevity we will use one of these as an example. תיקון מלה, meaning "refinement of expression" (cf. Rosin p. 142 note 5), appears four times in Lutzki 778 (above note 66). In three cases it is an explanation of one word, איפוא, stressing that this is not to be taken as an interrogative but only as "refinement of Expression". In 9:24, its first occurence in Job, the interpretation states: "איפא is a refinement of expression, like "now"!"; in 19:6 he lays down the rule "Every איפוא is for refinement of expression", and then again on 19:23: "איפוא — refinement of expression". Since איפוא occurs only five times in Job, this repetition covers a great percentage of its occurences. Two further notes should be made. 1) In the interpretation of 9:24 the method is exactly the same as the one revealed in the commentaries on Qoheleth and the Pentateuch (cf. below p. 38ff.): the linguistic detail is explained separately at the

rather, evidence of an exegetically significant recognition of certain phenomena, especially of parallelism. The fact that the poetic principle of "parallelismus membrorum" was known to Rashbam and was employed in his commentaries, has been pointed out by the scholars who have dealt with his exegesis[70], even though the full scope of Rashbam's application of that principle in his exegesis of Biblical poetry has not yet been investigated. One should not wonder, then, that Rashbam took pains to notice cases of parallelism in his commentary on the poetic parts of the Pentateuch[71], in his commentary on Qoheleth[72], and most extensively of all, in his commentary on Job. Parallelism, and the varied but consistent terminology connected with it, are an integral part of Rashbam's exegesis.

On the other hand, "parallelismus membrorum" was not one of the exegetical principles of Kara. For the purpose of control, Kara's commentaries on Qoheleth and Jeremiah were examined — both regarded as authentic compositions[73], and both dealing with texts which offer ample opportunity for the application of this principle. Nowhere in these commentaries are any of the above-mentioned terms ever found. For the more limited purpose of our context, the absence of these expressions from

---

end, while the conclusions of that explanation are already incorporated in the interpreta-tion of the verse. 2) The explanation of איפוא in this manner is characteristic of Rashbam. In his commentary on Gen. 27:33 he states explicitly that איפוא is a "refine-ment of expression" (תיקון לשון), an interpretation which is probably directed as polemic against Rashi in Gen. 27:33, 37. In the commentary of Kara on Job תיקון מלה occurs only once, on 6:7, in the interpretation of the word כדוי. The relationship of this com-mentary to Rashbam cannot be ascertained, as the commentary of Job 6:6-7 is missing from Lutzki 778. It is clear that the consistent use of Lutzki 778 is independent of Kara and is directly connected with Rashbam, in both content and exegetical method.

70 Cf. *inter al.* Rosin, p. 143-144; Melamed I, p. 466; Kugel, p. 174ff. and below pp. 51f. Kugel's excellent work is dedicated to the phenomenon of parallelism, and he deals in some detail with Rashbam's attitude towards it. However, even though he regards Rashbam's position on the matter as significant (cf. *par ex.* p. 180), the issue is not dealt with in its full scope.

71 Cf. *inter al.* on Gen. 49:3, 5, 9, 11, 22, 23, 24, 26; Ex. 15:2, 6, 11, 16; Num. 23:7; Deut. 32:5, 10, 23.

72 Cf. below, pp. 51-52.

73 Ahrend, Job, pp. 181-183.

the commentary on Qoheleth is of greater significance than their absence from Jeremiah, as the use of כפל מלה in Qoheleth was the starting point of our discussion on this point. While the various terms describing parallelism occur in Rashbam's commentary on Qoheleth almost twenty times, and among them also כפל מלה, כופל מלתו and מלה כפולה[74], no reference to that phenomenon is ever made in Kara's commentary on Qoheleth, and never is any of these expressions used. Moreover, the word מלה, which is the core of the matter, is never found in Kara's commentary on Qoheleth. The conclusion seems inevitable: the terms mentioned above cannot be regarded as characteristic of Kara. They are inherent in Rashbam's exegetical principles, literary judgement and style, and should be used as a criterion of his work.

Our examination of the various arguments put forward against the authenticity of Rashbam's commentary on Qoheleth has actually resulted in new considerations tending to confirm Rashbam's authorship. However, these are not the decisive factors. The attribution of the commentary to Rashbam is decided not in the negative way but in the positive: by the examination of the specific characteristics and methods of the commentary itself.

As the following exposition will show, the commentary on Qoheleth is a unified and harmonious composition. It has a clear exegetical method, followed systematically throughout and reflected in both content and form; it has its own particular style and terminology and it reveals a well-defined world-view and clear-cut religious concepts. The commentary as a whole bears the seal of one creative mind.

The identity of the author is betrayed by the striking similarities between this commentary and Rashbam's idiosyncratic interpretations exemplified in his commentary on the Pentateuch and in the extant remnants of his other commentaries. The common exegetical method, attention to linguistic details, specific grammatical concepts and emphases, unanticipated attention to the literary aspects of the biblical text, vocabulary and style, and the most surprising similarity between the most minute exegetical details, all point to one conclusion — that the author of our commentary is

74 Cf. Japhet, *Tarbiz* XLIV p. 87 notes 95-101.

Rashbam. Some of these common features were indicated by Rosin, who made extensive use of the commentary in his study of Rashbam's exegesis[75]; we have already pointed out some of these elsewhere[76]; some came to light through the discussion concerning the authenticity of our commentary; some are referred to in the following discussion[77], and there are more. Only the assumption of a common author can account for the close relationship and interdependence revealed by the close study of these commentaries. We may, therefore, conclude that a reliable tradition underlies the copyist's superscription on the first page of our commentary that it is "a commentary by R. Samuel".

Before concluding, two more points relevant to our discussion should be made. First, one should not confuse authenticity with purity of transmission. All medieval biblical commentaries underwent a long process of transmission and in no case are we even close to their autographs. The commentaries were later the object of intense preoccupation and study and were frequently recopied. Many of the copyists were scholars in their own right, who did not hesitate to interfere with the text by constantly glossing and editing it, thus adding to the routine errors caused by the ordinary course of transmission. Glosses, modifications, omissions and the like, are therefore to be expected in our Qoheleth commentary, as well as defects traceable to the process of transmission; nonetheless, it seems that the reworking of our commentary is in fact rather limited. Since only one manuscript of the commentary survived, the distance (if any) between our Ms. and the original work cannot be fully ascertained.

Second, the controversy over the question of authenticity should not deflect attention from the main issue, which is of course the commentary itself. The name of Rashbam adds, no doubt, to its prestige, and the study of the commentary from the angle of his authorship contributes also to the elucidation of Rashbam's overall exegetical approach and methods, but the principal value of this commentary is not to be assessed by authorship. It is an important composition in its own right, adding dimension to the work of the great exegetical school in medieval northern France.

75 Cf. above note 11.
76 Japhet, *Tarbiz* XLIV pp. 88-94.
77 Cf. *inter. al.* below, p. 42, and note 107.

b. The Unity of the Commentary

A most important feature of the commentary is its integrity, its unified nature being evident in its form, method and message. The basis of this unity lies probably in Rashbam's understanding of the nature and essence of the book of Qoheleth itself. He regards Qoheleth as a unified and harmonious literary composition, neither a collection of isolated matters, nor, on the other hand, just another segment of biblical literature. Rashbam's point of departure can be described, then, as literary in nature, considering the book of Qoheleth as a separate, and at the same time complete, literary work[78].

This view is expressed directly at the outset in the exposition of the literary framework of Qoheleth. Rashbam was the first to realize that the book of Qoheleth is set within a framework, consisting of the book's first two verses and the last seven. According to him these verses were written by "those who edited it (the book)"[79]. Commenting on 1:2 he says:

> These two verses "the words of Qoheleth" "Vanity of vanities" (1:1-2) were not said by Qoheleth but by the person who edited the words as they stand.

and then to 12:8:

> Now the book is completed; those who edited it speak from now on.

In these extremely important critical remarks Rashbam is both grasping the literary setting of the book[80] and recognizing its present form as the

---

78 The difference between this approach and that of the homiletic literature is not in degree but in principle. Cf. I. Heinemann, *Darkhei Ha'agadah*[2], Jerusalem 1954 esp. pp. 56ff. and cf. below p. 48 and note 124.

79 Rashbam uses the verb סד״ר, the Rabbinic equivalent of biblical and modern ער״ך. Cf. J. Levi III, p. 481ff.; E. Ben-Yehuda, III, pp. 3972ff.

80 This view is accepted by virtually all modern scholars, although most would regard only 1:1 and 12:9-14 as secondary. The fact that it was stated for the first time by Rashbam is mentioned by Ginsburg, pp. 42-43, but we have not found it noted anywhere else. Wildeboer, p. 112, attributes this view to Doederlein and so does Gordis, p. 73 and 349ff. For the status of these verses in the book of Qoheleth cf. *inter al.* Barton p. 44; Hertzberg pp 35-42; Ginsberg p. 10; Rankin, p. 1 and 12; Galling pp. 55, 89-90; Zimmerli pp. 143, 249ff. On the other hand, C.H.H. Wright, *The Book of Koheleth*, London 1883, speaks about "the unity of authorship of the book and the epilogue, which has never been called in question until comparatively modern times", p. 439.

result of "editing". Moreover, "those who edited it" did more than give the book its present form. In their short statements at the beginning and end, they summarized the message of the book, thus revealing the principle of the book's editing and becoming its interpreters. Next, in his comment on 1:2, Rashbam says:

> "Vanity of vanities" — he had given his mind to inquire and search out the affairs of the world and had found them all to be futile.

According to Rashbam's understanding of the structure ot the book, these are the words of the editors, and in the same spirit he explains their words in 12:8:

> All that goes on in the world is utterly futile, said Qoheleth.

By repeating the same phrase at the beginning and conclusion of the book, and by the specific wording of this phrase, the editors summed up the message of the book in a nutshell.

The idea that "all is vanity" could be expressed in two different ways. One is that of an abstract, epigrammatic saying, employed at the beginning and conclusion of the book. The other is followed throughout the book, as Qoheleth is shown painstakingly going through all his experiences, describing them in detail, re-living them and summarizing each of them with the same painful verdict: "this, too, is vanity". Rashbam was aware of both ways. He acknowledged the abstraction, understanding it as the editors' words, and followed the hard trail of Qoheleth's experiences. The phrase "this is vanity", in different variations, recurs twenty-four times in the book[81], and Rashbam makes explicit reference to practically all of them. In each case he expounds how Qoheleth's specific experience leads him to the conclusion that "this is vanity". At first glance this seems to contradict Rashbam's famous economy of words and brevity of expression. But this is his way of doing full justice not only to the book's theme but also to its specific literary form.

---

81 1:1, 14; 2:1, 11, 15, 17, 19, 21, 23, 26; 3:9; 4:4, 8, 16; 5:9; 6:2, 9; 7:6; 8:10, 14 (twice); 11:8, 10; 12:8. Similar to it is רעיון רוח in 1:17. The word הבל in other usages is found also in 4:7; 5:6; 6:4, 11, 12; 7:15; 8:14; 9:9. Cf. also, with slight changes, *Tarbiz* XLIV p. 76 note 24.

c. The Classification of Exegetical Categories and the Structure of the Commentary

As mentioned already, the unified character of the commentary is expressed in its form and exegetical principles. Although no theoretical presentation of principles and methodological premises is to be found in the commentary[82], such principles are nevertheless in evidence and can be discerned through their actual application in exegesis.

Rashbam's interpretations can be grouped under three headings according to the specific aspect of the text to which they relate: contents and meaning, language and literary form. The first of these is the most common and anticipated. Rashbam gives the meaning of the text, stressing the important points, unveiling the hidden nuances incorporated in the poetic language and enlarging upon obscure aspects[83]. His manner in these comments is quite consistent, although the interpretations are sometimes rather detailed and lengthy, and sometimes quite short. The presentation of content and meaning is achieved in a fluent discourse marked by a tendency to use words from the biblical text as part of the interpretation. The phrasing of the discourse is remarkably purposeful and the words, both the text's and Rashbam's own, are carefully chosen. Some aspects of these interpretations will be referred to below[84].

The second group is the linguistic. Rashbam's commentaries contain numerous discussions of various linguistic problems: etymologies[85], grammatical forms[86], syntactical constructions[87], semantic clarifications[88] etc., all brought to bear on the meaning of the text. This aspect of Rashbam's exegesis is well known and much celebrated; it seems that

---

82 Sporadic methodological statements are found in his commentary on the Pentateuch; best known are those on Gen. 1:1; 37:2 and Ex. 21:1 (for more detailed references cf. Rosin pp. 80ff) in which he seeks to define his own method of "literal meaning" (פשט) and his deviation from both the accepted traditional interpretations and the commentary of his grandfather. These are, however, only selected aspects of his methods.

83 For example cf. his interpretations on 1:5-6, 9-10, 11 etc.

84 P. 42ff.

85 Cf. to 1:14, 17 etc.

86 1:13, 16, 17; 3:18; 5:9 etc.

87 2:1; 3:14-15 etc.

88 2:1, 6, 8, 12, 16; 3:9 etc.

scholars tend to define his work as practically restricted to this area[89]. Rashbam's linguistic interpretations amount to a rather general linguistic outlook, another expression of which is to be found in his Grammar.

In his linguistic interpretations Rashbam tends to focus his attention upon certain particular points, to which he returns almost consistently. His didactic principle is that of analogy, which he applies in a most systematic way[90]. The linguistic interpretations can be clearly identified as Rashbam's work, both by content and by method, even when his name is not mentioned, but one should bear in mind that, although well recognised, they constitute only one facet of his work.

Rashbam's emphasis on linguistic analysis is related, no doubt, to what he regards as his most important goal, namely to reveal the "literal meaning" of the text[91]. Therefore he does not hesitate to follow his linguistic conclusions to their very end, no matter how extreme it may be. No other exegete of the French school has matched his standards of linguistic sensitivity and insight.

The third group is the least recognized and least expected. In general, medieval Jewish exegesis paid but little attention to literary aspects of the biblical text[92]. Rashbam is an exception to the rule and rather "modern" in his approach. We have mentioned above his opinion concerning the structure and composition of the book of Qoheleth, and further examples of his insights into the book's literary aspects will be presented below[93].

---

89 Cf. Ahrend, p. 46.

90 For example 1:14: "רעות רוח" ... and רעות is from the verb רעה just as דמות is from דמה (Ms.רמה), ראות from ראה, ענות from ענה." Or, again on 1:17 "ורעיון" ... just as one says רעיון from רעה, צביון from צבה, אביון from אבה, עליון from עלה and הגיון from הגה so one says רעיון from רעה meaning: desire". Rashbam uses didactic considerations to justify the use of analogy. In his grammar book he says: "We possess a short way of teaching those who make mistakes how to learn one word from another. When a grammarian errs in the grammar of a word, in its inflection and its root, what letters are basic to the word, what letters are formative and from what root it is derived, he should compare it to words that are clear to him and similar to that word; from this he will understand the rule of the word which he could not make out" (*Daikuth*, p. 44).

91 Cf. below, p. 59ff.

92 Cf. Simon, p. 151

93 P. 48ff.

The classification of Rashbam's comments into different categories, far from being a late, modern and artificial imposition, is actually realized in Rashbam's work itself. He himself was aware of the diverse spheres of exegesis as well as the specific contribution of each aspect to the final product; he deals with each on its own merits but his aim is the synthesis of all. Rashbam's awareness of the distinct exegetical spheres is not expressed explicitly or directly, but is embodied in the structure of his work.

As mentioned above, the usual form of the interpretations is the discourse: in a continuous and fluent presentation, comprising complete sentences and written in a brief and precise idiom, the meaning of the interpreted unit is given. As a result of careful and well-calculated choice of words, many details of the given text are elucidated in the course of the presentation, without making interruption for a specific reference. However, not all the details can be incorporated into the discourse; some require more explicit treatment or broader discussion, which would tend to disturb the flow of the commentary if introduced *in loco*. Rashbam solves this problem by means of a simple technique: he postpones the discussion of detailed linguistic matters until the end of the presentation, where he deals with them individually and with due attention to detail. At the same time he incorporates the results of these linguistic discussions into the continuous presentation itself[94]. In this way, each matter is presented fully, without interruption, and yet the details receive the attention they deserve. A similar method is applied by some modern series of biblical commentaries, such as the ICC or KAT, where the discussions in smaller type provide the necessary analytical basis for the main commentary.

To be sure, such a division of the interpretations is not to be found in every verse. For the sake of brevity and economy, all unnecessary verbiage is avoided, so that in certain cases only a linguistic detail is discussed, and it is assumed that the consequences for the meaning of the verse will be obvious, while in other cases the continuous presentation is regarded as sufficient. Nevertheless, whenever such a division does exist, the order of the interpretations is fixed, almost without exception: first comes the

---

94 The method was pointed out and demonstrated by S. Japhet, *Tarbiz* XLIV, pp. 78-79; 80-84.

general interpretation, and then the isolated details, discussed in order[95]. This fixed external feature of the commentary is a clear expression of Rashbam's awareness of the distinctive character and function of exegetical categories[96].

Comments which refer to literary aspects are in general less frequent and handled less consistently. Usually, however, they come first, as in 1:11; 3:9; 8:10 etc. The commentary on 1:2 provides an interesting example. It opens with a detailed note about the specific form of parallelism exemplified in the verse[97]; it goes on with an observation about the origin and function of the first two verses in the broader context of the book[98]; only then does Rashbam refer to the meaning of the verse, which can become clear after these preliminary literary notes.

The same order is followed in the use of the recurring expression "a doubled phrase", or "a parallel expression", found in various forms more than twenty times in the commentary on Qoheleth[99]. A "doubled phrase"

---

95 For example, cf. 1:8; 2:2; 3:9, 18; 4:2; etc.

96 The distinctive character and function of the linguistic sphere is demonstrated clearly in the attempt to write a "grammatical commentary" to the Bible, the beginning of which comprises the second part of Rashbam's grammar book and which deals, indeed, only with linguistic matters (cf. above, p. 17). Comparisons between the existing parallel parts of Rashbam's commentary on the Pentateuch and his grammatical commentary are very instructive for understanding Rashbam's concept of his task as exegete.

97 This specific form of parallelism, known today as "climactic parallelism", "staircase parallelism" or "the expanded colon", was first pointed out by Rashbam. It has recently become quite prominent in the study of biblical poetry, since it has been found in Ugaritic, as well as in other Ancient Near Eastern literatures. (Cf. the systematic survey and analysis by S.E. Loewenstamm, "The Expanded Colon in Ugaritic and Biblical Verse" *JSS* 14 (1969), pp. 176-196; E.L. Greenstein, "Two Variations of Grammatical Parallelism" *JANES* 6 (1974) p. 96 n. 47 for extensive bibliography, and recently, idem, "One More Step on the Staircase", *UF* 9 (1977), pp. 77-88, Kugel p. 35ff. Rashbam was wont to demonstrate this parallelism with fixed examples. Ps. 92:10; 93:3; Ex. 15:6, and Qoh. 1:2. (cf. his remarks to Gen. 49:22; Ex. 15:6 and Qoh. 1:2). These verses came to be known later as "the verses of Samuel" (פסוקי שמואל), cf. Berliner, pp. IX-X and *MWJ* VII (1880), p. 189.

98 Above, pp. 34-35.

99 Cf. on 1:6, 15, 17, 18; 2:3; 3:16; 4:8, 13; 5:9; 6:3; 7:12, 12; 8:10; 9:9; 10:10, 20; 11:10; 12:6, 11, 12 and *Tarbiz* XLIV p. 87 notes 95-101.

can sometimes refer to a synonym or a repetition of one word[100], but its most frequent use is as a description of *Parallelismus Membrorum*. Here too, the structure of the interpretation is predetermined: immediately after the lemma comes a statement that the part of the verse under discussion is a "double"; this is followed by an interpretation of the text, which usually refers to the specific wording and points out the particular way in which it "doubles" the previous part[101].

Recognition of the formal principles which govern the commentary is essential to its understanding. A major facet of this recognition is the demarcation of the *exegetical units*.

The learned reader of medieval exegesis expects the commentary to provide a verse-by-verse interpretation of the biblical text, but as far as the commentaries of Rashbam are concerned this expectation is misplaced and misleading. The above discussion has already made abundantly clear that Rashbam did not merely follow the text, word by word or verse by verse, but marked out the scope of the exegetical unit before turning to its interpretation. Of course, in many cases the exegetical unit corresponds to the verse and no tension arises between the two. Still, there are many cases in which the unit exceeds the verse, comprising two or more verses. These units must be clearly distinguished if the commentary is to be correctly understood.

For the delimiting of the units two criteria may be used. One is the external distinction between exegetical spheres: a cluster of linguistic discussions after a more general presentation of meaning is a clear sign of conclusion. When such a cluster contains details from several verses, this clearly indicates the scope of the unit. According to this criterion the following units exceed the scope of one verse: 4:10-11; 4:15-16; 6:3-4; 7:16-18; 7:21-22; 7:27-28; 8:6-7; 8:10-13; 9:9-10[102]; 9:18-10:1; 10:8-9; 11:5-6; 12:2-5; 12:6-7; 12:12-14.

100 On 8:10; 9:9; 11:10.

101 Cf. on 1:6, 15, 18; 4:8 *et al.* In three instances the remark "double" is not followed by an explanation (2:3; 3:16; 10:20). In one case only, 10:10, the statement "this verse is a double" is found at the end of the interpretation, but it denotes a repetition of message (of 9:18) rather than a parallelism.

102 In fact, the exegetical unit comprises vss. 7-10, but the linguistic details at its end relate only to vss. 9-10.

The prevailing mode of continuous, fluent presentation provides the second criterion of demarcation. In many instances the interpretation relates in one uninterrupted discourse to a section exceeding one verse in length, and no hiatus can be introduced without interfering with the syntactical continuity. According to this criterion the following units exceed the scope of one verse; and, as might be expected, the list contains almost all the units which were determined also by the previous criterion: 1:5-6; 1:9-10; 1:12-13; 2:13-14; 2:20-21; 2:22-23; 3:2-8; 3:14-15; 3:19-20; 4:7-9; 4:10-11; 4:15-16; 5:3-4; 5:12-13; 5:15-16; 6:1-2; 6:3-4; 7:16-18; 7:21-22; 7:27-28; 8:6-7; 8:10-13; 9:1b-3[103]; 9:7-10; 9:14-15; 9:18-10:1; 10:5-6; 10:8-9; 11:2-3; 11:5-6; 11:7-8; 12:2-5; 12:6-7; 12:11-14[104].

d. Conclusion: "Glosses" or Exegetical Composition?

An important conclusion of the above discussion pertains to the general character of Rashbam's commentaries. In his introduction to Rashbam's commentary on the Pentateuch, Rosin states: "Rashbam wrote his commentary on the margins of his Bible and the first scribe, who calls himself 'the young one' ... when he copied Rashbam's words into a

103 The division of verses in this instance seems to deviate from MT. The words הכל לפניהם are in MT at the end of vs. 1, while they are referred to in the commentary as the beginning of vs. 2. Cf. *Tarbiz* XLIV, p. 78.
104 In his edition of the commentary, Jellinek attempted to "overcome" these units by forcing the text into what he regarded as the proper order, namely a verse by verse continuity. He used several devices, for example 1) beginning the interpretation without a lemma (1:10; 12:3); 2) printing Rashbam's words as lemmata (1:13; 6:2; 9:3; 11:3); 3) breaking a sentence in the middle (2:14; 11:6); 4) omitting the number of a verse as if it is not explicated, although its interpretation is given together with that of the preceding verse (3:3-8; 4:11; 5:4; 6:4; 7:22; 8:7); 5) leaving isolated elements where they are found but without providing the numbers of the verses to which they belong (7:16; 8:10-13; 10:1; 12:4-5; 12:11-14). In spite of these efforts, the continuities could not always be suppressed and Jellinek presented the following as enlarged units: 2:20-21, 22-23; 3:14-15, 19-20; 4:7-8, 15-16; 5:12-13, 15-16; 7:27-28; 8:10-11; 9:7-10, 14-15; 10:5-6, 8-9; 11:7-8.

separate book added the lemmata to make Rashbam's interpretations intelligible . . ."[105]. Faithful to the prevailing view concerning medieval exegesis in general, Rosin regards Rashbam's work as a glossary — a series of notes written in the margins of the biblical text to accompany the reading and the study of the text.

Our investigation of the commentary on Qoheleth has clearly shown that the commentary is by no means a glossary! It is a well-structured, premeditated composition, the writing of which is guided by a literary insight into the book of Qoheleth. As we have seen, the exegetical units are clearly delimited, the scope and wording of each interpretation are carefully determined, and the interpretations are presented in a fixed order according to their categories.

It seems that the same principles were also applied in the commentary on the Pentateuch. Unfortunately it is only with difficulty that they can be deciphered now. In his edition Rosin "corrected" all deviations from the biblical order, which he regarded as scribal errors over many generations. As the only Ms. of that commentary has been lost, the only way to reconstruct the original, is through Rosin's notes which refer to these "corrections"[106]. Even so, the traces of Rashbam's method can still be found even in the present edition[107].

e. Some Features of the Exegetical Presentation

The main body of the commentary consists of what we have called the "continuous, fluent discourse", which records the content and meaning of the biblical passage. At first glance such a manner of presentation would seem rather commonplace and unremarkable. A closer look reveals a composition showing full awareness of every word and consistent application of fixed forms and principles.

105 Rosin, Pentateuch p. XXXVI; also Rosin p. 91.
106 Rosin, Pentateuch, pp. XXXVI-XXXVII.
107 Units which are longer than a verse are *inter al.* Gen. 1:6-7; 18:2-5 (or 1-5); 23:2-4, 18-20; 28:6-8; 34:7-8; 37:2-5, 15-19, 40-43; Ex. 3:11-12; 6:14-15; 21:3-5; 24:1-16 (18); Lev. 9:23-24; 10:1-3; Num. 17:27-28; 20:10-11; 30:2-3; 31:49-54; Deut. 7:7-8, 9-12; 9:25-28; 20:2-5; 26:5-10.

We have mentioned above that while certain details are discussed separately at the end of the discourse, the conclusion of this discussion are already incorporated in the main body of the interpretation. However, a separate handling of each detail would result in a complete disintegration of the commentary, and the synthesis then might risk becoming pointless repetition. In order to avoid such extremes — disintegration of the commentary on the one hand and needless repetition on the other, many of the details are handled in the course of the general interpretation, without drawing attention to the fact with specific lemmata. These details include difficult words, grammatical forms, syntactical constructions, and the like. The most common mode of such explanations is the use of a synonym or an equivalent to the element being interpreted, while preserving the text's structure and line of thought. The observant reader will discover the equivalent quite easily and will be able to appreciate Rashbam's exegetical achievement, whereas the superficial reader will notice only a general statement of meaning, a paraphrase of the biblical text.

This mode of interpretation is combined with another feature of the commentary. Rashbam, like every commentator, treats certain points with special attention. These points are heterogeneous and may belong to any sphere — a religious idea, a semantic precision, a linguistic feature, etc. One of the ways in which their importance is emphasized is through a repetition which strives for completeness. Certain matters attract the commentator's attention and he relates to them repeatedly. We have mentioned above the consistent manner in which the phrase "this, too, is vanity" is handled in the commentary[108] and we will demonstrate this further with several examples, from different exegetical spheres.

The first example is a linguistic detail — the particle כי — because, for, hence, etc. Rashbam attaches great importance to the understanding of particles in their specific nuances. The importance of the particle כי in the commentary on the Pentateuch was already recognized by Rosin[109], but its distinction in the commentary on Qoheleth is due as much to the book's style as to Rashbam's inclinations: within the book's limited scope the

108 P. 35.
109 Rosin p. 87 note 2; p. 90 note 5; p. 149.

particle כי appears almost ninety times, twice in every five verses. Nowhere in the commentary is it explained separately[110], but it does receive some sort of attention in the commentary in all but ten of the ninety cases. On more than sixty occasions it is assigned an explicit equivalent, usually שהרי (for), sometimes ש (that), sometimes רק, אלא (but), and לפי (so that)[111]. Thus, the way in which כי is dealt with demonstrates two features of the commentary, mentioned above: the actual interpretation of various details in the course of the running commentary by replacing them with synonyms, without drawing special attention to the interpretation, and the consistent repetition of certain elements, striving to make them absolutely clear. The attention given to כי in the Pentateuch, coupled with the consistent focus on it in Qoheleth, makes this awareness a characteristic feature of Rashbam's commentary.

Another example of the same phenomenon from a different area is found in the phrase תחת השמש = under the sun, which is broadened to include the word "sun" in other expressions. The phrase is a peculiarity of Qoheleth's

---

110 This is said explicitly in Gen. 18:15: "Most instances of כי after לא mean אלא (but, except) because כי has four meanings: if, perhaps, but, for," and again in Deut. 20:19: "Every כי after לא means אלא". The rule about the four meanings of כי is cited in the name of Resh Lakish in BT, Rosh Hashanah 3a.

111 These are the equivalents: 1) Represented by שהרי — 1:18; 2:10, 12, 16, 21, 22, 23, 25, 26; 3:17, 19, 19, 22, 22; 4:10, 14, 14, 17; 5:2, 3, 6, 7, 19; 6:4, 8, 11, 12; 7:3, 6, 7, 9, 10, 12, 20, 22; 8:6, 7, 12, 16; 9:1, 4, 5, 9, 10, 11, 12; 10:4; 11:1, 2, 6, 8, 10; 12:3; 2) represented by רק, אלא — 5:6, 10, 19; 6:2; 3) represented by לפי — 2:17, 17; 9:3; 4) represented by ש — 8:17; 9:7; 11:9. 5) The word כי itself is repeated in the explanation — 2:24; 3:12, 22; 5:1, 5; 7:13, 18; 8:3, 6, 15; 9:4, 11; 12:5, 13, 14; 6) no equivalent 3:14; 4:4, 16; 5:17; 8:7. Most of the cases where כי is passed over in the interpretation are those in which it appears more than once in one verse and not all its occurrences are noted (8:7; 9:5; 11:8).

language[112], recurring about thirty times in the book. Rashbam explains the phrase twice, in a succinct and straightforward way; in its first occurrence in the book, in 1:3:

> "Under the sun" — because there is nothing hidden from its heat he uses this expression — the same as if it were written "under heaven".

and then again, in 2:18:

> "under the sun" — like "under heaven".

In addition to these clear statements the phrase is constantly referred to in the interpretations with the equivalent בעולם = in the world; very few instances are left uninterpreted[113]. Furthermore, other phrases including the word "sun" such as 7:1 (לרואי השמש) 11:7 (לראות את השמש)[114], 12:2 (עד אשר לא תחשך השמש) are explicated by the expression בעולם = in the world.

One might ask whether the intensive treatment of "under the sun" is specific to this phrase and motivated by polemic considerations, endeavouring to establish the "literal meaning" as against the homiletic[115]. However even if there is a polemic component in the interpretation of "under the sun" it cannot explain the insistence on supplying the meaning of the phrase where no polemic is necessary. It seems that what is at work

---

112 The question of its origin is not yet settled in biblical scholarship. Until quite recently it has been explained as of Greek origin, cf. Barton, p. 32; with the rise of "Phoenicianism" it came to be regarded as of Phoenician origin. Cf. M.J. Dahood, "Canaanite-Phoenician Influence in Qoheleth" *Biblica* 33 (1952) p. 203; Y. Avishur, *Phoenician Inscriptions and the Bible*, Jerusalem, 1979, p. 29 (Hebrew) but the debate is still going on. Cf. Ginsberg, pp. 43-45; R. Braun, *Kohelet und die fruehhellenistische Popularphilosophie* (*BZAW* 130) Berlin–New York, 1973, pp. 49–51.

113 It has an equivalent in the following: 1:9, 14; 2:18, 20; 3:16; 4:3, 7; 6:12; 8:15, 17; 9:3, 6, 9, 11, 13; 10:5.

114 It seems that Rashbam has noticed here, without explicitly stating it, the metaphorical use of "sun" as the symbol of the living world. רואי שמש — "those seeing the sun", are the living, and so on. Cf. also Ginsberg, p. 44 note 2.

115 Principally against Rashi, who combines the literal and homiletical principles of exegesis in an interesting way. He explains תחת as "substitute", which is a legitimate meaning of the word (*BDB,* תחת 2b, p. 1065) but explains שמש homiletically as "Torah". Accordingly, the meaning of the whole verse of 1:3 would be: "Any labour which a man puts in place of the Torah — what profit does it have?". Cf. also Gelles, pp. 89-90.

here is an exegetical principle which is executed with great consistency. The same principle can be discerned in the explanation of other words and terms, such as עמל, טוב, יתרון etc. In all of these the method used by Rashbam is adapted admirably to the literary quality of the book of Qoheleth itself: the peculiar or characteristic key-terms are systematically referred to with almost complete thoroughness.

It is probably this effort to preserve the flow of discourse, while still making reference to specific details in the process, which gives rise to another feature of this method of interpretation. In many cases Rashbam applies a special technique: he preserves in the commentary both the biblical word and its equivalent; but rather than separating them by some explanatory particle such as 'namely', 'meaning', 'such as', 'i.e.' or the like, they are connected by a conjunctive *Waw*. Externally, then, the two words are presented as copulative, one serving as an addition to the other; in fact they are in a kind of apposition: each of the two words is an equivalent of and replacement for the other, but they are combined by means of a conjunction. The presence of both words is a result of exegetical technique and does not indicate any addition in meaning. As a rule, one of the words is the biblical one, the other is its equivalent; while the order is flexible, more often than not the biblical word is the first of the two.

This phenomenon, once noticed, appears repeatedly. We shall demonstrate with a few examples. Some sayings in Qoheleth are constructed according to the popular wisdom form "better is ... than ..." (... מ ... טוב)[116]. Rashbam usually explained the phrase "... מ טוב „by its equivalents in Rabbinic Hebrew, משובח יותר (4:3, 9, 13) and מוטב לו לאדם (7:2, 3, 5). However, in commenting on 7:1, "A good name is better than precious ointment", Rashbam opens with "טוב ומשובח שם יותר ... טוב", which, if translated literally would mean: "better and better is a good name ... than"; the same phrase recurs in the second part of the verse with a change in the order of the words[117]. It is clear, then, that the

---

116 4:6, 9, 13; 5:4; 6:3, 9; 7:1, 2, 3, 5, 8, 10; 9:16, 18; Cf. lately, G.S. Ogden, "The 'Better'-Proverb (Tob-Spruch), Rhetorical Criticism and Qoheleth" *JBL* 96 (1977), pp. 489-505.
117 The use of these two words with a conjunction is also found in the interpretations of 5:4; 7:10; 9:16.

'waw' is not copulative but explicative, and the presence of the two words is dictated by the exegetical technique.

The next example is of greater significance to the understanding of the commentary; it is עמל, one of the key words of Qoheleth, usually interpreted and translated as "toil"[117a]. Rashbam explains the word as referring primarily to the fruits of toil, namely money (ממון), riches (עשר) and the like[118]; only rarely does he equate it with work itself[119]. In 2:18 the lemma עמלי is explained by "ואת עשרי" which literally means "*and* my riches"; in 2:19 the interpretation is "... or a fool, in which case עמלי *and* עשרי shall fall from his possession into the possession of others". At first it appears, then, that these are two different words, each denoting a different idea, their conjunction enriching the meaning of each. In fact, however, עמל means "riches", as determined by the immediate context, and by a thorough reading of the whole commentary. The two words are used synonymously. One is the word from the biblical text, and the other an explanation which brings to light its precise semantic nuance.

The instances in which this practice is applied are very numerous; as occasional examples we could cite 1:4 (עומדת וקיימת)[120]; 1:5 (שואף ומהיר; לא ימצא ולא ;בעתו וזמנו) 3:11 (עמל וטורח); 3:9 (הווה ויש לו); 2:22 (בא ושוקע) ;(סחורתם ועמלם) 4:9 (אין ותהו ;מקרה אחד ומנהג אחד) 3:19 (עשה ותיקן ;ידע) and so on[121].

The results of this technique are twofold. On the one hand we have a sort of stylistic redundance, a result of the intensive use of synonyms which might seem practically meaningless for purposes of expression. On the other hand, the exegetical aspect profits from the clear presentation of

---

117a The RSV consistently translates it as "toil".

118 On this point Rashbam is followed enthusiastically by Ginsberg, cf. ibid pp. 13-15 and throughout the commentary.

119 As, for example, on 6:7.

120 The biblical word is emphasized.

121 It seems that other conjunctive particles serve in the same way, although more sporadically. A case in point is the commentary on 2:19, which says: "ומי יודע על בני שיבוא אחרי אם יהיה חכם או <u>וישלוט בכל עמלי שיתקיים עשרי בידו</u>". Underlined with one line are the words of the biblical text which are here incorporated in the running presentation; underlined with two lines is the explanation of these words, opening with שׁ, which should in this case be translated in view of its function, "namely".

synonyms which serves to establish precision without interrupting the flow of the discourse[122].

f. Treatment of Literary Aspects of the Text

As already mentioned, Rashbam stands out against the background of medieval exegesis in his awareness of and attention to literary features of the biblical text[123]. It seems that two factors are conducive to this awareness. One is a profound sensitivity to form, which is abundantly exemplified throughout his work and which goes beyond textual and linguistic aspects to include literary expressions in form. Thus, not only the content is regarded as significant, but also the form in which it is presented and which constitutes one facet of its expression. The other factor is the recognition of the literary composition as such: an independent whole, the only context in which the details are to be understood. In this respect Rashbam's divergence from traditional homiletical literature is so fundamental that it warrants description as a break with this tradition[124]. We have already mentioned some of Rashbam's observations on literary matters; we shall now demonstrate with a further selection of examples.

122 Avineri has recognized the existence of this *"Waw explicativum"* in Rashi's commentaries both to the Bible and the Talmud and has correctly traced its origins to Biblical and Rabbinic Hebrew, cf. Avineri, II p. XXVIII, Gesenius §154a note (b.). It seems however that in Rashbam's work it developed into an important exegetical tool and a characteristic stylistic feature. On the bearing of this technique on the translation, cf. below p. 83.

123 Rosin has pointed out some examples of such observation in Rashbam's commentary to the Pentateuch; he did not, however, define the literary aspect *per se,* and presented in one place matters which belong to differing categories (ibid, p. 84 note 3).

124 Cf. above pp. 37. A well-known example of Rashbam's deviation from accepted, traditional views is his bold interpretation of Gen. 1:5, where he regards the day as beginning in the morning, and not the previous evening. The most important point, however, is not this detail, but the exegetical principle. His point of departure is the actual literary context, namely Genesis 1; the meaning of any part of the chapter is determined within that specific, limited literary context, and not — as is the case with the accepted view — in the vast context of Jewish literature as a whole. (On Gen. 1:5 cf. U. Simon, Ibn Ezra p. 137). For some remarks on the question of context, cf. also Greenberg.

The book of Qoheleth is composed of smaller literary units. The exact scope of these units, their order and inner relationships are discussed at length in all modern commentaries on the book[125]. Rashbam was aware of this inner structure and tried to bring it to light, although not in a consistent manner.

Rashbam regards the first two verses of the book and the last seven as a literary framework in which the words of Qoheleth are set[126]. He then presents 1:3-2:26 as a complete literary unit in which one basic theme is being developed to a climax. Thus he establishes the context in which the details are clarified, providing the key for understanding the section.

In the interpretation of 1:3 he delineates the scope of the literary unit: "All these words refer to (the statement) below: There is nothing better for a man than that he should eat and drink etc. (2:24) which is to say that all this human endeavour is futile and there is nothing good for a man to do for his enjoyment except to drink and to be happy with his lot".

He returns repeatedly thereafter to the issue of context; in his interpretation of 1:6 ("Therefore it is said: 'What does man gain'" (1:3)), 1:7, 11; 2:11 and 15.[127]

Thus, through an explicit statement at the beginning and a technique of constant and repeated reference, the context is clearly marked out, from 1:3 to 2:26; only through reference to that context may each of the details be correctly interpreted.

The same goal, namely the delineation of the unit as the relevant context for interpretation, is attained by other methods as well. One is a repetition of certain elements — of language or content — throughout a section, as a

---

125 Cf. the general survey in Rankin, pp. 7-12; also A.G. Wright, "The Riddle of the Sphinx: the Structure of the Book of Qoheleth", *CBQ* 30 (1968), pp. 313-334; idem, "The Riddle of the Sphinx, Revisited: Numerical Patterns in the Book of Qoheleth", *CBQ* 42 (1980), pp. 38-51; M. Zer-Kavod, "Studies in Kohelet", *Beth Mikra* 18 (1973), pp. 182-197; 280-281.

126 Cf. above, pp. 34-35.

127 Cf. also Salters, Observations, pp. 57-58.

kind of *leit-wort*[128]. An example is provided by the commentary to 11:9-12:7[129].

This section juxtaposes the two ends of man's life, youth and old age, with a clear-cut conclusion, stated at the outset: enjoy your life while you are still young! The section is structured in an interesting way: its first part is built of a series of seven imperatives — rejoice, let your heart cheer you[130], walk, know, remove, put away, remember (11:9-12:1a); its second part, attached to the first, is built upon a threefold repetition of "before" (עד אשר לא 12:1b, 2, 6). The point of departure for the interpretation of the section is 12:1: "remember . . . your Creator in the days of your youth", which is the turning point between the two parts. This verse is the pole to which the whole second part is tied, both syntactically and in content, and it is related to the beginning of the section by being the seventh consecutive imperative and by repeating the phrase "in the days of your youth", found at the beginning. Rashbam understands the meaning of the section as focused around two themes: "let your heart cheer you in the days of your youth" and "remember your Creator in the days of your youth" — while you are still young, enjoy yourself and repent! do not put off any of these things to the dark days of old age[131]. Starting from this point, Rashbam repeats the key-idea of the section several times, in a way which clearly reveals its inner structure.

In his interpretation of 12:1 he says: "Before the time of evil comes, the time of old age . . . you should be zealous to repent before this". Then, on

---

128 M. Buber, *Werke* II, München 1964, pp. 1131ff.

129 Many modern commentators share Rashbam's view regarding the delineation of units at this point and the integrity of 11:9ff, although some of them differ regarding the conclusion of the unit, where they include 12:8. Cf. Hertzberg pp. 204ff.; Zimmerli pp. 242ff.; Gordis pp. 166-199; Rankin p. 83; Ginsberg on 11:9 and 12:5 and others.

130 Strictly speaking, this is not an imperative but a jussive. One should ask, therefore what is the expressive value of such a change within the framework of the whole pattern.

131 Critical scholars tend to regard both 11:9b and 12:1a, or just one of these verses, as secondary, attributable to a "Chasidic glossator", cf. Barton p. 185 and Rankin pp. 8, 84. Alternatively, some would regard בוראך in 12:1a as a scribal error for בארך or בורך (meaning either cistern on grave, cf. Barton p. 195; Galling pp. 88-89; Scott pp. 254-255) or for בראך (Ginsberg, p. 129).

12:2-5: "... before the world becomes dark and gloomy for you ... you should repent" and further "before darkness after darkness happens to you you should be zealous to return to the Holy One", and again: "Before all these things happen to him in his old age he should repent", and then, as a conclusion, on 12:6: "Before all these things he should repent".

Although the unit is not explicitly mentioned, it is clearly presented as such, and it becomes a closed context for the purpose of interpretation.

Another aspect of the same approach is revealed in the attempt to clarify the relationships between the units, and through them the development of the argument. This is exemplified in the commentary on Qoheleth in two places in a similar way. The first comment on 3:9 is "This is related to 'but to the sinner he gives the work of gathering' (2:26)", in other words, 3:9ff is a continuation of the theme of 1:3-2:26. The intervening section, 3:1-8, is a kind of intercalation, the subject matter of which is necessary for the development of the argument presented in 3:9ff. Thus both 3:1ff and 3:9ff are continuations of 2:26, 3:1-8 as a side issue standing very much on its own, and 3:9ff as a continuation of the main line of thought. The same structure is suggested in ch. 8, where the unit, starting with 8:10 is regarded as a continuation of 7:23-25 while what intervenes is an intercalation; it follows in a way the discussion of 7:23-25, but its contribution to what comes after is not specified[132].

Rashbam's sensitivity to form and to the special nature of poetic language have led him to recognize the phenomenon of parallelism and to differentiate some of its forms. As this subject requires special treatment which will be undertaken elsewhere, we will restrict ourselves here to some general observations.

No fixed, unified terminology is applied in the description of parallelism, but the most common phrases are those constructed with כפל = double[133]. By this very definition, a major premise is expressed: that the two parts of one verse, or two consecutive verses, have the same contents and thus each

132 A similar example is afforded in his interpretation of Deut. 33:1, cf. Japhet, *Tarbiz* XLV, p. 81 note 46.
133 Above p. 24ff. On the terminology cf. Japhet, ibid, pp. 86-87; Grossman, *Tarbiz* XLV, (1976) p. 339-340; Japhet, *Tarbiz* XLVII pp. 244-245.

one can be interpreted by the other. The impact of such an approach on exegesis cannot be overestimated[134], and polemical echoes may indeed be detected in many instances.

The classification into synonymous, antithetic and synthetic parallelism, which has been prevalent since Lowth[135], should not of course be expected in Rashbam's analysis. It is, however, noteworthy that two of these classes were actually recognized by him[136]. His point of departure being exegetical, it is the synonymous parallelism which receives the most attention[137], but when exegetical conclusions are to be drawn from an antithetic parallelism, it is clearly described[138].

Parallelism, according to Rashbam, is not confined to the verse. On the one hand he discerns parallelism between two consecutive verses[139] and on the other he describes as parallel units smaller than a colon[140]. In addition, Rashbam was the first to recognize and describe "stairway parallelism", an example of which is found in Qoheleth[141].

The last feature to which we would refer is Rashbam's discernment of a certain phenomenon in Qoheleth, the existence (or at least the extent) of

134 Cf. especially G.B. Gray, *The Forms of Hebrew Poetry*, 1915 (republished by KTAV, 1972), pp. 19ff; Kugel, pp. 96ff.

135 R. Lowth, *Lectures on the Sacred Poetry of the Hebrews,* 1835 (translated from the Latin of 1753), Vol. II, pp. 24ff.

136 A new attempt to explain the phenomenon of Parallelismus Membrorum, criticizing Lowth's categories, is the recent study of Kugel, pp. 1-95.

137 Cf. on 1:6, 15, 18; 3:16; 4:8; 5:9; 6:3; 7:12 (bis); 8:10; 12:6, 11, 12.

138 An interesting example is provided by the interpretation of 4:13. For Rashbam the word מסכן is problematic; reflecting on its meaning he says: "I cannot interpret it as "wise", to see it as synonym of ... חכם ... because there is a Tipha accent beneath מסכן to separate it from וחכם. 'Youth' is related to 'old', 'poor' is related to 'than a king'; and 'wise' is related to 'and foolish'". In other words, the colon "better is a poor and wise youth" is in the form of an antithetic parallelism to "than an old and foolish king"; therefore the word מסכן cannot be explained as "wise" — as he would have wished to do, in view of other passages, but as an antithesis to "king". Another consideration in this direction is provided by the cantillation signs: the Tipha accent under מסכן separates it from חכם and therefore the two words are not to be regarded as "double", namely as mutually interpretative, one explaining the other.

139 Cf. on 2:1-2; 7:11-12.

140 1:17; 2:3.

141 1:2; cf. above, pp. 23-24.

which is not a matter of general agreement. This is the use of quotations. The book of Qoheleth is notorious for its contradictory statements, a fact which very nearly led to its excision from the Scriptures. One solution to the problem of inner contradictions was offered by Gordis, who suggested that this is due to Qoheleth's literary technique of using quotations, some of which are cited for the express purpose of argument and refutation[142]. Rashbam preceded Gordis in observing the existence of quotations in Qoheleth, but his motives and guidelines are purely literary, devoid of any apology.

Some of the quotations are explicitly suggested by the text, as in 1:10[142a], while others are indicated by other means. In 4:8 the quotation is recognized by the change of person. Here Rashbam supplies the necessary hypothetical question: "For he should reckon: for whom am I toiling so much and depriving myself of enjoyment?" In 2:14 and 3:15 there is a shift in literary form, as a proverb-like saying is introduced: in 2:14 "The wise man has his eyes in his head but the fool walks in the darkness" and in 3:15 "That which is — already has been, that which is to be — already has been, and God seeks what has been driven away". Rashbam regards the two sayings as quotations and prefaces 2:14 with "therefore this is what is said", and 3:15 with "for they may say". A change of both person and literary form is found in 12:11ff. According to Rashbam, 12:8-14 are the work of the editors who state in vs. 10 "The Preacher sought to find pleasing words and uprightly he wrote words of truth". What follow, in vss. 11ff., are the words of Solomon, quoted by these editors in order to illustrate their point. Thus, the interpretation of vss. 11ff. begins with the words: "And this is what king Solomon used to say".

The last two instances, 8:12 and 9:3b, are found in one pericope with a specific theme — the problem of just retribution — and they are stylistically connected. 8:10ff poses the problem: retribution is late (8:11) unjust (8:14) and the same fate befalls all (9:2). But, in the midst of these harsh words an opposite view is expressed in an entirely positive statement: "Yet I know that it will be well with those who fear God because they fear

142 Gordis pp. 95-109, where he cites all of his other works on the subject.
142a The first part of the verse is translated in the RSV as a question, but the words "See, this is new" are still understood as a citation after: "it is said".

before him but it will not be well with the wicked . . ." (8:12b-13). These words, so divergent in tone and atmosphere from the whole section, are often regarded by critical scholars as a secondary reworking[143], while they are most welcome by conservative commentators, for whom they provide the proof of Qoheleth's positive attitude and adherence to traditional values.

Rashbam is aware of the dissonant views expressed in 12b-13 but, contrary to what we might expect, he regards the divergent conservative statement as a quotation. According to him, the words of Qoheleth in 8:11b, "The heart of the sons of men is fully set to do evil" are the preamble of a quotation; he presents them thus: "Men presume to do evil *and they say:* what does one lose etc.". The following two verses (12-13) are, then, the words of these evil men. While 12a is a statement of fact, 12b-13 are said in wonder and doubt and therefore are negative: "For I do not even know[144] that it will be well with those who fear God . . .". Rashbam's interpretation restores the unity of the section while sharpening and highlighting the theological problem it raised.

A parallel structure is suggested by Rashbam for Qoheleth 9:3b, which is an almost exact repetition of 8:11b. Consistently, he regards the words: "also the hearts of men are full of evil, and madness is in their hearts while they live" as a preamble to a quotation comprising the last words of the verse, "and after that they go to the dead". Rashbam opens his interpretation of these last words with "for they say to themselves", and explains them at length.

Common to all of the above sections is a certain linguistic or literary factor which led Rashbam to posit the existence of a quotation. The linguistic and literary integrity of the text were, then, the determinative

---

143 Cf. the table in Rankin p. 8 and his interpretation on pp. 71-72.

144 The paraphrase of MT, "כי גם יודע אני", is in Rashbam's words: "שהרי אף איני יודע". Since the equivalence with the MT is perfect in three of the four words (כי = שהרי; גם = אף; יודע) the deviation in the fourth, אני — איני which turns the positive into a negative statement, is puzzling. The question is, then, whether a different *Vorlage* is to be assumed, or whether this is how Rashbam understood the sentence after the opening of "כי גם", (Jellinek "solved" the difficulty by harmonizing the text with the MT).

factors; whatever the theological consequences might be, they were accepted.

g. The Lemma (דבור המתחיל)

An important feature of medieval Jewish commentaries is the lemma — דיבור המתחיל, a phenomenon which has not as yet received proper attention, and which we should discuss briefly here[145].

The use of lemmata, while not a universal and mandatory feature of biblical exegesis, is a natural consequence of the particular format of ancient Bibles. Without chapter division or numbering of verses, reference to ancient Hebrew Bibles was rather difficult[146]. In the absence of other aids, a verse was referred to by its opening words — whether or not the interest of the person making reference lay in that part of the verse. Thus, while absolutely essential in certain cases, the lemmata are superfluous in others, when different devices are used for reference or when a commentary is written in the form of glosses on the margins of the biblical text. Indeed, Rosin viewed Rashbam's commentary on the Pentateuch as composed in this way, and only "the first scribe ... when he copied Rashbam's words to a separate book added the lemmata"[147]. The same view was held by Berliner regarding Rashi's commentary on the Pentateuch: "Rashi wrote his commentary on the margins, and afterwards came scribes, each according to his way and wish, and added the lemmata"[148]. Both scholars, then, regarded the lemmata as completely secondary and only naturally found them inconsequential to Rashi's or Rashbam's exegetical work[149].

---

145 For some remarks regarding Rashi's practice cf. Avineri II, p. XXVI.

146 C.D. Ginsburg, *Introduction to the Massoretico-Critical Edition of the Hebrew Bible,* 1896, republished by KTAV, New York, 1966, pp. 25ff. and of course the facsimile editions such as *Pentateuch. Prophets Hagiographa Codex Leningrad B 19a,* Makor Publishing, Jerusalem, 1970; *The Aleppo Codex,* Magnes Press, Jerusalem, 1976.

147 Rosin, Pentateuch p. XXXVI, also Rosin p. 91.

148 Berliner, p. XVI.

149 Consequently, Rosin felt perfectly free to deviate from the Ms. in any matter concerning the lemmata, and freely altered their order and wording in order to conform with MT. Cf. Rosin, Pentateuch pp. XXXVI-XXXVII, above, p. 42.

Our previous conclusion, that Rashbam's commentary on Qoheleth is a coherent, carefully built exegetical composition and not a collection of glosses, as bearing also on the problem of the lemmata. It follows that they can no longer be regarded as a secondary addition to the commentary, but must be seen as an organic and relevant part of it. The guidelines for their use should, therefore, be made as clear as possible.

The lemma serves primarily as a reference in exactly the same capacity as the numbers of chapter and verse in modern commentaries. It generally comprises the first words of the biblical passage; these are meant as a reference only, and are not necessarily the very words which are discussed in the commentary itself. The scope of the biblical passage is decided by the commentator: it can be a verse, a part of a verse (especially when the verse is composed of distinct independent parts), or a unit longer than a verse[150]. Lemmata vary in length, but they tend to be short, mostly comprising between two and four words which form an intelligible linguistic unit. In general, the lemma is detached from the interpretation; with very few exceptions the separation is indicated, in addition to the syntactical structure, by a dot. This is the equivalent of a weak break, like the modern comma or colon[151].

A second category of lemmata includes such words and phrases as are the explicit subject of the explanation. These are mostly exegetical details which do not refer beyond themselves[152]. These lemmata are usually even shorter than the first group and might consist of only one word. Within the specific structure of Rashbam's commentaries, many of these lemmata are found at the end of the exegetical units, where the details are discussed one by one[153].

150 All the examples concerning the lemmata were taken from one chapter, chapter 4: in 4:2 the lemma is "ושבח אני", but the whole verse is subsequently interpreted; in 4:6 the interpretation is divided into two parts, each following a lemma; the first "better is a handful of quietness" stands for the first colon and the second, "than two hands full of toil" stands for the second. In 4:7 the lemma "Again, I" is followed by the interpretation of a verse and a half, etc.

151 On the punctuation system of the Ms., cf. below, pp. 73-74.

152 See, for example, the following lemmata: 4:2 — עדנה; 4:4 — skill; 4:9 — a good reward; 4:12 — יתקפו; 4:13 — poor; 4:14 — הסורים.

153 In ch. 4 the rule applies to vss. 2, 10-11, 12, 13, 15-16.

In addition to these two categories, where the lemmata are clearly separated from the interpretation and easily distinguishable, there is a third group which represents a specific exegetical technique. Here the interpretation is constructed as a syntactical continuation of the introductory lemma, and the two form one continuous sentence[154].

For example: in 2:9 the lemma is "So I became great and surpassed"; the interpretation then proceeds "in wealth, doing all these things etc.". It is clear that the biblical words serve in a double capacity: besides indicating the reference, they also form a part of the interpretation itself[155]. In other cases the procedure is somewhat more complicated. After the lemma comes a short explanation, which refers in fact only to a detail or a precise nuance; then the verse goes on as a new lemma, followed by the interpretation proper. For example: in 1:7 the lemma is — "to the place where the streams flow" and the interpretation proceeds: "to that place, today", referring in fact only to one matter: to the interpretation of "flow" as present tense, and not as an iterative; the verse then continues as a new lemma, "there they flow again" — and only here the main interpretation of the whole verse begins[156]. There are several variations in the use of this technique but its main feature is the fact that the interpretation is a direct continuation of the lemma, which thus serves in a double capacity, and both lemma and commentary are integrated in one sentence.

The origin of this technique seems to have been in the practice of glosses, where the interpretative words were affixed to the text itself. However, its persistence and use in an exegetical composition can be explained by the striving for economy and brevity, which is a marked feature of Rashbam's work. Surprisingly enough, this technique is not frequent in Rashbam's commentary on Qoheleth and it is the other two functions which dominate.

Another quite surprising aspect of the lemmata is the great number of deviations from MT. Disregarding the regular changes of the "defective" spelling of the MT to a "fuller" one, which occur about eighty times in the lemmata alone, there are over forty instances of various divergences from MT in the lemmata in our commentary. Their nature varies — there are

154 Cf. Avineri II, p. XXV for some remarks regarding Rashi's practice.
155 Similarly 2:3 (third lemma); 3:12, etc.
156 Similarly 4:1b; 5:3 etc.

differences of spelling[157], additions of *Waw copulativum*[158], changes or addition of prepositions[159], omissions of words[160], etc.

What are the reasons for these deviations, and to whom are they to be attributed? Not all of them can be classified with certainty, as there is always a 'wide range of possibilities in these matters. Still, some basic features are clearly distinguishable.

A very small percentage probably represents real variant readings — the *Vorlage* used by the commentator being different from MT[161]. Although few in number, these have bearing upon the whole problem of transmission in medieval Mss. On the other end is another group of deviations which should be attributed to the scribe(s) who made similar mistakes in both the lemmata and the commentary. These include not only errors which are orthographically obvious[162], but also those cases in which the subsequent interpretations relate to the MT and not to the lemma as actually written[163].

However, all these cases, in which the changes are certainly not to be attributed to the commentator, amount to only a part of the deviations; there still remains a large number of cases which are best explained as originating with the commentator himself. Here the deviation seems to be a result of the influence which the living language and the exegetical process exert on the phrasing of the lemmata. These include the additions of *Waw*

---

157 Cf. 5:15; 7:23 (Ms. זו MT זה); 12:11 (Ms. מסמרות MT משמרות).

158 1:17 (MT רעיון); 3:21 (MT מי); 6:5 (MT גם);7:19 (MT החכמה);8:3 (MT אל); 8:14 (MT יש); 9:1 (MT גם); 10:5 (MT יש); 12:5 (MT יראו).

159 1:8 (MS. לשמוע MT משמע); 5:1 (Ms. את MT על); 8:6 (Ms. על כל MT לכל); 12:9 (Ms. לדעת MT דעת).

160 2:18 (Ms. עמלי MT את עמלי); 2:24 (Ms. אין טוב שיאכל MT אין טוב באדם שיאכל); כי גם האדם (Ms. 9:12 MT וראיתי את כל מעשה האלהים ואראתי את כל המעשה); 8:17 (Ms. עד אשר לא תחשך השמש MT עד לא תחשך השמש); 12:2 (Ms. כי גם לא ידע האדם MT את האדם); 12:14 (Ms. כי את כל מעשה MT כי את מעשה).

161 One of these i.e., אחריו instead of MT אחרי in 2:18 was already pointed out by Rosin, p. 59 note 2. Cf. the edition *ad loc*. The other possible variants are 8:10 (Ms. הלכו MT יהלכו) and 8:15 (Ms. ושבח אני MT ושבחתי).

162 E.g., 4:14 (Ms. פסורים MT הסורים);5:7 (Ms. שמור MT שמר); 12:4 (Ms. לכל MT לקול); 12:5 (Ms. והתחתים MT וחתחתים); 12:5 (Ms. כאביונה MT האביונה).

163 Such as 2:7 (Ms. שהיה MT שהיו); 7:14 (Ms. טוב MT בטוב);7:26 (Ms. ומוציא MT ומוצא); 9:1 (Ms. ולבור MT ולבר); 12:4 (Ms. וישאו MT וישחו).

58

copulativum, the alterations of prepositions and other particles and above all the contraction of the opening phrase by omitting words while preserving the lemma as an intelligible linguistic unit[164].

The conclusion to be drawn from these facts transcend the realm of the lemmata and concern the status of the biblical texts incorporated into the commentary *vis à vis* the biblical Mss. proper. It would seem that the rigorism and meticulousness observed in handling the biblical Mss., and the careful attention paid to every sign and detail no matter how small, were not carried through into the commentary, either by the scribe or by the commentator. The differing standards would account not only for the many deviations in the lemmata, but also for the loose way in which biblical quotations were cited[165] and for the inaccuracy of the vowel-signs[166]. In the framework of the commentary all these are regarded as means to the end of interpretation; they are cited to perform a specific task and as long as this task is performed their accuracy *per se* is not made an issue. Thus biblical Mss. and commentaries on biblical texts should be regarded as two distinct spheres from the point of view of transmission. The rigorous rules applied in the one case are not automatically carried over to the other, in spite of their common subject matter.

h. "Literal Interpretation" and Rashbam's Attitude Towards his Predecessors

Perhaps the most well-known feature of Rashbam's work is his conscious, determined and successful effort to interpret according to the "Peshat" — the "literal meaning"[167]. Most familiar are his programmatic

---

164 To the references in notes 158-160 the following could be added: 3:19 (Ms. כי מקרה כי מקרה בני האדם MT אחד; the phrasing of the Ms. is probably influenced by ומקרה אחד להם, found later in the same verse); 3:19 (Ms. ורוח אחד להם MT ורוח אחד לכל); 4:16 (Ms. שגם MT כי גם).

165 Cf. Salters, Variant Readings, pp. 85-90.

166 Cf. below, pp. 71-72.

167 Cf., *inter al.,* Rosin pp. 77-81; Poznanski, pp. XL-XLIII; Lifshitz pp. 190; Kamin, pp. 300-303; Gelles, pp. 123-127, 132-133 etc.

statements to that effect, found in his commentary on the Pentateuch[168].
What is the evidence of the commentary on Qoheleth in this respect?

It whould be stated at the outset that the distinction between "Peshat"
and "Derash", i.e., between the "literal" as opposed to the "homiletic"
meaning, is not a determination between "correct" and "incorrect". As
emphasized lately by both Kamin and Simon[169], this distinction is between
two different methods of exegesis, based on different principles and aiming
at different goals.

No programmatic statements are found in the commentary on Qoheleth.
Even the phrase "פשוטו של מקרא"[170] is found only twice, in 3:2-8 and, with
a slight difference, in 8:10-13. In both places it appears alone, with no
further elaboration, and serves as a kind of recommendation for the
proposed interpretation of the unit[171]. In itself the phrase has polemic
overtones, but in its two occurrences the polemic edge is not specified, nor
are the exact views against which it is directed. The absence of any
programmatic statement can be explained by two factors, one of which is
the nature of the material. In a commentry on the Pentateuch the "literal
meaning" might not only deviate from traditional homiletic views but might
actually conflict with normative halachic precepts. A clear statement of

---

168 Berger, pp. 13ff. and throughout his study. Cf. especially his introductions to the interpretations of Gen. 1:1; 37:2; Ex. 21:2.

169 Kamin, pp. 1-16; Simon, pp. 133-135.

170 On its origin, its meaning in the Talmud and its use by Rashi, cf. Kamin, pp. 38-50; 77-
108. The references in Rashbam's commentary on the Pentateuch are collected by
Rosin, p. 80, notes 2-6.

171 According to Rashbam all the "times" cited in 3:2-8 are included in the rule, stated at
the end: "a time for war and a time for peace". Exceptions to the rule, says Rashbam
are "a time to be born" and according to פשוטו של מקרא — "a time to keep silence and
a time to speak". Thus, the statement "פשוטו של מקרא" concerns here only the exclu-
sion of vs. 7b from the general rule which governs the whole unit. It is interesting to
note, however, that the understanding of 3:2-8 as a series of examples of the rule of vs.
8b is already found in the Midrash (cf. Yalkut Shimeoni, II, section 1068, and with
variation in Qohelet Rabbah, III, 4). As far as we can see the words "פשוטו של מקרא"
in this context have no specific polemic intention. In 8:10-13 Rashbam introduces the
interpretation with the words "וכן פתרונו לפי פשוטו" — "this is its explanation according to its literal meaning", but this is followed by a straight interpretation without
explicit polemic points.

intentions, methods and attitudes is thus almost required. Qoheleth is, of course, a different matter. The subject-matter of Qoheleth is not in the realm of the Halacha, and the traditional, homiletic interpretations of the book are *a priori* on a different level of authority. A new exegetical approach would be simply another effort to cope with the book's message, and its conclusion might influence one's religious world view, but there would be no immediate results for the halachic practice. The second factor seems to be of a more personal and psychological nature. It seems that Rashbam has reached a certain degree of conviction which allows him to follow his own principles without the need for polemic or self-justification. Thus, in the absence of direct statements, the issue must be deduced from the work itself.

Several pertinent points have come to light in the course of our discussion. They all point to the same conclusion: the commentary on Qoheleth is an unflagging effort to achieve a clear, if implicit, goal: the "literal meaning". However, some further words on the problem are in order.

One of the terms used by Rashbam to define the literal meaning is אמתת פשוטו[172] which can be understood in two different ways. According to the first the two nouns of the construct state are mutually descriptive, as a noun and an adjective, and the meaning would then be "the literal, true meaning". According to the second, the two nouns are in the genitive, and the definition would mean "the truth of the literal meaning", that is, there is a "truth" in the exegetical level of "Peshat" and this "truth" is the goal of the exegete's efforts, the only interpretation which is the "literal meaning". The understanding of the literal meaning as אמתת פשוטו is the origin of one of the leading characteristics of Rashbam's commentaries, i.e. that a text has only one, single meaning. This principle is applied with absolute consistency throughout the commentary on Qoheleth. A word, a phrase, a verse — when found in a given context — can have one and only one interpretation. Thus the practice which is so common in Jewish exegetical tradition, including medieval commentators, of suggesting several possibilities for interpreting a given text, is completely absent from

172 In his interpretation of Lev. 10:3.

Rashbam's works. According to his view as our knowledge progresses, an interpretation might be found incorrect or deficient, needing to be replaced or supplemented as the case might be; but there can never be two correct interpretations of one text. Thus, the commentator's burden of responsibility is weighty indeed, for it is the single truth of the "literal meaning" of Scripture which he is called upon to reveal.

In order to realize this goal Rashbam summons up a fine sensitivity to and knowledge of language, an unusual insight into the realm of literary expression, an awareness of the nuances of textual transmission[173], an acquaintance with the world of his day and appreciation of the varieties of human experience as a source of knowledge, and the broadest familiarity with everything Jewish. All these are guided on the one hand by a clear and conscious awareness of the boundaries of context, both linguistic and literary, and of the legitimate sources upon which one may draw — and on the other hand by an unfailing willingness to accept whatever conclusions may arise from these methods of interpretation.

In the framework of his method, what is Rashbam's attitude toward the vast exegetical tradition which preceded him? Regarding the homiletic tradition a preliminary methodological distinction is necessary, that is, a distinction between the Midrash as a body of literature, the fruit of a long history of literary creativity, and the Midrash (or Derash) as a method of interpretation. Not everything in the vast "Midrashic" literature is to be categorized as "Midrash" according to its methodological presuppositions. It seems that such a distinction is recognized also by Rashbam. He does avail himself of the homiletic literature, but the interpretations he adopts can be defined as literal[174]. However, his use of Rabbinic and homiletic sources is not frequent, and only rarely does he mention his sources by name[175].

---

173 Cf. Rosin p. 59 note 2; S. Esh, "Variant Readings in Medieval Hebrew Commentaries: R. Samuel Ben Meir (Rashbam)", *Textus* 5, 1966, p. 84ff.

174 An example of this type is the interpretation of 3:2-8, mentioned in note 171.

175 After commenting on 5:7 Rashbam says: "It is similar to an Aggadic Midrash (מדרש אגדה) on Ex. 33:13". The implied reference is to BT, Berachot, 7a. In three places Rashbam illustrates his interpretation with sayings taken from Rabbinic sources, without giving a specific reference. In 5:1: "And so did the sages say" (citing Mishna,

All explicit references to earlier literature are positive in nature; in the whole commentary on Qoheleth there is no overt controversy with the homiletic tradition. Similarly, none of Rashbam's predecessors is ever mentioned, either with approval or disapproval. Although his interpretations themselves are influenced, no doubt, by the works of his predecessors[176] and may be better understood by realizing Rashbam's attitude, whether positive or negative, *vis à vis* these works, no explicit reference is ever made. In a very austere way he permits the matter to speak for itself, through an exegetical effort aimed at achieving the "truth of the literal meaning".

i. "Contradictory Statements", Joy, Vanity and Wisdom in Qoheleth

The book of Qoheleth differs in several respects from the other books of the Bible. Its existence and, more specifically, its enumeration among the Scriptures, have posed a serious problem to many generations of traditional Judaism. Its sayings have been described as contradictory, contrary to the Law, and conducive to heresy[177]. Much of the homiletic effort put into the interpretation of the book was devoted to a smoothing over of these difficulties. Having denied himself the comforts of homiletics, how did Rashbam cope with the book's message, and how was it integrated into his traditional Jewish outlook?

Aboth, 1:17); in 5:10: "As our Rabbis said" (citing from BT, Ketuvoth, 103a.); and in 10:8-9: "like what our Rabbis said" (citing from BT, Pesachim,28a.). In 7:24 he mentions "Merkavah mysticism' and "the Book of Creation" as examples of wisdom which is beyond human grasp, but he does not elaborate on these works. In 2:8 there is reference to a Rabbinic phrase "a chest, a box or a cupboard" (שידה תבה ומגדל) with the introductory word "כמו", generally used for biblical references. (Referring to Mishna Sabbath,16:5 *et al.*). Cf. also Salters, Observations pp. 55-56.

176 Principally Rashi. Rashbam's attitude to the actual exegetical work of his grandfather is quite complex; we cannot do it full justice by a comparison of their commentaries to Qoheleth alone. The whole range of Rashi's work has to be considered (cf. for example, below, note 190), a task which is beyond the scope of this work.

177 Cf. Mishna Eduyoth,5:3; Mishna Yadayim,3:5; Tosefta Yadayim,2:14; BT, Shabbath, 30b; ibid. Megillah,7a; Aboth de R. Nathan,ch. 1; Pesikta de Rab Kahana,piska 8; Qoheleth Rabbah,1:4. Cf. Gordis pp. 41-42.

A detailed answer to this question would entail a superfluous repetition of almost all of Rashbam's work; we will restrict ourselves, then, to one aspect of the question — that of contradictory statements. Most prominent among these are Qoheleth's dicta concerning wisdom, joy and God's justice. Having referred briefly to the last topic[178], we will deal here with the first two only.

In the Babylonian Talmud, Shabbath, 30b, we find: "Rab Judah, son of R. Samuel b. Shilath said in Rab's name: The sages wished to hide the Book of Ecclesiastes because its words are self-contradictory . . . And how are its words self-contradictory? It is written: "anger is better than play (שחוק)" (7:3) but it is written: "I said of laughter (שחוק) it is to be praised" (2:2). It is written "Then I commended joy (שמחה)" (8:15) but it is written: "and of joy (שמחה) (I said) What doeth it" (2:2)[179].

שחוק, always translated by the RSV as "laughter", is found in four places in Qoheleth, in two of which it is paralleled with שמ"ח[180]. Accordingly, Rashbam regards the two roots as partially synonymous, שחוק being always negative whereas שמ"ח is either negative or positive. שחוק is "the merriment of the house of feasting" (on 7:3), which should be understood as "frivolity" rather than as "laughter"[181]. It is the way of life of the fool: "Fools are attracted to and are anxious to go to the house of mirth, and this mirth leads them to sin" (on 7:7), therefore "a man should keep away from fools and the frivolity of their words" (on 7:6). The search for happiness through wine and pleasures was among the experiments

---

178 Above, pp. 53-54, and also below, p. 67.

179 Earlier in the passage there is a reference to Qoheleth's contradictory statements about death: "Thou, Solomòn, where is thy wisdom and where is thy understanding? It is not enough for thee that thy words contradict the words of thy father, David, but that they are self-contradictory! Thy father David said 'The dead praise not the Lord' (Ps. 115:17) whilst thou saidest 'Wherefore I praised the dead which are already dead' (Qoh. 4:2) but yet again thou saidest 'for a living dog is better than a dead lion' (Qoh. 9:4)" (BT Shabbath, 30a).

180 2:2; 10:19. The other two are 7:3, 6. Altogether שחוק is found fifteen times in the Bible, only in one other instance does it parallel שמ"ח: Prov. 14:13.

181 This equation is found in the saying of R. Akiba: "שחוק וקלות ראש מרגילין לערוה" — R. Akiba said: Jesting and levity accustom a man to lewdness (Mishna, Aboth, 3:14). Cf. also Ginsberg, pp. 66, 96-97.

which Qoheleth undertook in the course of his quest for meaning; his verdict was unequivocal: שחוק is mad! Contrary to the Sages in Shabbath 30b but in concordance with the usage of Qoheleth, Rashbam understands מהולל in 2:2 not as "praiseworthy" but as exactly the opposite, as "mad"[182]. Qoheleth's message regarding שחוק is consistent and simple: it is madness and folly.

The verb שמח and the derived noun vjna express one of the *leit-motifs* of Qoheleth: the idea of the one and only good in man's life. In its seventeen occurrences in Qoheleth[183] it has, according to Rashbam, two basic meanings. One is negative, parallel to שחוק and denoting the hollow joy of the tavern, the merriment produced by wine. In 7:2-7 Rashbam follows Qoheleth in enlarging upon this kind of "joy". The antithesis to "the house of mourning" in 7:2 is "the house of feasting" (בית משתה) while in 7:4 it is "the house of mirth" (בית שמחה). The equation of "mirth" with "feasting" determines its value and explains the strong repudiation. When Qoheleth describes his experiments he reaches clear conclusions regarding this kind of "joy": "and of pleasure (שמחה) (I said) 'What use is it?'" (2:2).

On the other hand there is joy, or happiness, as God's greatest gift to man[184]. Regarding the nature of this 'joy' Rashbam makes his point very clear, by following the method he employs in all important matters, namely repetition. For him, happiness and joy are the opposite of hedonistic pursuit. Joy is man's contentment with his lot, his satisfaction with what he has and his ability to enjoy the fruits of his work. Qoheleth's dictum: "to eat, to drink and to rejoice"[185] is presented by Rashbam as: "eating and drinking and rejoicing, to be happy in his lot"[186]. Extravagant pleasures, the hedonistic pursuits, are included in the experiments of Qoheleth which are declared to be "vanity". The happiness which Qoheleth recommends is

---

182 Cf. its use in 1:17; 2:12; 7:7, 25; 9:3; 10:13, and Barton p. 88, Gordis, p. 215. It seems that its use is similar to that of Rabbinic שוטה, denoting both "fool, foolish" and "mad".

183 2:1, 2, 10 (twice), 26; 3:12, 22; 4:16; 5:18, 19; 7:4; 8:15 (twice); 9:7; 10:19; 11:8, 9.

184 Cf. on 5:18 as well as on 3:13.

185 8:15. The RSV has here: "to eat and drink and enjoy himself". Cf. also 2:24; 3:12-13; 5:17; 9:7ff.

186 On 8:15. Similarly on 1:3; 3:22; 5:17, 18, 19; 9:7-10.

fully in keeping with Rashbam's view: the acceptance and enjoyment of one's allotted portion in life as God's gift.

The contradictory expressions of Qoheleth include his references to wisdom, both regarding its value (2:13 versus 2:15-16) and attainability (1:16 versus 7:23-24). Rashbam's stand on this topic is stated explicitly. According to him, Qoheleth is referring to two kinds, or degrees, of wisdom — the distinction between them being marked also by linguistic precision. One kind is "the common wisdom", "in which there is no depth", "which the world needs"; the other is "the profound wisdom, which men neither need nor are conversant with" (on 2:3, 13). The "ordinary wisdom" secures the successful management of mundane life, the conduct of personal and public affairs. It is the practical "know-how", accessible and beneficial. The "profound wisdom", on the other hand, is beyond man's powers and therefore unattainable. It does not center on man but on God and tries to penetrate the mysteries of his acts: "acts of the Holy One which he does in the world — why he does them" (on 1:18). Its scope includes the secrets of creation and the mystical worlds[187]. Its pursuit, with no prospects of attainment, is a source of sorrow and pain (on 1:18).

According to Rashbam, the difference between the two levels of wisdom is indicated linguistically as well. The "ordinary wisdom" is put in the definite state, while the "profound" is referred to in an indefinite manner[188].

Of significance in this context is the special treatment of the word הבל — "vanity". The most prominent of Qoheleth's terms, it recurs often also in the commentary[189], usually without an explicit explanation. The use of synonyms like תהו (emptiness, void, on 5:2, 5 etc.), ריק (void, on 5:2) רוח (wind, on 5:5) רעה (evil, on 11:8), and the constant contrast with יתרון (advantage, on 2:1, 11; 3:21 etc.) and its synonyms, benefit and profit (שכר, ריוח) make its basic meaning quite clear, while the nuances are left to

---

187 On 7:24. This is the only reference in Rashbam's works to the realm of early cosmological and mystical literature, represented by the "Merkabah Mysticism" (מעשה מרכבה) and the "Book of Creation" (ספר יצירה).

188 On 2:13. This linguistic distinction is not mentioned again.

189 Cf. above p. 35 on the treatment of the full phrase "this too is vanity". In addition to its frequent occurrence in the lemmata (over twenty times) it is often repeated in the commentary itself.

be determined by the respective contexts. Only in one context, however, does Rashbam refer explicitly to the meaning of הבל and it is at first surprising that its meaning there diverges from its general usage.

In the commentary on 8:10-14, the meaning of הבל is referred to three times, and its essence is: "I said that this also is vanity — I wonder and am amazed at this". הבל in this context is not "nothing and void", but "that which is hidden from men, which men cannot understand clearly". The passage deals with the problem of God's justice, which belongs to the realm of "profound wisdom" — "acts of the Holy One which he does in the world — why He does them". Here man cannot act as a judge. In the realm of "ordinary wisdom" on the other hand, an experience, a phenomenon, can indeed be declared as meaningless, worthless, because here man is qualified to judge. In the realm of "profound wisdom" there is no "vanity". Things may appear to be vanity and man may express his wonder[190], but the understanding of the phenomena, not to mention their causes, is beyond his powers. The "profound wisdom" is an unopened book.

As the whole sphere of God's justice is part of the "profound wisdom" and the guiding principles of retribution will remain forever hidden from man's knowledge — how should one conduct his life? For Rashbam the answer is very simple: in full conformity with traditional values and precepts. According to him Qoheleth's advice can be epitomized as follows: Believe in God, fear Him, keep His commandments, avoid sin, enjoy your lot when it is good and accept it when bad, and repent[191].

---

190 Although Rashbam does not specify the semantic path which led him to this interpretation, it seems to be as follows. One of the frequent synonyms of הבל is תהו. A long homiletic tradition connects תהו with the root תה"א, found only in Rabbinic literature and meaning "to gaze, marvel, wonder". On the famous והארץ היתה תהו ובהו of Gen. 1:2 we find in Genesis Rabbah 2:1ff, repeatedly "ישבה הארץ תוהא ובוהא" "The land was sitting marvelling and gazing". In his interpretation of תהו ובהו in Gen. 1:2 Rashi expresses a similar idea but uses the verbs "תוהא ומשתוממם", the same words used by Rashbam in Qoh. 8:10-14. It would seem, then, that Rashbam broadened the synonymity of הבל and תהו by attributing to הבל also the meaning of "marvel, wonder", traditionally assumed for תהו.

191 Cf., *inter al.* on 3:11-15; 7:13-14, 20; 9:4-5; 11:7-8; 12:1-5.

The world of Qoheleth as portrayed by Rashbam is unified and positive. We would even venture to say that the portrayal of Qoheleth could be a selfportrait of Rashbam. Drawn so powerfully to the quest for wisdom and to the joy of intellectual exploration, Rashbam has willingly bound himself to tradition. God's ways and demands are beyond man's power of comprehension and it is man's task to acknowledge his limits and to live by his faith.

CHAPTER THREE

THE EDITION

a. Major Shortcomings of Jellinek's Edition

Rashbam's commentary on Qoheleth is preserved in a single Ms. and since its publication by Jellinek in 1855 no other Ms., complete or fragmentary, has come to light. Yet, a new edition of the commentary is very much needed. Jellinek's edition is unreliable, and far from satisfying the standards of the modern reader. Some of its shortcomings were referred to in the course of the preceding discussion, and we will list here its major drawbacks.

1. The printed edition is not a reliable presentation of the Ms. and deviates from it in a large number of words. Some of these are probably just errors, the result of a wrong reading of the Ms. or of printing errors; others however, seem to be intentional changes, introduced consciously by the editor. These intentional changes vary: some are corrections of obvious mistakes found in the Ms; in others Jellinek "improved" the spelling or the language of the Ms, harmonized it with the Massoretic text, and the like. The most important point, however, is not the changes themselves but the fact that they are not brought to the attention of the reader, except in very few cases[1]. A brief survey of his way of dealing with one chapter, 12, will demonstrate this point.

---

[1] In only four instances in the entire commentary does he mention such a change (2:13; 3:18; 10:11; 12:2). The result is at best misleading, as it creates the illusion of a non-existent precision.

Ignoring for the time being deviations in spelling and abbreviations, we counted over thirty words in this chapter in which the printed edition deviates from the Ms.; only one of these is referred to in a nóte[2]. Without attempting a flawless classification, we may categorize the changes as mistakes made either by the editor or by the printer, harmonizations with the MT and intentional corrections.

Mistakes: vs. 4 נסתמו (Ms. אחר כך) אחר כן (Ms. יבוא) יבאו 2 .vs (Ms. סידרוהו) סידורוהו 8 .vs (³וה"י .Ms) והיא 5 .vs (ישפל .Ms) ישפיל (נסתתמו vs. 12 הן (Ms. הם).

Harmonizations with MT: vs. 2 עד אשר לא (Ms. עד לא) vs. 4 לקול (Ms. כי הולך (ויאנץ .Ms) בקול (וישאו) וישחו (לכל (Ms. קול) vs. 5 וינאץ (twice; Ms. (Ms. אל תירא) ואל תירא (Ms. ויראו והתחתים) ייראו וחתחתים (כי הוא הולך .Ms האביונה (Ms. כאביונה) vs. 6 על המבוע (Ms. על פניה) vs. 9 דעת (Ms. לדעת) vs. 11 משמרות 14 .vs (כי את כל מעשה (Ms. מסמרות) twice; Ms. (כי את מעשה).

Corrections: vs. 2 כמו (Ms. וזהו) vs. 3 שתהא (Ms. שתהיו) השינים (Ms. בשינים) vs. 3, 4, 5 זקנותו (Ms. זקנתו) vs. 4 שרים ושרות (Ms. שרים ושרים 5 .vs (Ms. הנקר') הנק"א 7 .vs (ויתאנץ .Ms) ויתרוצץ (תאוה .Ms) תאבה 6 .vs (הנקר' .Ms) הנק"א כמו 14 .vs (שבכולן .Ms) שכולן (המקרא .Ms) המקנה 11 .vs (הן .Ms) והוא (היא) (added).

In addition, there is a case of dittography in the Ms. (vs. 4) which Jellinek rightly omits but fails to mention.

Of the last group, some of the corrections are probably justified, as the scribe was far from perfect. Still, Jellinek's carelessness on the one hand, and his arbitrariness on the other, are quite apparent.

2. As is the case in other Mss. of the same period, our Ms. is not consistent in matters of plene and defective spelling, abbreviations and vocalization. Jellinek's general attitude to this seems to be that of "improvement", namely, an intention to produce a text which will better conform with the standards of his day. However, even this resolve is not

---

2   The word וזהו in the interpretation of vs. 2, arbitrarily changed into כמו. The change interferes with the flow of the interpretation and obscures its meaning. There is no attempt to justify it.

3   In this case the mistake makes the printed text unintelligible. Discussing the word אביונה Rashbam first explains the word אבין and then states that the final ה"י designates the feminine. In the printed text the second sentence makes no sense.

70

carried out consistently. In the matter of spelling his general preference is for a spelling which is more defective than the quite full one of the Ms.; consequently, the changes from plene to defective are very numerous, but still neither consistent nor systematic[4].

As to abbreviations, Jellinek's general tendency is to present the abbreviated words in their full form; in this he is almost consistent. Even here, however, there are exceptions, and occasionally abbreviations are left unchanged[5]. The regular abbreviation found in the Ms. of the word הקדוש — "the Holy One", into הק'[6] is retained in the printed edition.

On the other hand, Jellinek introduced into the text a convention which is foreign to the Ms.: the abbreviation of all words ending with the letters יה, a practice he holds to even within the lemmata[7]. This practice accords with the scribal conventions of Jellinek's own time, but as the Ms. shows is foreign to its scribe.

The inconsistency of the Ms. can be detected also in the realm of vowel-signs. The vocalized words belong to three groups: a) French glosses[8] b) words which are discussed from a linguistic, mainly morphological, point of view[9] c) words which might seem unclear without the vowel-signs[10]. This

---

4   In ch. 12 Jellinek omits vowel letters in ten words, such as זיקנה in vs. 1; בטילות in vs. 3, הציפור in vs. 4; ציביון in vs. 5 etc. but leaves untouched other words with similar full writing like החיצונים in vs. 4; בטילה in vs. 5, סידרוהו in vs. 8 etc. Among the changed words is אוזניו, which he prints as אזניו (vs. 9), but the same word אוזן is left unaltered in one of its occurrences in 1:8, etc.

5   Thus, to illustrate from ch. 12, the following words are abbreviated in the Ms. and written in full in the printed edition: vs. שנ', שנ', כעיני', לש'. 2, vs. 4 — ודוגמ', דוגמ', העול', vs. 11 — לומ' vs. 8 — לשר', כמ' vs. 7 — דוגמ', כמ', לשר, כמ', לשר — 5 החכמ'. However, in 12:13 the abbreviated וג' is turned into וגו' and in vs. 5 בלע' is left ulchanged.

6   The only exception is in 7:26, where the Ms. has הקדוש in full. This Jellinek abbreviates as well.

7   The following are abbreviated in ch. 12, vs. 1 — תהי', ותהי' (Ms. – תהיה, ותהיה) vs. 2 — ותהי', ויהי' (Ms. – ותהיה, ויהיה) vs. 5 — תהי', שתהי', יהי' (Ms. – תהיה, שתהיה, יהיה) vs. 7 — עלי' (Ms. – עליה) vs. 9 — שהי' (Ms. – שהיה) vs. 11 — הי' (Ms. – היה).

8   In the interpretations of 1:16; 6:12-13; 7:25; 9:1; 11:9.

9   In the interpretations of: 1:12-13, 14, 17; 2:13-14; 3:16, 18; 5:7, 9; 7:16-18, 19; 8:10-13; 10:17, 18; 12:11-14.

10 In the interpretations of 4:10-11, 12; 9:2-3; 10:18; 11:3.

categorization may indicate that the vocalisation was introduced by Rashbam himself as part of the interpretation, in spite of the fact that at times it deviates from that of MT. As a rule, Jellinek omitted the vowel-signs, but there are sporadic cases in which the signs are suddenly introduced[11].

3. Jellinek did not recognize the particular structure and style of the commentary; he made every effort to adjust it, as far as he could, to a verse by verse format, and tended to regard as lemmata many words and phrases which were indeed taken from the biblical text but not used as lemmata by the commentator[12]. These procedures interfere with the commentator's work, and greatly hinder the correct understanding and appreciation of his achievement.

4. Jellinek has provided his edition with almost no critical apparatus, not even for such simple matters as biblical references. The only element which receives full coverage is the transliteration and translation of the French glosses. Altogether, there are sixteen notes in the whole edition[13], as well as some occasional references.

b. Guiding Principles of the Present Edition

The fundamental point of departure of the present edition is a greater respect for both the commentator and the scribe(s) and a faithful presentation of their work. Thus, two rules are applied in dealing with the Ms. text: a) The text is reproduced as it stands, with its spelling, abbreviations, vocalization and the like. No attempt has been made to fill in the defective spelling, to reduce the plene, to fill out the abbreviations or to abbreviate the full. The vowel signs have been left as they are, even if they do not conform to Massoretic vocalization, and no other words have been vocalized. The only parts of the text that have not been reproduced are the various devices used by the scribe to preserve an even left margin, including

11 On 3:16; 5:7; 7:18.
12 Cf. above, pp. 38-41, and note 104.
13 Divided as follows: seven are interpretations of French glosses; four refer to a change introduced in the edition; two are references; two are explanations of obscure points and one is a proposal for a change which was not introduced in the text.

letters, signs and parts of words[14]. b) any necessary alteration of the text (cf. below) has been noted and pointed out.

Although interference with the Ms. has been reduced to a minimum, some changes were, nevertheless, required. These were made in the following cases:

1) The division into chapters and verses with their numbers was introduced into the text in order to facilitate the use of the commentary by the modern reader. 2) The lemmata were printed in a different type. 3) In cases of scribal errors which were noticed by the scribe and marked in the Ms. in one way or another — dots, strokes, marginal corrections and the like — the text was reproduced free of error and the scribal activity was taken note of in the apparatus. 4) In the case of obvious scribal errors which went unnoticed by the scribe but can be easily attributed to scribal activity — exchanges of similar letters, metatheses, dittographies, omissions and the like — the text was corrected and the change was referred to in the apparatus. In the less obvious cases the necessary change was proposed but not actually introduced into the text.

Special attention has been paid to two features of the Ms. which are very important for the correct understanding of the commentary: the punctuation, and the lemmata. The Ms. has a punctuation system of its own which comprises two signs: a dot, usually placed in the upper part of the line, after the word, and two dots, either vertical, like a colon (:) or horizontal, in the upper part of the line (··). While the dot-sign is used regularly, the two-dots sign is rather rare, and appears only seven times in the entire commentary[15].

The dot signifies a pause of varying length: from short, as a comma, to long, as full stop. Its use is not regulated by firm syntactical laws; it seems, rather, that whenever the writer (or the scribe?) feels that a pause is needed, a dot is introduced. There are, however, some basic rules which are followed quite systematically and can be detected. Most prominent are the introduction of a dot at the end of a sentence and at the end of a lemma. Two dots signify a longer pause, e.g., the end of a large section (a *Parasha*).

---

14 Cf. Beit Arié, p. 87ff.
15 At the end of the interpretations of 2:26; 3:1; 5:19; 6:12; 7:26; 12:7, 14.

The sign is sometimes accompanied by an empty space left in the line, accentuating the pause.

After much hesitation, we decided to introduce the punctuation system of the Ms. into the printed edition, and not to replace it with a modern one, which is itself already an interpretation. Only in very few cases, where the introduction of a dot seemed completely out of place, did we omit it. In dubious cases, arising from the condition of the Ms. and found mainly at the ends of lines, we used our judgement, feeling that the whole subject still awaits the treatment of a specialist.

The lemmata required special consideration. As pointed out above[16], the particular language of the commentary is created, among other things, by the admixture of the exegete's own words with phrases and parts of verses taken from the interpreted text and interwoven into the running commentary. Thus, not all segments of biblical text are lemmata, and to decide which ones are is not a simple task. An important tool in the delineation of the lemmata was the punctuation system of the Ms.: most of the lemmata are enclosed between two signs, a dot at the end of the preceding interpretation and a dot after the lemma, before the subsequent interpretation. However, the rule is not inviolate, and there is a considerable number of exceptions, especially regarding the second of these dots[17]. Our decision regarding the dubious cases was based in every case on the dynamics of the commentary and not on any external signs; only the lemmata were emphasized with a special type and not any other part of the verse in whatever other capacity.

Regarding the phrasing of the lemmata, we followed our basic rules stated above. Contrary to Jellinek we did not harmonize them with the MT, but merely noted the deviations in the footnotes[18]. We corrected the lemmata only in the very few cases of obvious scribal errors, mentioning the change, as always, in a footnote[19].

16 P. 42ff.

17 This is due not only to the loose practices of the scribes, but also to the specific nature of some of the lemmata, which are constructed as an organic part of the subsequent interpretation. Cf. above, p. 57.

18. On the many deviations from MT, cf. above, pp. 57-59.

19 Cf. the references in ch. two notes 101-102.

The text was provided with a critical apparatus, containing all necessary data for clarification of the editing procedures and all biblical and Rabbinic references. Jellinek's edition is at present the only available comparative material, but in view of its arbitrary nature and the fact that it is based on the same and only Ms., we saw no value in pointing out its readings when they differ from our edition. On the other hand, we mention in the footnotes all those cases in which the correction we propose was previously introduced by Jellinek.

The apparatus was not designed as an intermediary between the commentary and the reader. Therefore we refrained from any remark which is interpretative in nature and did not turn the apparatus into a supercommentary. Our views on the commentary are stated in the introduction; the text has been left to meet the reader's perusal on its own merits alone.

CHAPTER FOUR

THE TRANSLATION*

Our basic objective in the task of translation was to produce an accurate and reliable rendition of the Hebrew original in a clear, fluent and acceptable modern English. Without overstepping these guidelines we tried to preserve as much as possible of the form and style of the original[1]. There is no need to elaborate on the "inordinate difficulties involved in the undertaking"[2]. On the other hand, complete silence regarding these difficulties would also be unjustified[3]. In order better to equip the reader for judging our work, it seems desirable to offer some remarks concerning the problems we encountered, the solutions we suggested and the procedures we followed. Putting aside the problems of translation in general, we confine our remarks to matters immediately pertinent to our text, whose nature as an object of translation is determined by two factors: the specific

---

* Some sections of this chapter, dealing with the language of the commentary, are found in the Hebrew edition of our book, in the chapter entitled "The Language of the Commentary".

1 Cf. by contrast, the preface of M. Rosenbaum and A.M. Silbermann, in Silbermann, vol. 1.

2 S. Reif, *VT* 28, 1978, p. 379.

3 .This policy is followed by many of the existing translations of medieval commentaries; cf. *inter al.* M. Friedlaender, *The Commentary of Ibn Ezra on Isaiah*, vol. 1, London, 1873; S.R. Driver and Ad. Neubauer, *The Fifty Third Chapter of Isaiah according to Jewish Interpreters*, I-II, Oxford and London, 1874; R.G. Finch and G.H. Box, *The Longer Commentary of R. David Kimhi on the First Book of Psalms*, London, New York, 1919; C.B. Chavel, *Ramban Commentary on the Torah*, New York, 1971; J. Baker — E.W. Nicholson, *The Commentary of Rabbi David Kimchi on Psalms CXX-CL*, Cambridge, 1973.

variety of Hebrew in which it is written, and the particular character of the composition as a biblical commentary.

a. Notes on the Language of the Commentary

Ashkenazi Hebrew of medieval northern France is generally regarded as a development of Rabbinic Hebrew abundantly interwoven with biblical elements and subject to the influence of the local vernacular, Old French[4]. Of all varieties of Hebrew throughout its long history, this phase seems to be the least investigated. Important research has indeed been dedicated to the French aspect of this language — to the glosses interspersed in the writings of the French commentators, especially Rashi[5], and to the French-Hebrew Glossaries[6]. Only initial research, however, has been done on Rashi's language *per se,* and almost nothing on the language of his contemporaries and successors in northern France[7]. Thus, the preliminary linguistic work, bearing fruit *inter al.* in adequate grammar books and dictionaries, forming a solid basis on which a translation should be based, is to a great extent lacking in our case[8]. In the absence of preliminary research and necessary tools[9], the translator is often forced into *"ad hoc"* decisions, based on context, synonyms and antonyms, and on his general acquaintance wiht the author's ideas and attitudes. However, at times these may prove to be unsure ground upon which to base his decisions. We shall illustrate this point in further detail.

4 Goldenberg, p. 1635; Rabin, pp. 116-117.
5 Cf. A. Darmsteter, *Les Glosses française de Rashi dans la Bible,* Paris 1909; Raphael Levy, *Trésor de la langue des Juifs Français au Moyen âge,* Texas 1964; Raphael Levy, *Contribution à la Lexicographie française selon d'Anciens Textes d'Origine Juive,* Syracuse, 1960; Ahrend, Job pp. 120-159; Rosin, pp. 92-97; Berliner, pp. 453-465; Sarfati, and others. Cf. also next note.
6 M. Banitt, *Corpus Glossarium Biblicorum Hebraico-Gallicorum Medii-Aevi,* I-II, Académie Nationale des Science et des Lettres d'Israël, 1972, and a thorough bibliography on pp. 188-194.
7 Cf. mainly, Avineri, Rabin, Banitt and Sarfati.
8 Cf. the scant bibliography regarding this phase, Goldenberg p. 1661, and Kutscher, pp. 166-167.
9 In addition to the works already mentioned one should note the great Thesaurus of the Hebrew Language by E. Ben-Yehuda, which is of great help, although strictly speaking it is not a historical dictionary.

Introduction

A well-known feature of Rabbinic Hebrew in general, i.e., its "careless grammar"[10] and "general weakening of strict grammatical rules"[11], seems to gain prominence in French Ashkenazi Hebrew of our period. Obvious linguistic irregularities are quite common[12], mostly in the use of prepositions, particles in general, and in the realm of syntax. This phenomenon can be explained to a certain degree, by two most important characteristics of this variety of Hebrew: it is a mixed language, where biblical and Rabbinic elements are juxtaposed without recourse to a rigorous system, and it is a written, rather than a spoken idiom[13]. However, it seems that these characteristics cannot be solely responsible for the "irregular usages" or account for their multiplicity. The question is inevitably raised, whether these usages are indeed just "careless grammar"; are they not rather the result of various forces brought to bear on the language, giving it new direction? In the latter case one would hesitate to regard these phenomena as "irregularities" (which amounts to disregarding them), and prefer to consider them as reflecting the emergence of new rules. It seems to us that one such redirecting force would be the impact of the French vernacular, which deserves more attention than it usually receives.

The scholars who touch upon this issue are practically unanimous in the opinion that in comparison with the influence of Arabic and German on the Hebrew of Spanish and German Jews, the impact of Old French was rather limited[14]. It seems, however, that this attitude should be reviewed — without recourse to such comparisons, as is clearly implied in Banitt's

10 Goldenberg, p. 1642.

11 Ibid, p. 1640.

12 A large collection of irregularities in Rashi's use of gender and number is given by Avineri, vol. 4, pp. 362-453 (an alphabetical list, pp. 409-453). As examples from our commentary one could note such strange forms as תיוולדו, תמותו for the third person, pl. future (on 1:11), changes in gender, such as אומנות taken as masculine (on 10:8-9; already in Rashi on 9:9; on the probable Arabic influence as the cause for such renderings cf. Goldenberg, pp. 1628-1629). An unexpected plural for an abstract noun is מוסרים (on 7:21-22), נולדות (on 1:8); etc.

13 Cf. Rabin, pp. 107-113; Kogut pp. VII-VIII (Hebrew pp. 15-16); on its bearing on our problem, ibid, pp. Xff.

14 Avineri — "as nothing" (vol. 4, p. 358); Goldenberg — "much smaller" (p. 1635); cf. also Rabin, p. 117.

latest study[15]. This is true for Rashi's language and even more so for that of the following generations, to which our commentary belongs. A thorough linguistic exposition is of course outside the scope of this introduction, but some examples may serve to illustrate our general approach.

The noun עת is of feminine gender in biblical Hebrew. It is both feminine and masculine in the usage of Rashi, probably due to the influence of the French *tens* (*temps*), which is masculine[16]. In our commentary it is always masculine[17]. Some scholars have noticed the modification in the use of the accusative particle את and the accusative pronouns. Avineri notes the diminishing use of את in Rashi's language, but in accordance with his general approach, does not attribute it to the influence of French[18]. On the other hand, the very same phenomenon in Ashkenazi Hebrew is taken by Rabin as a clear indication of the influence of German[19]. In our commentary the use of את is greatly reduced; most of its surviving occurrences are in fixed idioms or due to the influence of the biblical text and the method of interpretation[20]. The use of the accusative pronouns אותו etc. as such, is greatly reduced and their place is taken by the pronominal suffixes[21]. אותו etc. are used mainly as demonstratives[22] or in the phrases

15 Banitt, pp. 130-136. The underestimation of the French element in our variety of Hebrew seems to have several causes. Almost the only part of it studied to any degree is the language of Rashi, the text of which is far from being reliable. Because of its high esteem and even sacredness among the following generations, its text has been constantly tampered with. "On avait toutes les raisons de l'épurer de ce qui pourrait apparaitre aux doctes copistes comme des erreurs" (Rabin, p. 114). The main work of Rashi's language, that of Avineri, is quite apologetic on this issue, cf. vol. 4, pp. 357-359 and throughout the work.

16 Cf. Banitt, p. 132. For the examples from Rashi, cf. Avineri, vol. 4, p. 439.

17 3:2, 11, 14, 15. The exception in 5:11 is determined by the combination of עת with שנה. Of the many occurrences of עת in our commentary, only in the above cases is the gender clearly pointed out.

18 Avineri, vol. 3, pp. 250ff.

19 Rabin, pp. 111-112.

20 For example: 1:8 — את הנולדות . . . ראה; 2:9-11 — את החיים; 2:17 — את החיות; 2:18 את עשרי; 3:11 — את הזמן; etc.

21 Cf. as examples, in 1:2 ומזכירו, לפרשה, וגומרה, אמרן, ומצאם.

22 Cf. *inter al.* אותו עושר (4:15) אותו דור, אותו מלך; (2:13) אותה חכמה (2:16); אותו חסרון; (5:11); אותו ממון (5:14, 17); etc.

אותו ש etc.[23], which are probably a development from the demonstrative but should be regarded as a calque of French *cel qui* etc.[24]. While the roots of this usage can be found in Rabbinic Hebrew, its proliferation, and the effect it has on the syntax in general, are to be attributed to French influence[25].

The same line of development can be discerned in the use of ש. According to Banitt, ש becomes an equivalent to the French *que* and takes on all its meanings: " '*afin que*', '*parce que*', '*pour que*', '*puisque*' "[26]. This example leads us to the still mostly uninvestigated field of semantics, which bears directly on the work of the translator. Several examples of "calque sémantique" have lately been adduced by Banitt[27]. It has been noted before that the frequent use of עשׂה, and the specific phrases constructed with it, are to be explained by the influence of the French '*faire*'[28]. Although the frequent use of מעשׂה, עניין and עסק in our commentary could be attributed to the prominence of מעשׂה and עניין in the book of Qohèleth[29], one should still ask whether their synonymity, their specific nuances and their use in certain phrases such as עניין העולם[30], מעשׂה עולם, תיקון המעשׂה etc. would not be better explained as equivalents to the French '*affaire*', and the phrases constructed with it. In the same way one may ask whether the frequent use of נהג, in the Qal, Hif'il and Hithpa'el, and its specific meanings is not affected by the French '*mener*'. One would even venture to ask whether preference given to some biblical prepositions over their Rabbinic equivalents is not determined by the analogy with the French.

---

23 Cf. *inter al.* אותו שסידר (1:2) אותן שיהיו (1:11); אותו שהיה (6:10); etc.
24 Cf. Banitt, p. 133.
25 Cf. Jastrow, v. אותו (p. 35); Avineri, vol. 3, p. 227. On the general phenomenon cf. Rabin, p. 112, who stresses that the influence of the vernacular is not expressed through completely new forms but through selection between already existing elements of language and shift of usage.
26 Banitt, p. 132.
27 Ibid, pp. 132-136.
28 Cf. Goldenberg, p. 1635.
29 Ginsberg, pp. 14-16.
30 מעשׂה עולם — 1:8, 12; עניין העולם — 8:10; תיקון המעשׂה — 4:4, etc.

Another quite complicated feature of this variety of Hebrew is the incorporation of biblical elements into its Rabbinic base[31]. The commentary on Qoheleth abounds with biblical elements which can be broadly classified into three groups: One includes those elements whose introduction is determined by the general preference of the language for certain biblical elements, such as forms, prepositions, words, and syntactical constructions, as against their Rabbinical equivalents. Another group includes the biblical citations which are incorporated into the flow of the language either literally or with slight changes, but are not identified as quotations — a technique which is found already in Rabbinic Hebrew and is quite common in the various branches of Ashkenazi Hebrew[32]. The use of these biblical phrases is determined by their rhetorical weight, and while the authors are probably aware of their origin, their incorporation into the language is organic[33]; in no way are they quotations in the strict sense of the term. The question facing the translator is whether to take cognizance of the biblical origin of these phrases by translating them according to an accepted English translation of the Bible, or to render them freely, as an organic part of the text. No strict rule is applicable in such cases, and their treatment is very much dependent on the general context and on the nature of each phrase.

The third group of biblical elements includes those which are occasioned by the more specific nature of our composition as a commentary on a biblical text, and even more so by its methods of interpretation. Thus, these elements directly affect the work of the translator and deserve particular attention.

b. Stylistic Features of the Commentary

One of the most common methods of interpretation is the fluent discourse, in which the essence of the text is presented[34]. Here, a kind of

31 There are probably several factors which contributed to it. Of these, the following have been mentioned: The origin of this variety in the Hebrew of the Jews in Italy, the influence of the liturgical poetry, the keen preoccupation with the Bible and a process of selection caused by the impact of the French vernacular. Cf. Goldenberg, p. 1636, Rabin, p. 107, Kogut, p. VII.

32 Cf. Goldenberg, pp. 1640, 1641.

33 For examples from Rashi, cf. Avineri, vol. 4, p. 323ff.

34 Cf. above, pp. 36, 42ff.

synthetic paraphrase is created, comprising the author's words, together with parts and pieces of the biblical text, all having the same status as components of the interpretation. The use of the biblical excerpts as organic parts of the interpretation enhances the brevity and economy of expression while at the same time focusing the reader's attention on the correspondence between the interpretation and the text. The fragments of text are often slightly modified, and adjusted to the grammar and syntax of the interpretation.

In neither the edition nor the translation were these textual fragments regarded as quotations. We acknowledged their origin by translating them as close as possible to the RSV[35], but we did not isolate them from the flow of the interpretation by any external signs, did not harmonize them with MT when they deviated from it, and did not introduce quotation marks.[35a]

35 The RSV has served as our English text all along, except for some instances, which are mentioned below.

35a The analysis of the language into its respective components is very instructive, but a full discussion is beyond the scope of the present study. However, the incorporation of biblical elements into the language of the commentary will be demonstrated here by a few examples, taken from the interpretation of the first three verses of the book. In the interpretation of 1:1 the sentence "because he gathered wisdom from all the people of the east" is a partial paraphrase of 1 Kg. 4:30 (Heb. 5:10), adapted to the present context. The first part of 1 Kg. 4:30 is replaced by "because he gathered (קיהל) wisdom", thus serving as an interpretation of the name Qoheleth (קהלת); the second part, however, is cited almost without change "of all the people of the east". The interpretation of 1:1 goes on with "and became wiser than any man" (ויתחכם מכל האדם) which, again, is a slightly changed citation of 1 Kg. 4:31 (Heb. 5:11) "For he was wiser than all other men" (ויחכם מכל האדם). The next lemma in 1:1, "King", is interpreted by one short sentence "who was king in Jerusalem". The words "king of Jerusalem" are taken over from the verse itself and the interpretation is made by adding two words: "who was". In 1:2, the interpretation following the lemma "vanity of vanities" is in fact a paraphrase of another verse in the same chapter. The interpretation starts with "he had given his mind to inquire and search out the affairs of the world" (נתן לבו לדרוש ולתור בעניני העולם), paraphrasing verse 13: "And I applied my mind to seek and search out ... all that is done under heaven" (ונתתי את לבי לדרוש ולתור ... על כל אשר נעשה תחת השמים). In 1:3, in the interpretation of the second lemma "what ... gain", the following components are incorporated and fully integrated into the interpretation: (1) a section of the verse itself — בכל עמלו שהוא עמל תחת השמש — "in return for all the labour in which he engages under the sun" (RSV — by all the toil at which he toils un-

A feature of the fluent discourse which has an impact on the translation is the abundant use of synonyms and equivalents as a method of interpretation[36]. In the flow of the interpretation isolated elements of the text, incorporated into the fluent discourse, are explained by synonyms or equivalents, preceded by a conjunction. The function of the biblical element in these instances is, in fact, that of a lemma — an object for interpretation; the conjunctive particle is to be understood, therefore, as an explicative. However, from the syntactical point of view the incorporation of these elements is so completely organic that there is no way of regarding them as lemmata, or even as quotations; formally and syntactically they are one with the interpretation.

We could find no single way of dealing satisfactorily with this phenomenon in the translation. An unflagging adherence to method in the translation would entail consistently preserving the two equivalents, presenting the conjunctive as an explicative, and pointing out the origin of the biblical elements. This could be done only at the cost of damaging the quality and clarity of the English. Therefore, no mechanical rules have been applied; each case has been treated on its own merits. Thus, only partial reflection of this method can be found in the translation; its full scope can be discovered only through the Hebrew original.

A matter which needed special consideration is Rashbam's attitude towards terminology — a matter in which he is heir to a long tradition. The clarification of meaning, which is the primary goal of the commentator, is

der the sun); (2) a citation, slightly changed, from another verse in Qoheleth: 8:13 וטוב לא יהיה לרשע is used here as וטוב לא יהיה לו; (3) a citation from the Mishna: Part of the saying of Aboth 5:21 שהרי סופו עבר ובטל is used as בן מאה כאילו מת ועבר ובטל מן העולם מן העולם "since at his end he passes out of the world". The interpretation of the lemma "under the sun" in 1:3 starts with "because there is nothing hidden from its heat he uses this expression". The words "there is nothing hidden from its heat" are a citation of Ps. 19:6 (Heb. 19:7). Two points should be emphasized again: the first is that all these elements integrate completely into the fluent language of the commentary and cannot be separated as citations without seriously damaging the linguistic texture. No translation can do them full justice. These examples are only a partial reflection of the phenomenon, and by no means exhaust the biblical elements in the interpretation of these verses or demonstrate in full the nature of its mixed language.

36 Cf. above, p. 43.

achieved not through exact, uniform terminology, but rather through variety and multiplicity of expression. One idea may be expressed in as many ways as the language would permit[37], thus unveiling the idea from every possible angle. Strict terminology is not adhered to even for the most technical matters[38]. The modern scholar, well versed in uniformity of terminology, is almost "naturally" inclined to interpret the variety of expression as "meaningful", i.e., as denoting variation of content, or as a result of different strata of authorship in the composition[39]. This inclination should be properly controlled in view of Rashbam's cultural environment.

Here, again, no absolutely uniform approach could be followed in the translation. Whenever there seemed to be no doubt that in the variety of expression only one idea is indeed indicated, we tried to transmit it in a uniform mode of expression. This applied mainly to the description of rules, principles of expression, grammatical terms, etc.[40] Otherwise we followed Rashbam's variety, trying to render nuances of meaning as faithfully as possible.

---

37 Thus, for example, the phenomenon of parallelism is described in our commentary in the following variations: כופל לשונו — "He duplicates his statement" (1:17; 2:3 etc.); לשון כפול — "a duplicated statement" (7:12); מקרא זה כפול הוא — "this verse is duplicated" (10:10); כפל לשון — "a duplication of statement" (12:7); מלה כפולה — "a duplicated expression" (1:6); כופל מלתו — "He duplicates his expression" (1:15; 3:16 etc.); כפל מלה — "a duplication of expression" (4:13; 8:10 etc.). An outstanding example from the commentary on the Pentateuch is the multiplicity of expressions for the description of the "literal meaning" — the basic method and goal of the commentary. The following are a partial list of these variations: לפי פשוטו; זהו פשוטו; משמע לפי הפשט; נראה לפי הפשט; לפי הפשט; זהו העיקר; לפי פשוטו; זהו עיקר הפשט; לפי פשוטו של מקרא; עיקר פשוטו כך; זהו עיקר פשוטו; לפי עמק פשוטו; כך עיקר פשוטו. Cf. Melammed, vol. I, pp. 458ff.

38 On Rashbam's terminology in linguistic matters, cf. Rosin, p. 128ff.

39 Cf. above, p. 23 on the discussion concerning the authenticity of our commentary.

40 For example: references to parallelism are usually described as "parallel expression"; the exact wording of the sentence they are included in is adapted to the sequence (cf. on 1:5-6, 18; 2:3 etc.); the phrase אחז לשון in its variations is translated as "He uses (an, this) expression" (1:3; 6:4 etc., but differently on 8:13); נופל בו לומר לשון — is usually translated "one may use the expression" (1:5-6, 8; 7:26 etc.). The phrase דקדוק מלה with its variations is translated as "literally", with the necessary adaptations to the sequence (cf. 7:19; 8:13; 9:1; 10:20), and so on.

Another, although related, stylistic feature is the constant repetition of certain words and phrases, with slight variations adapted to context, throughout the commentary. In this feature Rashbam is a faithful follower of Qoheleth[41], and the influence of repetition in the biblical text is probably one of the factors which led to its preponderance in the commentary. These repeated words and phrases are not technical terms, and their meaning is subject to a great variety of semantic nuance. To handle these expressions mechanically — rather an easy solution for the translator — would be to provide a given Hebrew word with the most suitable English equivalent, to be adhered to consistently throughout the commentary. Our policy has been to avoid this mechanical approach and to employ all the appropriate variety of semantic alternatives in order to convey as much as possible the shades of meaning intended by the original.

c. Points of Procedure

We shall conclude by presenting briefly the major lines of our procedures.

a. In matters of form the translation follows the Hebrew edition: in division into exegetical units[42], introduction of numbers for chapters and verses[43], presentation of lemmata in different script[44], etc. Only in the matter of biblical references does the translation deviate from the Hebrew edition: in order to enhance their availability they are added in brackets to the text and not included in the footnotes.

b. As a matter of principle we made every reasonable effort to render everything in the Hebrew text in English, and to avoid the use of Hebrew words, terms and expressions. However, in practice this rule could not be followed with absolute consistency. Not only are certain Hebrew terms, mainly grammatical, universally used for the description of that language, but for the sake of significance and clarity we used Hebrew phrases in other cases as well, as will become clear below.

---

41 On this feature in the language and style of Qoheleth, cf. Lauha, p. 9.

42 Cf. above, pp. 40-41.

43 Cf. above, p. 73.

44 Cf. above, p. 73.

c. As a rule, the translation of the lemmata has been taken from the RSV, but there are cases when this seemed impossible. (1) By its very nature a translation is also an interpretation, and the RSV is no exception. The sequence of Rashbam's interpretations after the RSV's lemmata is rendered problematical in two contrasting cases. One is when the correspondence between the interpretation of Rashbam and that of the RSV is so complete that Rashbam's comments appear superfluous and commonplace after the RSV's preceding lemmata. The other is the opposite: when the interpretation implied in the translation of the RSV is so divergent from that of Rashbam that no correspondence at all obtains between the lemma and the following interpretation. In neither of these cases did we follow the RSV; we either substituted another translation, accepted or free, or left the lemmata in Hebrew[45]. We referred to all deviations from the RSV in footnotes. (2) Certain interpretations, especially in the realm of grammar and semantics, are rendered unclear if preceded by an English lemma. The *raison d'être* of the interpretation, in the form or root of the Hebrew word, is not apparent if the lemma is rendered in English. One way of solving the problem is to add the required explanations to clarify the issue for the English reader[46]. Such procedure seemed rather subjective, and in fact, a kind of supercommentary, inserted into the text. We preferred to avoid such tampering with the commentary and to have the translation correspond to the Hebrew text. Therefore, the necessary Hebrew words were sometimes added in brackets[47], or more often, the lemmata themselves were presented in Hebrew[48]. (3) Due to the dynamics of translation there is no literal correspondence between the Hebrew MT and the RSV. As a result some words which serve as lemmata for Rashbam's interpretations are simply missing from the the English text, or are merely implied. In such cases we added the necessary lemmata, in English or Hebrew, as the case required, and referred to it in the footnotes[49].

45 Cf. in 1:11, 14, 17; 2:2, 6 etc.
46 Cf. Silbermann's method in the translation of Rashi.
47 Cf. 1:17; 3:9 etc.
48 Cf. 1:8, 12-13; etc.
49 Cf. 1:16 (saying); 2:3 (בטוב) etc.

d. The French glosses found in the commentary[50] have been transliterated from the Hebrew back to their supposed original Old French, although no hard and fast rules exist for such transliteration[51]. The English translations of the glosses have been given in the footnotes.

e. Another matter that should be mentioned is that of textual corruptions[52]. All the emendations that were actually introduced into the Hebrew edition were translated accordingly. Possible corruptions, which were pointed out in the footnotes, are not reflected in the translation.

f. The translation is accompanied by a necessary apparatus, the function of which is to clarify matters pertaining to the translation. It has been kept to a minimum and by no means has it been meant to be a super-commentary on the work of Rashbam. Some notes of this kind, however, seemed indispensable, and were introduced at the necessary points.

We stated above that the commentary on Qoheleth "is an important composition in its own right, adding dimension to the work of the great exegetical school in medieval northern France"[53]. We hope that the new edition of the commentary and its translation into English will provide the interested reader with the appropriate means for its study. We hope also that the commentary will take its rightful place as an important stage in the interpretation of Qoheleth, and as a source for a broader and deeper understanding of the spiritual world of the Jews in medieval northern France.

50 There are altogether eight short glosses, in 1:14, 16; 2:1; 5:12; 7:25; 9:1; 11:9; 12:5. Cf. Salters, French Glosses.
51 Cf. Ahrend, *Job,* pp. 120-122.
52 Cf. above, p. 73.
53 Cf. above, p. 33.

A COMMENTARY OF R. SAMUEL

CHAPTER 1

1   **The words of Qoheleth[1]:** Solomon is called Qoheleth because
he gathered wisdom from all the people of the East, and became
wiser than any man; also, in one place he is called Agur because he
collected wisdom[2], as it is said "The words of Agur son of Jakeh"
(Prov. 30:1).
king: who was king in Jerusalem.

2   **Vanity of vanities, says:** as yet he has said nothing except the
beginning of a statement; and he repeats his words in order to express his message as a general rule, and to state clearly that
everything is empty. This verse is like: "Not to us, O Lord, not to
us" (Ps. 115:1), "The floods have lifted up, O Lord, the floods have
lifted up" (Ps. 93:3), "For lo, thy enemies, O Lord, for lo, thy
enemies" (Ps. 92:9 (Heb. 10)), where (the author) first begins a
statement and mentions the Name, because he is eager to mention
the Name, mentioning it within his statement, and then he begins
his statement again in order to state it clearly. So here too, he mentions the name of Qoheleth at the beginning of the statement and

---

1 RSV: the Preacher.
2 Rashbam takes the name Qoheleth to be derived from *qhl,* meaning "assemble, gather",
and Agur to be derived from *'gr,* meaning "collect".

פרק א

א   **דברי קהלת.** שלמה נקרא קהלת על שם שקיהל חכמות מכל בני קדם
ונתחכם מכל האדם כי גם במקום אחד[1] נקרא אגור[2] מפני שאגר חכמות. שנ'
דברי אגור בן יקא.[3]

     מלך. אשר היה מלך בירושלים.

ב   **הבל הבלים אמר.** עדיין לא אמר רק תחילת מלה. וכופל לשונו לומר
לכלול ולפרש דברו שהכל הבל. מקרא זה דוגמ' לא לנו ‏‏‏﮲ ‏‏[4] לא לנו.[5] נשאו
נהרות ﮲‏' נשאו נהרות.[6] כי הנה אויביך ﮲‏ כי הנה אויביך.[7] שפותח תחילה
במלה ומזכיר את השם מחמת שהוא להוט להזכיר את השם ומזכירו בתוך
מילתו. ואחרי כן מתחיל בה לפרשה. וכן עתה מזכיר שם קהלת בתחילת

---

1   One expects אחר, but cf. the same usage on 7:11; 8:16.
2   Preceded by a dotted אחד. (The scribe has two modes of indicating deletion: one by a
    diagonal or horizontal stroke, the other by superlinear dots. In what follows the first
    mode is indicated as 'cancelled', the second 'dotted').
3   Prov. 30:1. MT — יקה, cf. BH *ad loc.*
4   The abbreviated form of the Tetragrammaton in this text is two *Yods* followed by a ver-
    tical uneven line. Cf. also on 7:7; 10:19.
5   Ps. 115:1.
6   Ps. 93:3.
7   Ps. 92:10 (Engl.92:9).

then he begins it again and completes it. These two verses, "The words of Qoheleth", "Vanity of vanities[3]", were not said by Qoheleth but by the person who edited the words as they stand. Vanity of vanities: he had given his mind to inquire and search out the affairs of the world and had found them all to be futile.

3   What . . . gain: all these words refer to (the statement) below: "There is nothing better for a man than that he should eat and drink etc." (2:24), which is to say that all this human endeavour is futile and there is nothing good for a man to do for his enjoyment except to drink and to be happy with his lot.
What . . . gain: what reward or gain has a man in return for all the labour in which he engages under the sun, since at his end he passes out of the world and it will not be well with him. In this context the statement is repeatedly referred to.[4]
under the sun: because there is nothing hidden from its heat he uses this expression — the same as if it were written 'under heaven'.

4   A generation goes, and a generation comes: for all die and return to dust.
but the earth remains for ever: *i.e.* endures, for it does not move from its place.

5-6   The sun rises: in the morning it rises in its place in the east; and in the evening it sets in the west; and it travels all night long — because it pants and hurries — until in the morning it arrives at the place where it rose today. Again, on the following day it rises there and travels during the day from the east towards the south, and goes via south and west until it turns and travels towards the north, and arrives at its place in the east.

3   *I.e.* 1:1-2, cf. Introduction, pp. 34-35.
4   The Hebrew is difficult and the meaning uncertain.

המלה. ואחרי כן מתחיל בה וגומרה. שתי מקראות הללו. דברי קהלת. הבל
הבלים. לא אמרן קהלת כי אם אותו שסידר הדברים כמות שהן.

הבל הבלים. נתן לבו לדרוש ולתור בעיניני העול׳ ומצאם כולם הבל.

מה יתרון. כל הדברים הללו מוסבים למטה על אין טוב באדם שיאכל
ג
ושתה וג׳ [8] לומ׳ כל אילו מעשי האדם הבל הם. ואין טוב מעשה להנאת האדם
רק לשתות ולשמוח בחלקו.

מה יתרון. איזה שכר וריוח יש לו לאדם בכל עמלו שהוא עמל תחת
השמש. שהרי סופו עבר ובטל מן העול׳ וטוב[9] לא יהיה לו. בעניין זה מוסבת
המלה בשיטתה.

תחת השמש. לפי שאין נסתר מחמתו אחז לש׳ זה. והרי הוא כאילו כתוב
תחת השמים.

דור הולך ודור בא. שכולם מתים ושבים אל העפר.
ד
והארץ לעולם עומדת. וקיימת שאינה זזה ממקומה.

וזרח השמש. לבוקר הוא זורח במקומו במזרח. ולעת ערב בא ושוקע
ה-ו
במערב. והולך כל הלילה מחמת שהוא שואף ומהיר עד שהוא מגיע לעת
בוקר במקומו אשר זרח היום. וגם למחר הוא זורח שם והולך ביום מן המזרח
לצד דרום והולך דרום ומערב עד שהוא סובב והולך אל הצפון עד שמגיע
במקומו במזרח.

---

8   2:24.
9   Ms. ושוב; cf. 8:13.

and goes round: when the sun is in the north and approaching the east one may use an expression indicating 'going round' and 'circling'.

round and round goes the wind: this is a parallel expression to "blows to the south and goes round", meaning that it circles all the points of the compass.

and on its circuits the wind returns: thus for ever it is repeatedly circling round in all its circuits, in that it continually travels all the points of the compass. But man is here today and in the grave tomorrow; all that he does stops, and he is remembered no more. Therefore it is said, "What does man gain" (1:3).

7   **but the sea is not full:** for if it were to fill up, the rivers would no longer flow into it.

to the place where the streams flow: to that place, today.

there they flow again: also tomorrow they continue to flow into the sea; for rivers do not abandon their habit and their flowing, but man abandons his habit and his ways in that he passes from the world. Everything is related to "What...gain" (1:3).

8   **All things:** all the events of the world are wearisome[5], for no one can tell or speak of them all.

the eye is not satisfied with seeing: for man always foresees and expects coming events.

nor the ear filled with hearing: the ear always listens and is eager to hear the things which happen in the world.

nor . . . filled: since the ear is hollow one may use an expression indicating 'filling'.

יגיעים: the meaning is the same as in עיף ויגיע (Deut. 25:18).

9-10   **What has been:** and what advantage has a man from all these things? Whatever has already taken place shall again take place in

---

5   The literal translation of יגיעים would be "weary", but it seems, from what follows, that Rashbam understood it as a transitive, rather than as an intransitive form.

וסובב. כאשר השמש בצפון שהוא קרב והולך לצד המזרח. נופל בו לומ'
לש' היקף וסיבוב.

סובב סובב הולך הרוח. מלה כפול' על הולך אל דרום וסובב לומ'
שהוא סובב והולך כל הרוחות שבעולם.

ועל סביבותיו שב הרוח. וכן חוזר וסובב חלילה לעולם בכל היקיפותיו
וסיבוביו שהוא שב והולך בכל הרוחות שבעולם. אבל אדם היום כאן ומחר
בקבר ומעשיו נפסקין שלא יזכר עוד. על כן נאמ' מה יתרון לאדם.[10]

ז והים איננו מלא. שאם יתמלא לא יהו הנחלים הולכים עוד אליו.
אל מקום שהנחלים הולכים שם היום.

שם הם שבים ללכת. גם למחר הם שבים והולכים אל הים שלא יניחו
הנחלים מנהגן ומרוצתן. אבל אדם מניח מנהגו ווסתו להיות בטל מעולמו.
הכל מוסב על מה יתרון.[11]

ח כל הדברים. כל מעשה עולם יגיעים הם. שאין איש יכול לספר ולדבר
כולם.

לא תשבע עין לראות. כי תמיד הוא רואה ומצפה את הנולדות.

ולא תמלא אוזן לשמוע.[12] תמיד אוזן שומעת ותאיבה לשמוע את
המעשים שנעשים בעולם.

לא תמלא. על שם שהאוזן חלולה נופל בה לש' מילואי.
יגיעים לש' עיף ויגיע.[13]

ט-י מה שהיה. ומה יתרון לאדם בכל אלה. מה שהיה כבר הוא שיהיה עוד

---

10 1:3. Ms. להאדם; a dot above the word signifies the redundant *He*.
11 1:3.
12 MT: משמע. Ms. probably influenced by לראות of the first colon.
13 Deut. 25:18.

the future; whatever has already happened shall happen again in the future; for there is nothing new under the sun. It might happen that there is a certain thing in the world of which a man may say to his friend: 'Look at that, it is a new thing in the world'. But his words are not true; for such a thing has already existed before our time.

11   **There is no remembrance of former ones⁶:** this is related to "what does man gain" (1:3).
of former ones⁶: there is no remembrance of men created before us in the world, for they are already dead, and memory of them has perished. And also the later ones, who will come into the world after us, will have no remembrance among those who will exist at the latter time, *viz.* in the later days of the latter ones. For they will all die and be remembered no·more. For if a certain man dies today there shall never be born another like him, since men do not resemble one another. But there is remembrance of the other dead creatures, for if some die today, others like them will be born tomorrow in the world; therefore, observers may say: 'This creature resembles such and such a creature which passed away'. From this we may conclude that the other creatures have remembrance, which is not the case with men. Therefore it is said, "What does man gain" (1:3).

12-13 **I Qoheleth:** for I was king, and because of my greatness my mind was free, and I applied it to inquiring and searching out by wisdom what goes on in the world. And I found out that it is an evil occupation which the Holy One has given to men to be occupied with.
עיניין: is from the *Lamed He* verb ענה, and so is לענות from ענה; therefore both may be used in one expression. Just as one says בניין from בנה so one says לבנות, קנינין from קנה לקנות, so one says עיניין, לענות from ענה. Both have the same basic meaning.

---

6   RSV "things" would not be appropriate in the light of the interpretation.

להבא. ומה שנעשה כבר הוא שיעשה עוד להבא. שאין דבר חדש תחת
השמש. שהרי יש לך דבר אחד בעולם שיאמר אדם לחבירו ראה זה דבר חדש
הוא בעול׳. ואין דבריו אמיתאין. שכבר היה לפנינו כדבר זה.

יא   **אין זכרון לראשונים.** מוסב על מה יתרון לאדם.[14]
לראשונים. בני אדם שנבראו לפנינו בעולם אין להם זכרון שכבר מתו
ואבד זכרם. וגם לאחרונים שיבואו אחרינו בעולם לא יהיה להם זכרון עוד.
עם אותן שיהיו לאחרונה. באחרית הימים של אחרונים. כי כולם ימותו ולא
ייזכרו עוד. שאם ימות אדם אחד היום. לא יוולד לעול׳ אדם כמוהו. שאין בני
אדם דומין זה לזה. אבל שאר בריות מתות יש להם זכרון. שאם תמותו אילו
היום. תיוולדו למחר דוגמתן[15] בעול׳. ועל כן יאמרו הרואים ברייה זו דומה
לברייה פלונית שעברה מן העולם. נמצא שיש להם זכרון לשאר בריות. מה
שאין כן באדם. על כן נאמר מה יתרון לאדם.[14]

יב-יג   **אני קהלת.** שהרי הייתי מלך. ומפני גדולתי היה לבי פנוי. ונתתיהו לדרוש
ולתור בחכמה במעשה עולם. ומצאתי שהוא עניין רע נתן הק׳ לבני אדם[16]
להתנהג בם.

עניין מהפעל של ה״י עָנָה וכן לַעֲנוֹת מן עָנָה. ועל כן הוא נופל על לשונו.
כאשר יאמר קיניין לקנות מן קנה.[16] בניין לבנות מן בנה. כן יאמר עניין
לענות מן ענה. לש׳ אחד לשניהם.

14   1:3.
15   Ms. דוגמתו. Cf. Jellinek.
16   Preceded by a cancelled *He*.

14   ורעות רוח[7]: and desire of the will. And רעות is from the verb רעה, just as דמות is from דמה, ראות from ראה and ענות from ענה. רוח: *talent* in French[8].

15   **What is crooked cannot be made straight:** for if a man has corrupted his deeds he cannot be as perfect in his deeds before the Holy One as he was at the beginning.

    and what is lacking cannot: he uses a parallel expression. If one has omitted anything, that omission can never be counted or numbered with that which remained.

16   **I said to myself:** *porpensai mei* in French[9].

    saying[10]: and so I said.

    surpassing all: more than all the wise men who were before me in Jerusalem, before I was born.

17   **and to know (ודעת):** is like 'and to know' (ולדעת). The same as in "to know (דעת)[11] what Israel ought to do" (I Chr. 12:32 (Heb. 33)), which is like 'to know' (לדעת)[12].

    madness (הוללות): is like "I said of laughter, 'it is mad'" (מהולל) (2:2).

    וסכלות[13]: wisdom. It is a parallel expression for "to know wisdom".

---

7   RSV "and a striving after wind" would not be appropriate in the light of the interpretation, cf. note 8.

8   In fact medieval French, which is the language of all the glosses. It means "will, desire, longing".

9   "I considered, reflected", cf. Salters, *French Glosses* p. 249.

10   The word is not represented in RSV.

11   Cf. The Hebrew text p. 4 note 3.

12   The point might seem superfluous in translation. Rashbam is demonstrating that two forms — the infinitive with *Lamed* and the infinitive without *Lamed* have the same meaning and function in the same way.

13   RSV "and folly" would not be appropriate in the light of the interpretation. Rashbam takes it to mean the opposite. Cf. also on 2:3.

יד   ורעות רוח. ורצון רוח. ורעות מן פעל של רָעָה. כמ' דמות מן דָּמָה. ראות
מן ראה. ענות מן ענה.
רוח. טלנט בלע'.

טו   מעוות לא יוכל לתקון. שאם עיוות אדם את מעשיו אינו יכול להיות
מתוקן במעשיו כבתחילה לפני הק'.
וחסרון לא יוכל. כופל מלתו. ואם חיסר שום דבר אותו חסרון אינו יכול
להיות עוד מנוי[17] וספור עם המותר שנשתייר.

טז   דברתי אני עם לבי. פֿר פֶנְשָׂיְימֵי בלע'.
לאמר. וכך אמרתי.
על כל. יותר מכל החכמים שהיו לפניי בירושלים קודם שנולדתי.

יז   ודעת. כמ' ולדעת. וכן דעת מה יעשה ישר'.[18] כמו לדעת.
הוללות. כמ' לשחוק אמרתי מהולל.[19]
וסכלות[20] חכמה. וכופל לשונו על לדעת חכמה.

---

17 A *Yod* is cancelled after the *Mem*.
18 I Chr. 12:33 (Eng. 12:32). MT: לדעת. On the deviation from MT, cf. Rosin, p. 59 n. 1
   (No. 0) and Salters, Variant Readings, p. 90.
19 2:2.
20 MT — ושכלות.

ורעיון: means 'desire' as in ורעות רוח. And just as one says צביון from צבה, אביון from אבה, עליון from עלה and הגיון from הגה, so one says רעיון from רעה meaning 'desire'.

18   **For in much wisdom:** for with his great wisdom he thinks deeply about what he observes, and as a result, is greatly vexed. **and he who increases:** a parallel expression. Because, as he increases superior wisdom and much knowledge, he thinks deeply about the acts of the Holy One which he performs in the world — why he does them — for he is unable to understand them. As a result of his many reflections he is vexed and suffers increasingly.

וְרַעְיוֹן.[21] לש׳ ריצוי. כמ׳ ורעות רוח. וכאשר יאמר צביון מן צבה. אביון מן
אָבָה. עליון מן עלה. הגיון מן הגה. כן יאמר רעיון מן רָעָה. לש׳ ריצוי.

יח   **כי ברוב חכמה.** שהרי ברוב חכמתו מחשב ומעמיק על ראות עיניו.
ומתוך כך כועס ברוב כעס.

ויוסיף. כופל מלה. שמתוך שהוא מוסיף חכמה יתירה. ודעת הרבה. מחשב
ומעמיק במעשיו של הק׳ שהוא עושה בעולם על מה הוא עושה אותם שאינו
יכול לעמוד עליהם. ומתוך רוב מחשבות׳ כועס ומוסיף מכאוב.

CHAPTER 2

1   **I said to myself:** *porpensai mei*[14].

Come now: that is what my heart said to me: 'Go on and enjoy yourself'.

אֲנַסְּכָה[15]: expressing 'royalty' and 'leadership'. I will conduct myself in royal gaiety, listening to the song of singing men and singing women, that I may be joyful and gay.

בטוב[16]: in laughter and joy.

But behold, this also was vanity: even this thing is worthless to me, for what advantage do I have in enjoyment and laughter?

2   **It is mad:** crazy.

of laughter: concerning laughter I said that it is crazy, and of enjoyment I said: 'What good does it effect and what avantage is there in it?' לשחוק which is masculine is related to וראה בטוב which is also masculine; ולשמחה is related to אנסכה בשמחה.

---

14 "I considered, reflected"; cf. also on 1:16.
15 RSV "I will make a test" derives the Hebrew form from נסה, while Rashbam derives it from נסך.
16. RSV renders the whole phrase ראה בטוב as "enjoy yourself" making it impossible to present the exact lemma.

102

א   [אמרתי אני בלבי]¹ פור פנשימיי².

לכה נא. וכך אמר לי לבי לכה נא. וראה בטוב.

אנסכה. לש׳ נסיכות וקצינות.³ אתנהג עצמי בנסיכות של שמחה לשמוע
קול שרים וקול שרות. למען אהיה שמח וטוב לב.

בטוב. בשחוק וששון.

והנה גם הוא הבל. גם דבר זה הוא לי להבל. כי מה יתרון לי בשמחה
ושחוק.

ב   מהולל. שוטה.

לשחוק. על השחוק אמרתי שהוא מהולל. ועל שמחה אמרתי מה זו טובה
עושה היא ומה יתרון בה. לשחוק שהוא לש׳ זכר מוסב על וראה בטוב. שגם
הוא לש׳ זכר. ולשמחה מוסב על אנסכה בשמחה.

---

1   The lemma is missing in the Ms.
2   The only case in our commentary where a French gloss is not followed by the remark
    בלע׳ — in a foreign language, i.e., in French. Cf. on 1:14; 1:16; 5:12; 7:25; 9:1; 11:9;
    12:5.
3   Preceded by the dotted word וקצות.

Of laughter; and of pleasure: the interpretation is: concerning laughter, and concerning pleasure, just as the phrase "as he has promised you" (Deut. 12:20 etc.) means "as he has promised concerning you", and "say of me he is my brother" (Gen. 20:13) means "say concerning me; He is my brother"[17].

3   **I searched with my mind:** I was searching and seeking within myself.

To cheer . . . with wine: to enjoy myself and to be merry with wine; like "and wine to gladden the heart of man" (Ps. 104:15).

my mind still guiding me with wisdom: in which there is no depth and which the world needs. And so is "ולאחז בסיכלות"[18] which is a parallel expression. But in "For in much wisdom" above (1:18), it is the profound wisdom, which men neither need nor are conversant with.

till I might see: for I do not know what to rely on that I might follow it.

what was good: what pursuit is good.

the few days of their life: during their life.

6   **צומח**[19]: means 'growing'.

7   **more than any that had been before me:** more than any man who was before me in Jerusalem, before I was born.

8   **and the treasure of kings:** the desirable treasures of kings.
and provinces: and the desirable treasures of the provinces.

---

17 The point Rashbam is making here concerns the effect and meaning of the *Lamed*. It is to be understood as "of, concerning". The same interpretation is reflected in RSV *ad loc* and Gen. 20:13.

18 RSV "and how to lay hold of folly" would not be appropriate in the light of the interpretation, cf. above, note 13.

19 The RSV translation "growing" would have rendered the interpretation superfluous.

לשחוק ולשמחה. פתרונו. על השחוק ועל השמחה. כמ' כאשר דבר לך.[4]
שפת' כאשר דבר דבר עליך. וכן אמרי לי אחי הוא.[5] אמרי עלי אחי הוא.

ג   תרתי בלבי. הייתי תר ודורש בעצמי
למשוך ביין. להתענג ולשמח עצמי ביין. דוגמת יין ישמח לבב אנוש.[6]
ולבי נוהג בחכמה. שאין בה עומק שהיא צריכה לעולם. וכן ולאחוז
בסיכלות. כופל לשונו. אבל כי ברוב חכמה שלמעלה[7] היא חכמה עמוקה
שאין בני אדם צריכין לה ואין רגילין בה.
עד אשר אראה. שאיני יודע על איזה דבר לסמוך ללכת בו.
איזה טוב. איזה עניין טוב הוא.
מספר ימי חייהם. בחייהם.

ו   צומח. לשון גידול.

ז   מכל שהיה[8] לפניי. יותר מכל אדם שהיו לפני בירושלים. קודם
שנולדתי.

ח   וסגולת מלכים. אוצרות חמדת מלכים.
והמדינות. ואוצרות חמדת המדינות.

4   Deut. 12:20 *et al.*
5   Gen. 20:13.
6   Ps. 104:15, MT: ויין.
7   1:18.
8   MT: שהיו. Cf. BH *ad loc.*

I got: I prepared for my needs, as in "and the calf which he had prepared" (Gen. 18:8), and so in "and she shall . . . pare her nails[20]" (Deut. 21:12).

שדה ושדות[21]: this is like שדה in the phrase שידה תיבה ומגדל (Mish. Shab. 16. 5 etc.); these are covered wagons for delight and beauty.

9-11 So I became great and surpassed: in wealth — doing all these things with my wealth and riches.

also my wisdom: I had wisdom as well. Yet both of them were, in my opinion, empty. So this is the poetic language of the section: for the three things which the Holy One has given to him — riches, wisdom and life — are empty; and below, he mentions life where it says: "So I hated life etc." (2:17).

I did not keep: I did not keep apart from them, for everything of significance which I saw, I made for myself.

for my heart found pleasure: for my heart was happy[22].

this was my lot[23]: this lot was mine.

And I turned[24]: to consider all these deeds, but I found them all empty. And that is what is said above, "What does man gain by all the toil etc." (1:3).

12 for what . . . the man: for what is the point in a man coming after the king to beg mercy and intercede for his life?

what he has already done: after his verdict has already been decided. For after the judgement is decided it is irrevocable. So it is futile that he should come to ask for pardon after the verdict.

---

20 In all the passages quoted the Hebrew verb is עשה, translated by the RSV as "get" (Qoh. 2:8) 'prepare' (Gen. 18:8) and "pare" (Deut. 21:12).

21 RSV "many concubines" would not be appropriate in the light of the interpretation.

22 The participle שמח is regarded by Rashbam (and RSV) as referring to the past.

23 RSV "reward", but cf. RSV 3:2; 5:17, 18.

24 RSV "and I considered" would not be appropriate in the light of the interpretation.

עשיתי לי. תיקנתי לצורכי כמ' ובן הבקר אשר עשה.⁹ וכן ועשתה את צפורניה.¹⁰

שדה ושדות. כמ' שידה תיבה ומגדל.¹¹ והן עגלות צב. לתענוג ולנוי.

ט-יא וגדלתי והוספתי. בעושר לעשות כל המעשים האלה ברוב עושרי וכבודי.

אף חכמתי. גם חכמה היתה לי. ושתיהן הבל בעיניי. וכן לש' צח של פרשה. כי גם אותן שלשה דברים שנתן לו הק' עושר וחכמה וחיים. הן לפניו להבל. ועושר וחכמה מזכיר במקרא זה שהן הבל. וגם את החיים מזכיר למטה. שנ' ושנאתי את החיים וג'.¹²

לא אצלתי. לא הבדלתי¹³ מהם שעשיתי לי כל דבר חשיבות אשר ראיתי.

כי לבי שמח. שהרי לבי היה שמח.

זה¹⁴ היה חלקי. חלק זה היה לי.

ופניתי אני. לתת לבי בכל המעשים האלה ומצאתים כולם הבל. וזהו שנ' למעלה מה יתרון לאדם בכל עמלו וג'.¹⁵

יב כי מה האדם. שהרי מה לו על האדם שהוא בא אחר המלך להתחנן לפניו ולבקש על נפשו.

את אשר כבר עשוהו. לאחר שכבר גמרו גמר דינו. שלאחר שנגמר הדין שוב אין לו תקנה. והבל הוא זה שבא אחר גמר דין לבקש חנינה.

9 Gen. 18:8.
10 Deut. 21:12.
11 Mish. Shab. 16:5 *et al.*
12 2:17.
13 Ms. הגדלתי; cf. Rashi *ad loc.* and Gen. 27:36.
14 MT: וזה.
15 1:3.

13-14 Then I saw: because I had applied my mind to this matter.
לחכמה: the *Lamed* has a *Pathah*. This is the common wisdom which the world needs and which is not profound. לחכמה is the same as לְהַחכמה — that wisdom with which we are conversant. But if *Lamed* is vocalised with *Hateph*[25] then the meaning of the word is profound and superior wisdom. Wisdom is likened to light, and folly to darkness; therefore this is what is said: "The wise man has his eyes in his head etc.", for he takes care to walk in the light and does not fall. But the fool walks in darkness and falls; nevertheless one is the same as the other, for they both alike die.

15 will befall me also: for I shall die just as one of the fools, so what gain do I have over him by virtue of my wisdom?
that this also is vanity: and therefore it is said: "What does man gain" (1:3).

16 of the wise man as of the fool: for neither one nor the other are remembered, for in time to come everything will have long been forgotten.
How ... dies: this is a great waste, that the wise man should die with the fool. In every place where איך occurs it is a rhetorical statement[26], as in "How (Babylon) has become a horror" (Jer. 50:23; 51:41), "How then have you turned degenerate and become a wild vine" (Jer. 2:21).

17 So I hated life: the vitality which the Holy One has given to me, which is one of the three things which the Holy One has given to me.
I hated: because I see nothing in my long life except that everything is vanity.

25 I.e. *Shewa*. Cf. Rosin p. 130.
26 The more common term is תמיהה מתקימת for "rhetorical question" cf. Avineri Vol. I, p. 1355.

יג-יד וראיתי אני. שנתתי לבי לדבר זה.

לחכמה. למ״ד פתוחה. היא חכמה הרגילה וצריכה לעולם. שאינה עמוקה.
לחכמה. כמ׳ **לְהַחכמה.** לאותה חכמה שאנו רגילין בה. אבל אילו תנקד[16]
למ״ד בחטף. אז תהיה נשמעת התיבה חכמה עמוקה ויתירה. חכמה נמשלה
לאור. וסכלות לחשך וזהו שנ׳ **החכם עיניו בראשו** וג׳. שמשמר עצמו ללכת
באור ואינו נופל. **והכסיל הולך בחושך** ונופל. וגם בכל זאת כזה כן זה שמתים
שניהם כאחד.

טו גם אני יקרני. שאמות[17] כאחד מן הכסילים. ואיזה ריוח יש לי בחכמתי
יותר ממנו.

שגם זה הבל. ועל כן נאמ׳ מה יתרון לאדם.[18]

טז חכם עם הכסיל. שהרי אין זכרון לא לזה ולא לזה. שכבר הכל נשכח
בימים הבאים.

ואיך ימות. הפסד גדול הוא זה שימות החכם עם הכסיל. בכל מקום שנ׳
איך. הוא דבר המתקיים. כמ׳ **איך היתה לשמה.**[19] **איך נהפכת לי סורי הגפן
נכרייה.**[20]

יז ושנאתי את החיים. את החיות שנתן לי הק׳ שהוא אחד משלשה שנתן
לי הק׳

שנאתי. לפי שאין אני רואה באריכות ימיי רק הכל הבל.

---

16 Ms. תבקר cf. Jellinek.
17 A dotted *Waw* after the *Alef* was omitted.
18 1:3.
19 Jer. 50:23; 51:41.
20 Jer. 2:21; MT: ואיך.

109

18   עֲמָלִי[27]: *i.e.* my riches.

which I toiled under the sun: like "under heaven" (1:13; 3:1).

after him[28]: he has been speaking about himself, for he does not wish to attach death curses to himself. (One should say that "after him (it)" refers to money.)

19   and who knows: about my son who will succeed me — whether he will be wise and have control over all that I have gained, namely that my riches shall last in his possession; or a fool, in which case my gains and riches shall fall from his possession into the possession of others.

This also is vanity: for if he is a fool, my gains will be lost from his possession; so the result is that I have toiled for it in vain.

20-21 So I turned about: therefore I turned to despair in my heart concerning all my gains; for you could have a man in the world, like me, who has troubled himself through wisdom, knowledge and skill to acquire money, yet the Holy One gives it to a man who has not troubled himself with it.

This also is vanity: the first man has troubled himself in vain.

22-23 What has a man: for what gain does a man have that he troubles himself about it? For all his days are painful and his whole manner fretful, because he figures out and tries hard to acquire money. Even at night, when he is lying upon his bed, his mind is not resting, because it is continually making plans that the money should not escape or disappear from his possession. And this is what is said below: "but the surfeit of the rich will not let him sleep etc." (5:12 (Heb. 11)).

27 RSV "my toil" would not be appropriate in the light of the interpretation; cf. Introduction, p. 47.
28 RSV "after me". In this case Rashbam may have had a different Hebrew text, cf. the edition *ad loc.*

יח   **את עמלי.**[21] ואת עושרי

שאני עמל תחת השמש. כמ' תחת השמים.[22]

אחריו.[23] היה אומר על עצמו לפי שאינו רוצה לתלות קללות מיתה בעצמו.
(ויש לומ' אחריו של ממון).[24]

יט   **ומי יודע.** על בני שיבוא אחרי אם יהיה חכם וישלוט בכל עמלי שיתקיים
עושרי בידו.[25] [או][26] סכל יהיה ויפול עמלי ועושרי. מידו ליד אחרים.
גם זה הבל. שאם הוא סכל יצא עמלי מידו. ונמצא שעל הבל עמלתי בו.

כ-כא   **וסבותי אני.** ועל כן סבותי ונתייאשתי בלבי על כל עמלי שהרי יש לך אדם
בעולם כמותי. שטרח בחכמה ובדעת ובכשרון לקנות ממון. ולאדם שלא טרח
בו הק' יתננו.
גם זה הבל. ועל הבל טרח בו הראשון.

כב-כג   **כי מה הווה לאדם.** שהרי איזה ריווח הווה ויש לו לאדם שהוא טורח בו.
שהרי כל ימיו מכאובים. וכל מנהגו בכעס מחמת שהוא מחשב ומחזר לקנות
ממון. וגם בלילה כשהוא שוכב על משכבו לבו אינו שוכב כי תמיד לבו חושב
שלא יברח ולא יסתלק הממון מידו. וזהו שנ' למטה והשבע לעשיר איננו
מניח וג'.[27]

---

21   MT — את כל עמלי.

22   1:13 *et al.*

23   MT — אחרי. The interpretation, which regards the third person as a euphemism for the
first person, shows clearly that Rashbam had indeed a different version than MT. Cf.
Rosin p. 59, n. 2 (Contra Salters, Variant Readings, p. 86).

24   Probably a gloss, cf. Introduction p. 61. Although suggesting a different interpretation it
still refers to the reading אחריו (cf. previous note).

25   Ms. בידי. Cf. Jellinek.

26   Ms. does not have the word, cf. the wording of the verse and Jellinek *ad loc.*

27   5:11 (Eng. 5:12).

24 **There is nothing better ... than that he should eat:**
there is nothing good in the affairs of man except that he eat and
drink and find enjoyment from the earnings of his money for which
he troubled himself. For this thing which is not vanity is from
Heaven; but all these things which I have related above, are all
vanity.

25-26 **for ... who can eat:** for who is he who deserves to eat and to
hasten to enjoy my earnings except me? Therefore one should eat
and drink and enjoy one's earnings.

For to the man who pleases him: for to the man who is
good before the Holy One, like me, the Holy One has given luck to
accumulate money for his needs and his pleasure; but to the sinner
the Holy One has given the task of accumulating money for the sake
of another who is good in his eyes, like "the wicked man[29] may pile
it up, but the just will wear it" (Job 27:17).

This also is vanity: the result is that it is for the sake of the wise
man that the sinner has troubled himself; therefore I ought to eat
and drink and to enjoy my earnings.

29 The quotation is somewhat free, cf. the edition *ad loc.*

112

כד   **אין טוב שיאכל.**[28] אין דבר טוב בעיסקי האדם אלא שיאכל ושתה
להראות לעצמו טובה בעמל ממנו אשר טרח בו. כי מן השמים הוא דבר זה
שאין בו הבל. אבל כל הדברים הללו אשר סיפרתי למעלה כולן דברי הבל
הם.

כה-כו כי מי יאכל. שהרי מי הוא שראוי לאכול ולמהר לשמוח בעמלי מבלעדי.
ועל כן יש לו לאכול ולשתות ולשמוח בטוב בעמלו.[29]

כי לאדם שטוב לפניו. שהרי לאדם שהוא טוב לפני הק׳ כמני נתן[30] הק׳
מזל לאסוף ממון לצורכו ולהנאתו. ולאדם חוטא נתן הק׳ עיניין לאסוף ממון
לצורך אחר שהוא טוב בעיניו. דוגמ׳ יכין רשע וצדיק ילבש.[31]

גם זה הבל. ונמצא שעל החכם טרח בו החוטא ועל כן יש לי לאכול
ולשתות ולשמוח בעמלי:

28 MT: אין טוב באדם שיאכל.
29 Ms. בעמלי, cf. Jellinek.
30 Ms. שנתן..
31 Job 27:17. MT: יכין וצדיק ילבש; cf. Salters, Variant Readings, p. 86.

CHAPTER 3

1   For everything there is a season: every event has its time
     and every matter under heaven has its appointed time — evil times
     and good times — to pay people their reward according to their
     deeds: payment of evil and payment of good, times appointed for
     evil and times appointed for good. He subsequently specifies the
     times.

2-8   a time to be born: on one occasion someone is born, on
      another someone dies.
      a time to plant: in time of peace.
      and a time to pluck up what is planted: in time of war.
      And thus all these 'times' are included in "a time for war" and "a
      time for peace", with the exception of "a time to be born", and also
      "a time to keep silence, and a time to speak" according to the literal
      sense of the verse. It is therefore written at the end as if to say: This
      is the general rule — "a time for war and a time for peace".

9   What gain has the worker: this is related to "but to the sin-
     ner he gives the work of gathering" (2:26) so as to say: since there
     are times for good and times for evil, and also for this sinner there is
     a time when he is gathering money, and a time when he loses
     possession of it to give it to the man who is good, what advantage
     has the one who gathers it in that he toils and troubles himself
     about this money, since he loses possession of it.

114

פרק ג

א **לכל זמן.** לכל המעשים יש להם זמן. ולכל חפץ אשר תחת השמים יש לו
עת. עתי רעה. ועתי טובה. לשלם לבריות משכורתם כפי פעלם. תשלום רע.
ותשלום טוב. עתים של רעה ועתים של טובה. ואחר כך מפרש[1] את העתים.

ב-ח **עת ללדת.** פעמ׳ זה נולד וזה מת.
עת לטעת. בעת שלום.
ועת לעקור נטוע. בעת מלחמה. וכן כל העתים הללו כלולים בעת
מלחמה ועת שלום. חוץ מעת ללדת. וחוץ מן עת לחשות ועת לדבר. לפי
פשוטו של מקרא. ועל כן נכתב בסופן. לומ׳ זה הכלל עת מלחמה ועת שלום.

ט **מה יתרון העושה.** מוסב על ולחוטא נתן עניין לאסוף.[2] לומ׳ אחרי
שעתות לטובה ועתים לרעה ועתים זה חוטא וגם זה עת שהוא אוסף ממון. ועת שהוא
יוצא מידו לתת אותו לאדם שהוא טוב. מה יתרון האוסף באשר הוא עמל
וטורח בממון זה אחרי שהוא יוצא מידו.

---

1   Ms. אפרש, cf. Rosin, p. 23, note 3b. Since the commentary does not go on to specify the
    "times", it seems that Rashbam is referring to Qoh. and not to himself.
2   2:26.

the worker (העושה): the gatherer, like "have gotten me (עשה) this wealth" (Deut. 8:17).

10   the business: the conduct.
to be busy: to conduct oneself.

11   everything: the Holy One has established all the appointed times, each one right and proper in its time and season.
also . . . eternity: the Holy One has also put time in the hearts of men that they may know and understand that there are times appointed for good and times appointed for evil. For man cannot discover or know the acts of the Holy One from the beginning to the end. For if all the times were for good or all for evil, man would not repent before the Holy One, because he would think: 'Since there is one fate in the world, either everything is for good, or everything is for evil, should I abandon my evil deeds for that, and what benefit would I get in my repentance?'
from the beginning to the end: from the beginning of the appointed time to the end of the appointed time.
that there is nothing better: in all these times and events than this: "than to be happy etc.". This is what has been said: "There is nothing better for a man than that he should eat and drink etc." (2:24).

13   God's gift: this gift is from Heaven: that he was given opportunity and luck to enjoy himself.

14-15 that whatever . . . does: all the appointed times, which are in the power of the Holy One.
and God has made: evil times and good times in order that men should fear him and repent. For they may say: 'Whatever already existed in former days, that times were alternating, exists now, today, the same pattern. And the same order and pattern which shall exist in the future, already have existed in days gone by. For the Holy One sought out the persecuted to give him the money for which his persecutor troubled himself.'

העושה. האוסף. כמ' עשה לי את החיל הזה.[3]

י העניין. המנהג.
לענות. להתנהג.

יא את הכל. כל הזמנים עשה ותיקן הק' כל אחד נכון והגון בעתו וזמנו.
גם את העולם. גם את הזמן נתן להם הק' בלבם של בני אדם ויבינו
שעתים שהם לטובה. ויש עתים לרעה. לפי שלא ימצא ולא ידע האדם את
המעשה אשר יעשה הק' מראש ועד סוף. שאם יהיו כל העתים לטובה. או
כולם לרעה. לא ישוב אדם בתשובה לפני הק'. לפי שיאמר בלבו. אחרי
שמקרה[4] אחד בעולם או הכל לטובה או הכל לרעה. על זה אניח רוע מעשיי.
ואיזו הנאה תגיע לי בתשובתי
מראש ועד סוף. מתחילת העת ועד סוף העת.

יב כי אין טוב בכל העתים ובכל המעשים הללו כזה כי אם לשמוח וג'. זהו
שנ' אין טוב באדם שיאכל ושתה וג'[5].

יג מתת אלהים. מן השמים הוא מתן זה שנתנו לו שעה ומזל לעשות טובה
לעצמו.

יד-טו כי כל אשר יעשה. כל העתים שבידו של הק'.
והאלהים עשה. עתי רעה. ועתי טובה. כדי שייראו מלפניו בני האדם
לעשות תשובה. ויאמרו מה שהיה כבר בימים הראשונים שהיו העתים
משתנים. עכשיו הוא קיים היום הזה אותו מנהג[6] ואותו סדר ומנהג שעתיד
להיות כבר היה בימים שעברו.[7] שביקש הק' את הנרדף ליתן לו את ממן זה
שטרח בו רודפו.

3 Deut. 8:17.
4 Ms. שמקרא, cf. Jellinek.
5 2:26.
6 Ms. מנהגי. Cf. Jellinek.
7 Ms. שעבר.

16   **Moreover I saw:** this thing in the world which is vanity.
      the place of justice: which is where righteous men are appoin-
      ted to execute justice.
      even there was wickedness (הָרֶשַׁע): a noun, like הרשע but
      the *Soph pasuq* changes the vocalisation of the *Resh* into a *Pathah*,
      as in ˙הללוהו בצלצלי שָׁמַע זֶבַח, זֶבַח (Ps. 150:5), where שָׁמַע has an
      'Athnah accent.

17   **I said in my heart:** concerning this I thought that the Holy
      One judges the righteous just as he executes judgement and justice
      upon the wicked. Because the righteous have sinned in a small num-
      ber of their actions they are expelled from their place and the
      wicked replace them. For every matter of the Holy One has an ap-
      pointed time in which to be fulfilled; and for every thing that a man
      does he is judged according to his deeds there, in the place in which
      he sinned. And the rule is that both righteous and wicked are judged
      alike.

18   **with regard to:** concerning men who sin, the Holy One is
      engaged in selecting them from the world, and he causes men to
      see[30] themselves that they are considered as beasts.
      לברם: this is the *Piel* of the root ברה. as in "I will purge out
      (וברותי) ... from among you ... those who transgress against me"
      (Ez. 20:38). Just as one says לכלם from לכלה as in בחימה לכלה
      (Ez. 13:13) — לעלה לעלם — so one says לברה לברם. It is in the
      Piel but the *Resh* cannot take a *Daghesh*. However, from לברות in
      the *Piel* one would say לברותם; likewise לכלות לכלותם, לכסות
      לעלות לעלותם, לכסותם. And it cannot be said to derive from בר; if

---

30 The insistence on the causative force of ולראות might reflect a vocalisation which dif-
   fered from MT, viz. וְלָרְאוֹת which would be an apocopated form of וּלְהַרְאוֹת.

טז   **ועוד ראיתי** זאת בעולם שהרי הבל.

מקום המשפט. שיש שם אנשים צדיקים קבועים לעשות משפט.

שמה הרשע. שבאים רשעים להכרית צדיקים ממקומם ויושבים תחתיהם.

ומקום הצדק כופל מלתו.

שמה הרשע. שם דבר כמו הרֶשע. אבל סוף פסוק פותח הרי״ש כמ׳ זֶבַח זַבַח.[8] הללוהו בצלצלי שמע.[9] שהוא באתנחתא.

יז   **אמרתי אני בלבי.** על זאת חשבתי לומ׳ שהק׳ שופט הצדיקים כמ׳ שהוא עושה דין ומשפט ברשעים. על אשר חטאו צדיקים במקצת מעשיהם נטרדו ממקומם ויבאו רשעים תחתיהם. שהרי יש עת לכל חפצו של הק׳ לקיים. ועל כל המעשה שעושה האדם שם ידונוהו לפי מעשיו במקום שחטא. והכלל[10] הוא שנידונין שניהם כאחד צדיק ורשע.

יח   **על דברת.** על אודות בני האדם שהם חוטאים. עוסק הק׳ לברותם מן העולם. וגורם הוא להם לבני אדם[11] לראות בעצמם שהם חשובים כבהמה.

לברם. משקל חזק גזרת וברות מכם הפושעים בי.[12] מן פעל של ברה. וכאשר יאמר לכלם מן לכלה. שנ׳ בחימה לכלה.[13] לעלה לעלם. כן יאמר לברה לברם. במשקל חזק. אבל רי״ש אינה יכולה להידגש. אבל מן לְבַרוֹת במשקל חזק יאמר לברותם כמו כן לכלות לכלותם לכסות לכסותם לעלות לעלותם.[14] ואינו יכול לומ׳ שיהיה מגזרת בר. שאם כן היה לו לומ׳ להבירם

---

8   Lev. 17:8 *et al.*   9   Ps. 150:5.   10 Ms. והכל.

11 Preceded by a cancelled *He*.

12 Ez. 20:38. MT — וברותי מכם המרדים והפושעים בי. cf. below note 14.

13 Ez. 13:13. cf. the next note.

14 The grammatical analysis seems to presuppose two variant readings in Ezekiel. Rashbam is starting from the two forms of the infinitive construct of ל״ה verbs in the Piel. Illustrated by the verb כלה, these would be כַּלֵּה and כַּלּוֹת; with prefixes and suffixes — לְכַלֵּם, and לְכַלּוֹתָם. On analogy to the first form Rashbam regards לְבָרָם as a suffixed infinitive construct of ברה in the Piel, its different vocalization determined by the *Resh*. וּבָרוֹת, in Ez. 20:38 would be the other form of the infinitive construct Piel of the same root. The variants, presupposed by Rashbam are וברות in Ez. 20:38 (MT וברותי) and לכלֶּה in Ez. 13:13. (We are grateful to Prof. Moshe Greenberg for drawing our attention to this matter). For another approach to the matter cf. Salters, Variant Readings, pp. 87, 89-90.

that were so it would have been להבירם in the *Hiphil*, likewise שב
סר להסירם, קם להקימם ,להשיבם.

that they are: what happens to them, for they are beasts.

19-20 For the fate . . . is the same: for the fate of man and the fate
of beast is the same fate. There is one rule, that both die in the same
way.

They all have the same breath: they have the same life
force.

and man has . . . advantage: the advantage of man over
beast is nothing and void.

for all is vanity: for both are equal; man and beast go to the
same place, for they came from the dust and shall return to the dust.

21   Who knows: is related to "and they all have the same breath"
(3:19), as if to say: Therefore I say that both have the same spirit,
because who knows that the spirit of man goes upwards and the
spirit of the beast goes downwards. This is why I say that they have
the same spirit and that everything is futile, for what advantage has
man over beast?

22   So I saw: I examined all sides and I saw that there is nothing better for man than this: that a man be happy in what he does, eating
and drinking and being happy in his lot; for this is a good portion for
him while he is alive. Because who shall bring him into the world after his death, that he may know and see his son who shall follow
him and inherit his property — whether that property will last in his
possession? Perhaps his son will be a fool and his property will not
last in his possession. Therefore it is good for a man to eat and
drink and to enjoy his life.

בלשון מפעיל.[15] כמו כן שב להשיבם קם להקימם. סר[16] להסירם

שהם. איזה מעשה מתקיים עליהם שהרי בהמה המה.

יט-כ **כי מקרה אחד**.[17] שהרי מקרה האדם ומקרה הבהמה מקרה אחד. ומנהג אחד הוא שמתים שניהם בעניין אחד.

ורוח אחד להם.[18] וחיות אחד להם.

ומותר האדם. יתרון האדם יותר מן הבהמה איין ותוהו הוא.

כי הכל הבל. ששניהם שוין אדם ובהמה ילך אל מקום אחד שהרי מן העפר היו לעפר ישובו.

כא **ומי[19] יודע**. מוסב על ורוח אחד לכל.[20] לומ׳ על כן אני אומ׳ רוח אחד לשניהם כי מי הוא שיודע שרוח האדם עולה למעלה ורוח בהמה יורדת למטה. ועל [כן][21] אני אומ׳ רוח אחד להם והכל הבל. כי מה יתרון לאדם יותר מן הבהמה.[22]

כב **וראיתי** חיפשתי בכל צדדין וראיתי שהרי אין טוב לאדם יותר מדבר זה אשר ישמח האדם במעשיו לאכול ולשתות ולשמוח בחלקו. כי זו היא מנה טובה לעצמו בעודנו חי. שהרי מי יביאנו בעולם לאחר מיתתו לדעת ולראות בבנו שיהיה אחריו שיירש נכסיו אם יתקיימו בידו. כי שמא בנו היה סכל. ולא יתקיימו נכסיו בידו. ועל כן טוב לו לאדם לאכול ולשתות ולשמוח בחייו.[23]

15 Ms. מפעול. Cf. Jellinek.

16 Ms. כד. Cf. Jellinek.

17 MT — כי מקרה בני האדם. The lemma seems to be a combination of the beginning phrase, as is shown by the following explanation, and the phrase ומקרה אחד which occurs later in the verse.

18 MT — לכל.

19 MT — מי.

20 3:19.

21 The word is missing in the Ms.

22 Ms. הבמה, cf. Jellinek.

23 Ms. בחיו, cf. Jellinek.

CHAPTER 4

1   **Again I:** furthermore I saw all the oppressed whose money was taken forcibly from them; they were weeping and had no one to comfort them by retrieving their money. And from their oppressors, who are powerful, they have no comfort. So he repeats his statement. And everything is empty, for what sin did one commit that his money was taken forcibly from him?

2   **ושבח אני:** is like ולשבח. I am wont to praise the dead who are already dead rather than the living who are yet alive, because the dead have already departed from all trouble and evil intrigue, but the living are still troubled by the frustrations of the world. **עדנה:** is like עד הנה.

3   **but better than both:** better than both of these is he who has not yet been in the world, for he has not experienced these evil things which are in the world.

4   **skill:** proficiency.
    that . . . a man's envy: which a man has of his fellow.
    This also is vanity: for why is he envious of him — of his wisdom and riches? What had he forcibly taken from him? If the

פרק ד

א   **ושבתי אני.** ועוד חזרתי לראות את כל העשוקים שנאנס ממונם מידם
והנה הם בוכים ואין להם מנחם להחזיר ממונם. ומיד עושקיהם שהם בעלי
כח אין להם מנחם. כך הוא[1] כופל[2] לשונו. והכל הבל. כי מה פשע זה שנאנס
ממונו מידו.

ב   **ושבח אני.** כמ׳ ולשבח ועוסק אני לשבח את המיתים שמתו כבר יותר מן
החיים שהם חיים עדיין הנה. שהמתים נפטרו כבר מכל צרה ומחשבה רעה.
אבל החיים עדיין טרודים בהבלי עולם.
עדנה. כמ׳ עד הנה.

ג   **וטוב משניהם.** זה הוא משובח יותר משניהם. את אשר עדיין לא היה
בעולם שלא ראה מעשים רעים הללו אשר בעולם.

ד   **כשרון.** תיקון המעשה.
כי היא קנאת איש שיש לו לאיש מרעהו.
גם זה הבל.[3] כי מפני מה הוא מקנא בו בחכמתו ובעושרו. איזה דבר אנס

---

1   Ms. היא, cf. Jellinek.
2   Ms. נופל.
3   Ms. has a ditt. of גם זה הבל.

Holy One has given him prosperity — why should the other envy
him? What crime has he committed by it?

5   **The fool folds his hands:** for he does no work with which to
       support himself.
       and eats his own flesh: because of this he has nothing to eat
       except his flesh which keeps degenerating, for he has done no work
       with which to support himself. Therefore a man ought to work in
       order to make a decent living.

6   **Better is a handful with[31] quietness:** it is pleasant and
       good for a man to have a handful of money with contentment so
       that he may make a decent living.
       than two hands full with[31] toil: for a little money is better
       for him than a lot of it with toil, for he would not make a decent liv-
       ing with it.

7-8   **Again, I:** I saw a further instance of futility in the world. You can
       have someone in the world who troubles himself and is anxious
       about his earnings; and he does not want to have a second man with
       him to help him, since the other would take his share of his goods
       and earnings.
       he has neither son nor brother[32]: he uses a parallel expres-
       sion. He does not want to have an associate to help him and to share
       with him. There will be no end to the toil of the solitary one, and he
       will not achieve his heart's desire. Also, his eye will not be satisfied
       with the sight of his riches. for he should reckon: 'For whom am I
       toiling so much and depriving myself of enjoyment?'
       This also is vanity: that he does not reckon in this way, but
       troubles himself and toils too much, and deprives himself of enjoy-
       ment.

31 RSV "of" would not be appropriate in the light of the interpretation.
32 The rendering of RSV here does not correspond to the Hebrew lemma.

וגזל ממנו. אם הק׳ נתן לו טובה מה יש לו לזה שהוא מקנא בו ומה פשע לו
בכך.

ה   **הכסיל חובק את ידיו.** שאינו עושה מלאכה להתפרנס בה.

ואוכל את בשרו. ואין לו מה יאכל בשביל כך. כי אם בשרו שהוא
מתנווה והולך לפי שלא עשה מלאכה להתפרנס בה. ועל כן יש לו לאדם
לעשות מלאכה למען יתפרנס בכבוד.

ו   **טוב מלא כף נחת.** נוח ומוטב לו לאדם שיהיה לו מלא כף ממון בנחת
כדי שיתפרנס בכבוד.

ממלא חפנים עמל שטוב לו ממון מועט מממון[4] גדול בעמל. שלא
יתפרנס בו בכבוד.

ז-ח   **ושבתי אני.** ועוד ראיתי בעולם מעשה של הבל. שהרי יש לך אחד בעולם
שהוא טורח ולהוט בעמלו. ואינו רוצה שיהיה עמו אדם שיני לסייעו שיקח
חלקו עם סחורתו ועמלו.

גם בן ואח אין לו. כופל לשונו. שאינו רוצה שיהיה לו ריע שיעזור לו
ויחלוק עמו. לא יהיה קץ לעמלו לאותו היחידי ולא ישיג תאות לבו. וגם עינו
לא תשבע לראות בעושרו. שיהיה לו לחשוב בעצמו למי אני עמל כל כך
להיות מחסר נפשי מטובה.

גם זה הבל. שאינו מחשב כל כך וטורח ועמל יותר מדיי. ומחסר[5] נפשו
מטובה.

---

4   Ms. ממק, cf. Jellinek.
5   Ms. ומסר.

9 **Two are better:** two men who associate with each other to handle their goods and earnings, are better than the individual who toils and busies himself alone.

a good reward: for they produce a great profit.

10-11 **For if they fall:** for if one or other falls, the one shall lift up his fellow; but woe is he who toils alone, for if he should fall, there would be no other to raise him up. Therefore woe to him who is alone. And if in cold days there are two, then they may warm each other if they both lie together; but if one lies alone how can he be warm? Therefore it is said: "Two are better than one" (4:9). **וַאִילוּ:** like אוֹי לוֹ. And so אי לך ארץ שמלכך נער (10:16) whose interpretation is "Woe (אוֹי) to you, O land".

12 **And though a man might prevail:** for if someone should come in from the street, as for example a thief or a robber, who would come in upon this man to rob him of his money — then if two men face him he would not be able to overcome them both, for he could have no victory over two men. And if there were three friends who associated together like a triple cord then they would indeed endure and would not be easily torn asunder. **יתקפו:** like in התוקף עבדו של חברו (BT, Baba Mezia 64b); and as it is said: "Thou art stronger than I, and thou hast prevailed" (חיזקתני ותוכל)[33] (Jer. 20:7).

13 **Better is a poor and wise youth:** a youth who is poor and wise is better than a king who is rich, old and foolish, who no longer knows or understands how to be careful and wise because he is a fool; like "For my people are foolish, they know me not; they are stupid children etc." (Jer. 4:22).

---

33 Rashbam seems concerned to equate the meanings of תקף and חזק.

ט   טוֹבִים הַשְּׁנָיִם. משובחים הם שני בני אדם שמתחברים זה עם זה לעסוק
בסחורתן ובעמלם יותר מן היחידי שהוא עמל וטורח ביחידות.
שָׂכָר טוֹב. שהם מוציאים ריוח גדול.

י-יא   כִּי אִם יִפּוֹלוּ. שהרי אם [יפול][6] או זה או זה האחד יקים את חבירו. ואוי
לו לאחד שהוא עמל יחידי שאם יפול ואין שיני להקימו. ועל כן אוי לו
ליחידי. ואם הם שנים בימות הצינה אז יתחממו אם ישכבו שניהם ביחד. ואם
הוא שוכב יְחִידִי[7] איך יחם. על כן נאמ' טובים השנים מן האחד.
וְאִילוֹ. כמ' אוי לו. וכן אי לך ארץ שמלכך נער.[8] ופת' אוי לך ארץ.

יב   וְאִם יִתְקְפוֹ הָאֶחָד. שהרי אם יבוא אחד מן השוק כגון גנב וְלִיסְטֵם[9]
שיבוא על זה לגזול ממנו ממונו. אילו שנים לנגדו ולא יכול נגד שניהם שלא
יהיה לו נצחון[10] עם שני בני אדם. ואם הם שלשה ריעים שנתחברו יחד[11] כמו
חוט משולש יתקיימו עד מאד ולא ינתקו מהרה.
יִתְקְפוֹ כמו התוקף עבדו של חבירו.[12] וכמ' שנ' חיזקתני[13] ותוכל.[14]

יג   טוֹב יֶלֶד מִסְכֵּן וְחָכָם. משובח הוא בחור אחד. שהוא עני והוא חכם.
יותר ממלך שהוא עשיר והוא זקן והוא כסיל שאינו יודע ומבין עוד להיות
זהיר וחכם. מחמת שהוא כסיל. דוגמת כי אויל[15] עמי אותי לא ידעו בנים
סכלים המה[16] וג'.

6   The word is missing in the Ms, cf. Jellinek.
7   The last letter is a *Waw*, cut in the middle by a stroke and a dot above it. The word is
    also vocalized. All these point to the scribe's efforts to restore the word after a wrong
    Waw was initially written.
8   10:16.
9   In an unusual way the final *Mem* is also vocalized.
10   Ms. נצחין, so also 9:11. The repetition of the same form may suggest that נצחין is not an
    error but rather a variant form of נצחון (cf. 10:10); however, such a form is not
    documented in the existing dictionaries.
11   Preceded by a cancelled *Beth*.
12   BT Baba Mezi'a 64b.
13   Jer. 20:7. MT — חזקתני cf. Salters, Variant Readings, p. 89.
14   Ms. ותלכל, cf. Jellinek.
15   Ms. אוי, cf. Salters, Variant Readings, p. 88f.
16   Jer. 4:22.

poor (מסכן): I cannot interpret it as 'wise', to see it as a synonym and a noun for 'wise man', like in המסוכן תרומה (Is. 40:20), הלאל יסכן גבר (Job 22:2), because there is a *Tipha* accent beneath מסכן to separate it from וחכם. "Youth" is related to "old"; "poor" is related to "than a king"; "and wise" is related to "and foolish"[34].

14 **from prison:** for this old and foolish king came out of the prison house, that is his mother's womb, to be the crown prince; so that royal honour fell to him after he was born. This poor and wise youth also came out of his mother's womb, and maybe today or tomorrow royal honour will fall to him as it fell to the other. The conclusion is that the youth is better than him, for he is wise, while that king is a fool.

הסורים: like האסורים, and therefore the *Samekh* does not have a *Daghesh*. Sometimes the *Aleph* drops out of a word as in לא יהל שם ערבי (Is. 13:20), where יהל is like יאהל.

in his own kingdom had been born: for even during the reign of this old, foolish king there is born to him a poor and foolish son like himself.

15-16 **I saw:** all the people who walk under heaven.

as well as . . . youth: this is the second one who was to become king in his father's stead, and is a fool like his father. And I saw that there was no end of all the people — the former generation who lived in the time of this man's father — for they were not happy with him because of his folly. That generation was before these later ones who are subjugated to this man's son who is poor and foolish. Nor will these later ones be happy with his son because of his great folly.

34 On Rashbam's understanding of this verse cf. Introduction, p. 52, note 138.

מסכן ואיני[17] יכול לפותרו כמו חכם. לעשותו כפל מלה ושם דבר של חכם.
כמ׳ המסוכן תרומה.[18] הלאל יסכן גבר.[19] לפי שיש בו תחת מסכן טיפחה.
להפליגו מן וחכם. ילד מוסב על זקן. מסכן מוסב על ממלך. וחכם מוסב על
וכסיל.

יד   **כי מבית הסורים.** שהרי מלך זקן וכסיל זה יצא מבית האיסורין מבטן
אמו להיות עתיד למלך.[20] שלאחר שנולד נפל לו כבוד של מלוכה. ילד מסכן
וחכם זה גם הוא יצא מבטן אמו. ושמא היום או מחר יפול לו כבוד של
מלוכה. כמ׳ שנפל לזה. ונמצא שהילד משובח ממנו שהוא חכם. ואותו מלך
כסיל הוא.

הסורים.[21] כמ׳ האסורים. ועל כן סמ״ך נרפי״ת. ופעמי׳ אלף נופלת מן
התיבה. כמ׳ לא יהל שם ערבי.[22] שהוא כמ׳ יאהל.

כי גם במלכותו נולד. שהרי[23] גם במלכותו של מלך זקן כסיל זה נולד לו
בן רש וכסיל כמותו.

טו-טז **ראיתי** את כל האנשים[24] המהלכים תחת השמים.

עם הילד זה שיני אשר עמד להיות מלך תחת אביו. והוא כסיל כאביו.
וראיתי שאין קץ לכל העם לכל אותו דור ראשון שהיה בימי אביו של זה
שהם לא היו שמחים עליו מחמת סכלות. שאותו דור לפניהם של אילו
אחרונים שהם משועבדים לבנו של זה שהוא רש וכסיל. וגם אילו אחרונים
לא ישמחו בו בבנו. ברוב כסילותו.

---

17 Ms. ואינו, cf. Jellinek.
18 Is. 40:20.
19 Job 22:2.
20 Preceded by two words, dotted and cancelled.
21 Ms. פסורים, cf. Jellinek.
22 Is. 13:20.
23 Preceded by a cancelled *Waw*.
24 Ms. המעשים.

this also is vanity: for they are foolish kings, and the generations are subjugated to them.

as well as the second[35] youth: his son who was born is
called "second" because he is a second foolish king, in place of his
father.

17   Guard your steps: watch your foot that you may walk in
(5:1) purity, in cleanliness and in humility. You should also go barefoot
when you go to seek God, to pray in the Temple, as it is said: "Put
off your shoes from your feet, for the place etc." (Ex. 3:5).

and near[36] to listen: and the Holy One will be nearer to you, to
listen to your prayer, than to the sacrifices of fools. For these fools
do not know to do good deeds, therefore they are ready to do evil.

35 Cf. RSV footnote *ad loc.*
36 RSV "to draw near" would not be appropriate in the light of the interpretation.

שגם[25] זה הבל. שהם מלכים כסילים והדורות משועבדים להם.

עם הילד השיני. בנו זה שנולד קורא שיני על שם שהוא מלך כסיל שיני תחת אביו.

שמור רגלך. שמור את רגלך שתלך בטהרה ובנקיות ובענוה וגם תלך יחף יז
כאשר תלך לדרוש אלהים להתפלל בבית המקדש. כעניין שנ׳ של נעליך
מעל רגליך כי המקום וג׳.[26]

וקרוב לשמוע והק׳ יהיה לך קרוב לשמוע תפילתך. יותר מנתינת זבחי
הכסילים. שהרי אינם יודעים כסילים הללו לעשות מעשים טובים. ועל כן הם
מזומנים לעשות רע.

25 MT — כי גם.
26 Ex. 3:5.

1 (2) **Be not rash with your mouth:** when you pray before him do not be hasty in your prayer, by uttering a lot of words before the Holy One. For he is in heaven; therefore you should fear him if you multiply words before him. Let there be few words lest you err by means of your many words. And this is what is said: "When words are many, transgression is not lacking" (Prov. 10:19). And also the sages said the same thing: "he that multiplies words occasions sin" (Mish. Aboth 1:17).

2 (3) **For a dream comes:** for this dream which a man dreams at night is due to his many transactions and ways which he thinks about during the day; this is what is said: "As you lay in bed came thoughts" (Dan. 2:29). But his dream is meaningless and empty. And so is the voice of the fool in his many words meaningless and void, for through the multitude of his words it is realised and recognised that he is a fool. Hence you should reduce the number of your words in order to shun folly.

3-4 **When you vow a vow:** to the Holy One in your prayer, do not
(4-5) delay paying it — for so is the custom to make a vow at the time of prayer — for the holy One has no use for fools who vow but fail to pay. Therefore I have said to you: "Whatever you vow, pay"; for better is he who does not vow at all than he who vows but fails to pay.

א **אל תבהל את¹ פיך.** וכאשר תתפלל לפניו. לא תהיה בהול בתפילתך
להוציא ריבוי דברים לפני הק׳. כי הוא בשמים. ועל כן יש להתיירא ממנו.
אם תרבה דברים לפניו ויהיו דברים² מעטים שלא תהיה נכשל ברוב דבריך.
וזהו שנ׳ ברוב דברים לא יחדל פשע.³ וגם כמ׳ כן אמרו חכמ׳ כל המרבה
דברים מביא חטא.⁴

ב **כי בא החלום.** שהרי חלום זה שאדם חולם בלילה ברוב⁵ ענייניו ומנהגיו⁶
שהוא מחשב ביום הוא. וזהו שנ׳ ורעיוני לבך על משכבך סליק.⁷ והבל וריק
הוא חלומו. וכן קול כסיל ברוב דבריו הם הבל⁸ ותוהו. שעל ידי ריבוי דבריו
נודע וניכר שהוא כסיל ויש לך למעט דבריך למען תתרחק מן הכסילות.

ג-ד **כאשר תדר נדר.** להק׳ בעת תפילתך אל תאחר לשלמו. וכן הוא המנהג
לנדור בשעת תפילה כי אין חפץ של הק׳ בכסילים שנודרין ואין משלימין.⁹

1 MT — על.
2 Possibly: דבריך.
3 Prov. 10:19. MT: יחדל for יכחד, cf. Salters, Variant Readings, p. 87.
4 Mish. Aboth 1:17.
5 Ms. has a ditt. of ברוב.
6 Ms. מנהיגיו. cf. Jellinek.
7 Dan. 2:29. On the deviation from MT cf. Salters, Variant Readings, p. 98.
8 Ms. הבל, cf. Jellinek.
9 Possibly: משלמין.

5 (6) **Let not your mouth:** increase words before the Holy One, with
your much talk, to the extent of leading you into sin for "he who
multiplies words occasions sin" (Mish. Aboth 1:17). And, after your
many words, do not say before the Holy One that the multiplicity of
your words was unintentional, for all your thoughts are well known
to him — that you multiplied words deliberately and wilfully. Why
should the Holy One be angry at the sound of your many words —
which are empty, void, mere nothing — and damage and destroy
your achievements, what you have accomplished, which is the essence of your deeds.

לחטיא: like להחטיא.

the messenger: is the messenger of the Holy One.

6 (7) **For when dreams increase:** for through many dreams,
vanities and much talk, men perish from the world; and this is what
is said: "why should God be angry etc." (5:5 (6))

but: but[37] fear God by not multiplying words.

7 (8) **If . . . oppressed:** if you see oppression of the poor and the
deprivation of judgement and justice — that is to say, someone rob-
bing the poor of his money, and someone depriving another of his
justice and distorting his judgement, in order that he may lose his
money — do not wonder at men's behaviour in these matters, for
there is someone who is higher in rank than the one who has forced
money from the poor and has distorted judgement and justice; he in
turn will rob the latter of his money.

higher ones over them: and there are men of high rank in the
world who are powerful and whose power is great over these high
ones; they also will rob them of their money, and distort the judgement and justice of these high ones who have robbed others. Thus
the Holy One handles and conducts his world. It is similar to the
homiletic interpretation on "show me now thy ways etc." (Ex.
33:13).

37 Rashbam interprets the Hebrew כי as "but". RSV follows the same interpretation.

ועל כן אמרתי לך את אשר תדור שלם. שהרי טוב ומשובח הוא מי שאינו
נודר כל עיקר. ממי שנודר ואינו משלם.

אל תתן את פיך להרבות דברים. לפני הק׳ ברוב שיחתך כדי להחטיא את   ה
עצמך. שכל המרבה דברים מביא חטא.[4] ולאחר ריבוי דבריך לא תאמר לפני
הק׳ כי שגגה אודות מרבית דבריך שכל מחשבתיך גלויות וידועות לפניו כי
במזיד ובזדון הרביתה דברים. למה יקצוף הק׳ על קול ריבוי דבריך שהוא
הבל ותוהו ורוח שיחבל וישחית את פעולתך ואת מעשה ידיך שהוא עיקר
ושורש מעשיך.

לחטיא. כמ׳ להחטיא.

המלאך הוא מלאכו של הק׳.

כי ברוב חלומות. שהרי ברוב חלומות והבלים ורוב דברים הולכים   ו
ונאבדים בני אדם מן העולם. וזה שנ׳ למה יקצוף האלהים וג׳.[10]
כי את. אלא את האלהים ירא שלא להרבות דברים.

אם עושק. אם תראה עושק של רש וגזל של משפט וצדק. שזה גזול לרש   ז
את ממונו. וזה גזול לחבירו את משפטו ומעוות את דינו. למען יפסיד ממונו.
אל תתמה על חפצם[11] של בני אדם בדברים הללו. שהרי יש גבוה אחר על
גבוה זה שאנס ממון רש ועיוות משפט וצדק שגם הוא יגזול ממונו של זה.
וגבוהים עליהם. ויש גבוהים[12] בעולם שהם חזקים וידם תקיפה. על
גבוהים אילו שגם הם יגזלו מהם ממונם ויעוותו משפטם וצדקם של אילו
גבוהים אשר גזלו לאחרים. וכן מגלגל ומנהיג הק׳ את עולמו דום׳ למדרש
אגדה של הודיעני את דרכיך וג׳.[13]

---

10 5:5.
11 The last *Mem* is preceded by a dotted *Yod*.
12 Preceded in the Ms. by a superfluous על which is probably a result of "vertical" dit-
    tography, cf. Jellinek.
13 BT Berakhot 7a on Ex. 33:13 (MT — הודיעני נא את דרכיך).

watches[38]: for the other high one waits for the first high one until his time comes to rob him of all his possessions, and to distort his justice.

גֵּזֶל: is a noun whose accent is on the last syllable; when it is in the construct state it is pointed throughout with a small *Pathah*[39] with its accent on the penultimate syllable גֵּזֶל; so also כפל[40], גֵּדֶר.

8 (9) **and the advantage of a land**[41]: for all men is the same, for they must all till the soil in order to live and make a living from the work of their hands. Even the king must be a farmer of a cultivated field. In that he commands his people, compelling them to till the soil for his needs, he is called a farmer.

9
(10) **He who loves money**: too much will never be satisfied with his money.

nor he who loves wealth: he uses a parallel expression, saying: and he who loves masses of money will nog get the great abundance that he covets.

this also is vanity: like the man who is busily engaged in acquiring too much money; for it should be enough if he is able to make a decent living without great wealth.

תְבוּאָה: the same as תבואה, just as לא תעבורי (Ruth 2:8) is like לא תעבורי, and תשמורם in the book of Proverbs (14:3) is like תשמורם.

---

38 RSV "watched" understands the syntax of the passage differently.
39 I.e. *Segol*, cf. Rosin p. 130.
40 Cf. note to the Hebrew text *ad loc*.
41 The RSV rendering here would not be appropriate in the light of the interpretation.

שׁוֹמֵר.[14] שממתין גבוה השיני לגבה הראשון שתגיע שעתו לגזול את כל אשר לו ולעוות משפטו.

גֵּזֶל. שם דבר הוא וטעמו למטה. וכשהוא דבוק ננקד כולו בפת"ח קט"ן. וטעמו למעלה גֶזֶל. וכן כפל[15] גֶּדֶר.

ח   וִיתְרוֹן אֶרֶץ בכל בני אדם הוא שווה שיש לכולם לעבוד אדמה למען[16] יחיו ויתפרנסו מעמל ידיהם. ואף המלך. יש לו להיות עובד אדמה לשדה נעבד. את שהוא מצווה לעמו להכריחם לעבוד אדמה לצורכו בכך נקרא הוא עובד אדמה.

ט   אוֹהֵב כֶּסֶף יותר מדיי לא יהיה מעולם שבע ממונו.

וּמִי אוֹהֵב בֶּהָמוֹן. כופל מלתו לום' ומי שהוא אוהב המונו של ממון. לא תבוא אליו שפעת מרבית ממון כמה שהוא חומד.

גַּם זֶה הָבֶל. כאדם שהוא עוסק וטורח לקנות ממון יותר מדיי[17] כי דיי לו אם יכול להתפרנס בכבוד בלא הון רב.

תְבוּאָה. כמ' תבואה[18] וכן לא תעבורי.[19] כמ' לא תעבורי. וכן תשמורם בספר משלי[20] כמ' תשמוֹרֵם.

---

14 Ms. שמור, cf. Jellinek.

15 The word is not vocalized. No such word, which would illustrate the indicated phenomenon, is found in the Bible. It could be either a scribal replacement of another word (such as כבד), or the Rabbinic word כָּפֵל*, which is found only with the suffix. (cf. Ben Yehuda, V, p. 2495).

16 Ms. למעלה.

17 Preceded by a cancelled *Mem*.

18 The word should be vocalized with a *Holem*, as is indicated by the interpretation, as well as by the following vocalized examples.

19 Ruth 2:8.

20 Prov. 14:3.

10   **When goods increase:** prosperity is great and increases in the
(11)   possession of a man as money increases. Because he is excessively
       engaged in acquiring a lot of money, corresponding to that money
       which is great there are many consumers of it, and he spends his
       money. For his needs are as numerous as his earnings, as our
       Rabbis have said: "The blessing of a house consists in the numbers
       of its inmates" (BT Baba Bathra 144b).
       and what gain: what advantage and gain has the owner of this
       great wealth? Why does he trouble himself about it so much? He
       gets no pleasure from it except the sight of it, in that he sees the
       wealth in his possession, but he has no profit or gain from it.

11   **Sweet is the year**[42] **of a labourer:** the year and time of a
(12)   farmer is good because he can eat the fruit of his farming, whether
       little or much.
       but the surfeit of the rich: who has great abundance and
       much wealth — those riches do not let him sleep. For he is always
       thinking about his money lest it be lost, as it is said above: "even in
       the night his mind does not rest" (2:23).

12-13 חוֹלָה**:** *enferme* in French[43].
(13-14) **riches were kept:** and hidden away for the owner's needs, but
       to his misfortune, not for his benefit. When he busied himself ac-
       quiring money he planned to obtain it for his benefit, but it turned
       out to be to his misfortune. For sometimes a man is killed or cap-
       tured for his money, and those riches are lost in an evil venture, so
       that he does not enjoy his money. After this when he possesses
       nothing, he begets a son and has nothing to give him, to bequeath to
       him or to leave as an inheritance.

---

42 RSV: sleep. The MT has שְׁנַת, which could be construct of שָׁנָה (year) or שֵׁנָה (sleep).
43 Weak, sick.

ברבות הטובה. כטובה רבה וגדלה[21] ביד האדם ברוב ממון. מחמת שהוא ‎**י**
עוסק יותר מדיי לקנות ממון הרבה כנגד אותו ממון שהוא גדול רבים לו
אוכלים ומוציא ממונו. שלפי שהוא משתכר רבים צרכיו. כמ׳ שאמרו[22]
רבותי׳. ברכת הבית ברובה.[23]

ומה כשרון. מה יתרון וכשרון לבעליה של טובה גדולה זו על מה הוא
טורח על כך יותר מדיי אין לו בה הנאה רק ראות עיניו שהוא רואה את
הטובה בידו. ואין לו ריווח ושכר בכך.

מתוקה שנת העובד. טובה היא שנתו ועתו של עובד אדמה שהוא יכול ‎**יא**
לאכל מעבודת קרקעו אם מעט אם הרבה.

והשבע לעשיר. שיש לו שובע גדול והון רב. אותו עושר אינו מניח לו
ליישן. כי תמיד הוא מחשב בממונו שלא יאבד כמ׳ שנ׳ למעלה וגם בלילה לא
שכב לבו.[24]

יב-יג חולה. אֶנְפְרִמא בלעז. ‎**יב-יג**

עושר שמור. ומוצנע לצורך בעליו. לרעתו ולא לטובתו. כאשר טרח
לקנות ממון חשב לקנות לטובתו ונהפכה לו לרעתו שפעמים שהוא נהרג או
נתפס בשביל ממונו ונאבד אותו עושר בעניין רע שלא נהנה מממונו[25]
והוליד בן אחרי כן שאין בידו מאומה. שאין לו מה יתן לבנו להורישו
ולהנחילו.

---

21 Preceded by the dotted גדולה.

22 Ms. שאמרנו, cf. Jellinek.

23 BT Baba Bathra 144b.

24 2:23.

25 Ms. ממונו.

14
(15) **As he came from his mother's womb:** poor and needy —
for he had nothing at the time of his birth — so will he return naked
and wanting to his grave, taking nothing with him; for his money
has been lost.
שׁיולך: is like שׁיוליך.

15-16 **This also:** this too is a grievous evil among all these things (men-
(16-17) tioned) above. Just like that fact, namely, that he was wanting, poor
and naked when he came into the world at the time of his birth, so
will he depart from the world at his death.
and what gain has he: in all this, his money, for which he
troubled himself and laboured in vain? This is not the only thing
that happened to him; for in addition, throughout his days, while he
was still alive, he ate in darkness and was full of much vexation,
sickness and anger, due to his many deliberations as he was acquiring his money.

17
(18) **Behold, what I have seen:** behold, this thing which I have
seen is right: that it is good for a man to eat and drink and enjoy his
gains, that he should be happy with his lot while he is still alive,
from the gains for which he has troubled himself during his life,
that is, from the money which the Holy One has given him.
for this is his lot: this thing is his portion, and you have no better thing than this, and this is what is said above: "There is nothing
better for a man than that he should eat and drink etc." (2:24).

18
(19) **Every man also:** of all these things which men do, this one is by
far the best. Because for the man to whom the Holy One has given
wealth, and the power to control his wealth, to enjoy it and to take
his share of it so that he is happy in his lot and with his gains —
this is a significant gift to him, given to him by Heaven.

יד‏ **כאשר יצא מבטן אמו.** עני ורש שלא היה לו כלום בשעה שנולד. כן
ישוב ערום וחסר לקברו שלא ישא בידו מאומה. כי אבד ממונו.

שיולך. כמ׳ שיוליך.

טו-טז‏ **וגם זו.** [26] אף זאת רעה חולה. בכל אילו[27] שלמעלה כל כנגד אותו עניין
שבא לעולם בשעה שנולד חסר ורש וערום כן הולך מן העולם בסופו.

ומה יתרון לו בכל אילו ממונו שטרח ועמל על חנם. ולא זו בלבד הגיע לו
שהרי אף בכל ימיו בעודנו חי אכל[28] בחושך ונתמלא כעס הרבה וחולי וקצף
ברוב מחשבותיו כשהיה קונה ממונו.

יז‏ **הנה אשר ראיתי אני.** הנה דבר זה נכון אשר ראיתי שטוב לו לאדם
לאכול ולשתות ולראות טובה בעמלו שיהיה שמח בחלקו בעודנו חי מעמלו
אשר טרח בו בחייו. מאותו ממון שנתן לו הק׳.

כי הוא חלקו. דבר זה הוא חלקו. ואין לך דבר טוב יותר מזה. וזה שנ׳
למעלה אין טוב באדם שיאכל ושתה וג׳.[29]

יח‏ **גם כל האדם.** אף על כל המעשים הללו שעושים בני האדם מעשה זה טוב
ומשובח יותר מכולם שכל האדם שנתן לו הק׳ עושר ונתן לו יכולת לשלוט
בעושרו לאכול וליטול חלקו ממנו שיהיה שמח בחלקו ובעמלו נתינת מתנה
חשובה היא לו שנתנו לו מן השמים.

---

26 MT — ‏זה.

27 It seems that the word was first written as ‏אולו; the *Waw* was then cut in the middle and
the *Alef* vocalized with a *Chirek*, cf. above ch. 4 note 7.

28 Ms. ‏הכל.

29 2:24.

19
(20)
For . . . not much: for not many days after his death, no one will remember him for the money which he left, nor for the works which he did during his life. After his death he will not even have [remembrance] from that man to whom he bequeathed his property and money.

because God: but the Holy One gave him this money in order that he might sing and be glad of heart and happy in his lot during his life.

מַעֲנֶה‎: is *Hiphil* and denotes rejoicing and singing, as in ותען להם מרים (Ex. 15:21) and וענתה השירה (Deut. 31:21).

יט   **כי לא הרבה.** שהרי לא הרבה ימים שלאחר מיתתו לא יזכור אותו הזוכר
על ממונו שהניח ועל מעשיו שעשה בימי חייו. שאפי׳[30] לא יהיה לו בעולם
לאחר מיתתו. מאותו אדם אשר הוריש לו נכסיו וממונו.

כי האלהים אלא הק׳ נתן לו ממון זה למען יהיה משורר ושמח בלבו.
ולהיות שמח בחלקו בחייו.

מענה. לש׳ מפעיל. והוא לש׳ שמחה וזימרה. כמ׳ ותען להם מרים.[31] וענתה
השירה.[32]

---

30   The subject of the sentence is obviously missing; probably זכרן.
31   Ex. 15:21.
32   Deut. 31:21.

1-2   **and it lies heavy:** and it is a great evil upon men: a man to whom the Holy One has given great riches but who has neither ability nor power to enjoy them; but a stranger, who has taken no pains with them, will enjoy them. This is a case of futility, for why did the other man trouble himself about it?

3-4   **If a man begets:** up to a hundred children — that is the one whose money was consumed by a stranger — and lives many years.
so that the days of his years are many: he uses a parallel expression. (The man) who lived many years and whose soul was not satisfied with what wealth he had, and even at the time of his death was not handed over for burial — I said of him that the abortion, which has not seen light and was not born alive, is better off than he. For he entered the world in obscurity and left in darkness, and his name is covered in darkness — for the entire circumstances of the man whose money was lost and who was not handed over for burial, were in obscurity and darkness, since he did not enjoy himself; but the abortion had neither good nor evil.
If a man begets a hundred: since, at the end of the verse, he mentions the abortion whose birth is despised and loathsome, he uses an expression referring to many significant births of a hundred children.

5   **moreover it has not seen the sun:** although the abortion

פרק ו

א-ב   ורבה היא. ורעה רבה היא על האדם. איש שנותן לו הק׳ עושר גדול ואין
לו יכולת ורשות שיאכל ויהנה ממנו. אלא איש נכרי יאכלנו שלא טרח בו. זה
מעשה הבל. כי על מה טרח זה בו.

ג-ד   אם יוליד איש זה שאכל איש נכרי ממונו עד מאה בנים ויחיה שנים
רבות.

ורב שיהיו ימי שניו. כופל מילתו. שהיו ימי שניו רבים ולא היתה נפשו
שביעה מן הטובה שבידיו ואף לעת מיתתו לא ניתן לקבורה. אמרתי עליו
שהנפל אשר לא ראה אור ולא נולד חי משובח יותר ממנו שהרי הוא בא
בעולי׳ בהבל. והלך מן העולי׳ בחשך ושמו מתכסה בחושך שכל אדותיו[1] של
זה שאבד ממונו ולא ניתן לקבורה היו בהבל ובחושך שלא ראה בטוב. אבל
נפל זה לא היה לו לא טוב ולא רע.
אם יוליד[2] איש מאה. לפי שמזכיר בסוף המקרא הנפל שלידתו[3] בזוייה
ומאוסה אחז לשונו בלידות[4] רבות וחשובות של מאה בנים.

ה   גם שמש לא ראה. שנפל זה לא ראה[5] כלום ולא ידע מאומה. ואעפ״כ

---

1   Ms. אדותיי, cf. Jellinek.
2   Ms. יוליד, cf. Jellinek.
3   Ms. שילדתו.
4   Ms. בילדות.
5   Ms. באה. cf. Jellinek.

145

did not see anything and did not know anything it is better off than he; for the abortion saw neither good nor evil, whereas this man saw nothing but evil all day.

moreover it has not seen the sun: as "like the untimely birth that never sees the sun" (Ps. 58:8 (Heb. 9)).

6   **Even though he should live:** if this man lived two thousand years and did not enjoy himself, it would be of no good to him, since everyone goes to the same place.

7   **All the toil of man is for his mouth:** for he does not busy himself unless it concerns his eating.
yet his appetite is not satisfied: since every day he desires food.

8   **For what advantage:** for what advantage in the world has a wise man over a fool, in that both live and exist in the world alike; therefore I said: "Everything is futile".
what does the poor man have who knows: how did the poor man start inferior to the wise man, for he knows how to conduct himself in the world with the rest of the living, like one of the wise men?

9   **Better is the sight of the eyes:** you may have a man in the world for whom the sight of his money — viewing and observing it — is better than eating and satisfying his appetite. This too is vanity.

10   **Whatever has come to be has already:** he who was a mighty man, famous, and known to be important and mighty, will be unable, at the time of his death, to argue and fight with the angel of death who is stronger than him. Therefore I said: "Everything is futile".

משובח הוא יותר ממנו. שלא ראה נפל זה לא טוב ולא רע וזה לא ראה. רק רע כל היום.

וגם[6] שמש לא ראה. כמ'[7] כנפל בל יחז שמש[8]

ו   ואילו חיה. ואם חיה זה[9] אלפים שנה ולא ראה בטובה אינו משובח כלום. שהרי אל מקום אחד הכל הולכים

ז   כל עמל האדם לפיהו. שאינו טורח כי אם על אודות אכילתו. וגם הנפש לא תמלא. שבכל יום ויום הוא מתאווה לאוכל.

ח   כי מה יותר. שהרי מה יתרון לחכם יותר מן הכסיל בעולם ששניהם חיין ועומדין בעולם כאחד. ועל כן אמרתי הכל הבל.

מה לעני יודע. באיזה דבר התחיל עני זה גרוע מן החכם. שהרי הוא יודע לילך בעולם עם שאר החיים כאחד מן החכמים.

ט   טוב מראה עיניים. יש לך אדם בעולם שטוב לו ראות עיניו בממונו שהוא רואה ומסתכל בו יותר ממה שהוא אוכל ומשביע את נפשו גם זה הבל.

י   מה שהיה כבר. אותו שהיה גבור ונקרא שמו ונודע שהוא אדם חשוב[10] וגיבור. בשעת המיתה לא יוכל לדין ולהלחם עם מלאך המות שהוא תקיף ממנו. ועל כן אמרתי הכל הבל.

---

6   MT — גם.

7   The emendation is supported by two considerations. On the one hand, the introduction of וג' after a lemma and before an interpretation is extremely rare (in our commentary it is found only once, in 12:13, where it is really part of the lemma). On the other hand, quotations are usually preceded by a word of introduction (שנאמר, לשון, כמו) but וג' is not one of these. The emendation of וג' into כמ' solves both difficulties.

8   Ps. 58:9. MT — נפל אשת בל חזו שמש. The citation is inaccurate but the points of contact with our verse are, nevertheless, clear.

9   Ms. זו.

10   Preceded by a cancelled *Waw*.

11   The more words: for there are words in the world in that men
      speak many words which bring man to poverty, for "he that mul-
      tiplies words occasions sin" (Mish. Aboth 1:17). So what advantage
      is there in a multitude of words? Therefore I said: "Everything is
      futile".

12   For who knows: for who is the one who knows what a man
      should do in this world? If he had known to choose the right thing
      he ought to have done it. But people do not act this way; for they
      spend their futile life like a passing shadow, as they do not want to
      walk in the right path; therefore they die before their time. But one
      ought to practise good works, for who is to tell what will happen in
      the world after his death and to his sons who will succeed him?
      Therefore he should practise good works, so that his sons after him
      might find blessing.

יא **כי יש דברים.** שהרי יש דברים בעולם שמדברים בני האדם רוב דברים
שמביאים את האדם לידי עניות. שכל המרבה דברים מביא חטא.[11] ומה
יתרון ברוב דברים. ועל כן אמרתי הכל הבל.

יב **כי מי יודע.** שהרי מי הוא אשר יודע. איזה דבר לו לאדם לעשות בעול'
הזה שאילו היה יודע לבחור מעשה הטוב היה לו לעשות. והם אינם עושים כך
שהם עושים ימי חיי הבלם כצל עובר שאינם רוצים לילך בדרך הטוב. ועל כן
הם מתים קודם זמנם. ומעשים טובים יש לו לעשות. אשר מי הוא שיגיד מה
שיהיה אחרי מותו בעול' ולבניו אשר יהיו אחריו. ועל כן יש לו לעשות
מעשים טובים למען אשר ימצאו בניו אחריו ברכה.

---

11 Mish.Aboth 1:17.

CHAPTER 7

1   **A good name is better than precious ointment**[44]: much better is a man's good reputation than the good oil of the balsam tree, whose fragrance spreads; for we find in one place an explicit text which mentions (both) and compares reputation with good oil, "your name is oil poured out" (Song of Songs 1:3), so do not be surprised at both being mentioned together and compared in this verse.

and the day of death, than the day of birth: much better is the day of a man's death than that of his birth, because in the day of his death his evil deeds cease, and he sins no more; whereas the day of his birth is evil for him for he is born for trouble, as it is said: "but man is born to trouble" (Job 5:7). Further, since there is no man who does not sin, the day of a man's birth is evil for him.

2   **It is better to go:** it is better for a man to go to a house of mourning than to a house of feasting, for the house of mourning is the final point in the death of every man, and a living man, going there, sets his thought and mind upon human death and as a result he refrains from sinning; but when he goes to be merry in the house of feasting, he sins as a result of his merrymaking.

44. The Hebrew word שמן may mean "oil" or "ointment".

א   **טוב שם משמן טוב.** טוב ומשובח שם טוב של אדם יותר משמן טוב של
אפרסמון שריחו נודף. לפי שמצינו במקום אחד מקרא מלא שהמשיל והזכיר
שם לשמן טוב. שנ' שמן תורק שמך.[1] ואל תתמה על אשר נמשלו והוזכרו
שניהם במקרא זה יחד.

ויום המות מיום הולדו. ומשובח וטוב יום מיתתו מיום לידתו. שביום
מיתתו פוסקים מעשיו רעים ולא יחטא עוד. אבל יום לידתו רע הוא לו כי
לעמל נולד. שנ' כי אדם לעמל יולד.[2] ועוד בשביל שאין אדם אשר לא יחטא
רע הוא לו יום לידתו.

ב   **טוב ללכת.** מוטב לו לאדם. שילך לבית אבילות יותר מאשר ילך לבית
משתאת[3] כי בית אבילות הוא סוף מיתתו של כל אדם. ואדם חי שהולך שם
נותן מחשבתו ולבו על מיתתו של אדם. ומתוך כך הוא מונע מלחטוא. אבל
כשהוא הולך לשמוח בבית המשתה מתוך שמחתו חוטא.

---

1   Song of Songs 1:3.
2   Job 5:7.
3   A strangely defective spelling.

3   **Sorrow is better than laughter:** better is sorrow for a man
— for he is a thinker and reflects upon the matter of death which is
the end for all men, and does not make merry — than that he
should engage in the merriment of the house of feasting. For due to
a sad countenance, which he has because he reflects on the matter
of death, his heart becomes glad, for he will not sin.

4   **The heart of the wise is in the house of mourning:**
(wishes) to go there, for in this way they set their minds upon the
day of death and do not sin.
but the heart of fools is in the house of mirth: and they
sin as a result of their merrymaking, for they do not set the fear of
God before their eyes.

5   **It is better . . . to hear:** it is better for a man to listen to the
rebuke of a wise man and so to become wiser, than it is for a man to
listen to the song of fools, where he shall not learn or hear anything
but folly.

6   **For as the crackling:** just like the sound of thorns — which is
heard when they are kindled as they are placed and burned beneath
a bronze pot in order to cook a dish in it, but the fire from those
thorns is not as significant as the fire from other wood — so is the
frivolity of the fool with his many words, for he utters with his voice
things which are devoid of all rhyme or reason, of all reproof or
wisdom.
this also is vanity: like the other vanities mentioned above.
Therefore a man should keep away from fools and the frivolity of
their words.

7   **Surely oppression makes the wise man foolish:** this is
related to "but the heart of fools is in the house of mirth" (7:4), as if
to say, fools are attracted to and are anxious to go to the house of
mirth, and this mirth leads them to sin and iniquity. Therefore wise
men should keep away from fools, because the fool who is full of
folly and oppression makes the wise man mad, that is, turns him

ג   **טוב כעס משחוק.** מוטב לו לאדם כעס שהוא בעל מחשבות לחשוב
בעניין המיתה. שהוא סוף כל האדם ואינו שמח. יותר ממה שהוא עוסק
בשחוק של בית המשתה. שהרי ברוע פנים שיש לו מחמת שהוא מחשב
בעניין המיתה. ייטב לבו שלא יחטא.

ד   **לב חכמים בבית אבל.** ללכת שם שמתוך כך נותנים לבם על יום המיתה
ואינן חוטאין.
ולב כסילים בבית שמחה. ומתוך שמחתן הן חוטאין. שאינן נותנין
פחד אלהים נגד עיניהם.

ה   **טוב לשמוע.** ומוטב לו לאדם שישמע גערתו של חכם ועל כן יחכם יותר.
מאיש שומע שיר כסילים שלא יבין ולא ישמע שם רק דבר כסילות.

ו   **כי כקול.** שהרי כקול הקוצים שנשמע בשעת הבערת דליקתן שנותנים
ומתבערים תחת סיר⁴ של נחשת. כדי לבשל תבשיל שבו. ואין אש של אותן
קוצים אש חשובה כשאר אש של שאר עצים. כן שחוק הכסיל ברוב דבריו
שהוא משמיע בקולו דברים שאין⁵ בהן טעם וריח⁶ ודבר תוכיחה וחכמה.
וגם זה הבל. כשאר הבלים הנאמרים למעלה. ועל כן יש לאדם להתרחק
מן הכסילים ושחוק של דבריהם.

ז   **כי העושק יהולל חכם.** מוסב על ולב כסילים בבית שמחה.⁷ לומ׳
הכסילים הם משוכים ולוהטים ללכת בבית השמחה ואותה שמחה מביאתן
לידי חטא ועון. על כן יש להתרחק לחכמים מן הכסילים. שהרי הכסיל שהוא

---

4   Ms. שור (Or already סור?) cf. Jellinek.

5   Ms. שהן, cf. Jellinek.

6   Ms. וריוח, cf. Jellinek.

7   7:4.

into a fool, and he loses the wise mind which is a gift to a man from the Holy One; so the wisdom of the wise man is turned into folly. **oppression:** the fool is called 'opression' because he is full of folly and oppression; like וחטא עמך (Ex. 5:16) where the people are called 'sin'.

gift[45]: wisdom is called a gift, as it is said: "For the Lord gives wisdom" (Prov. 2:6).

8   **Better is the end of a thing**[46] **than its beginning:** than the beginning of a word[46]. For at its beginning its secret is not yet known, nor is it revealed until the end; so the listener should listen and pay attention and not open his mouth until he has heard.

the patient in spirit is better: he controls his anger and wrath more than he who is haughty and quick-tempered. With regard to the man who is (patient) it is appropriate to use the phrase ארך רוח expressing the idea of length, for he is slow to anger and it does not give him pain; he contains his mild anger and keeps silent. And, since this expression is suitable with respect to the man who is not bad-tempered, it is fitting to call him who is quick-tempered גבה רוח.

9   **Be not quick to anger:** subdue your nature lest you become angry, because anger is with the fools who are bad-tempered.

10   **Say not, 'Why were . . .':** do not say, "what are the things which are done in the world now", for you should not wonder or question about them, stating that in regard to what was done, former times were much better than the present times. For it is not out of wisdom that you have asked about this matter, but out of great

---

45 RSV "bribe" would not be appropriate in the light of the interpretation.
46 The word דָּבָר can either mean "thing", as RSV has understood it, or "word" as Rashbam understood it.

מלא כסילות ועושק יהולל חכם לעשותו כסיל ומאבד את לב החכמה[8] שהיא מתנה לאדם מן הק׳. ונהפכה חכמת החכם לכסילות.

העושק. הכסיל קורא עושק על[9] שם שהוא מלא כסילות ועושק. דוגמ׳[10] וחטא עמך.[11] שהעם קורא חטאת.

מתנה. חכמה[12] קורא מתנה כעיני׳ שנ׳ כי ← יתן חכמה.[13]

ח **טוב אחרית דבר מראשיתו.** יותר מראשיתו של דבר. שהרי בראשיתו לא נודע ולא נגלה סודו עד באחריתו. ויש על השומע[14] לשמוע. ולהטות אוזן שלא יפצה פה עד אשר ישמע.

טוב ארך רוח. שהרי מאריך אפו וחרונו יותר מאותו שהוא גבה רוח וכועס מהרה. באדם שהוא   [15]   נופל לומ׳ ארך רוח. לש׳ אריכות שמאריך על אודות כעסו ואינו חושש בו וסובל מיעוט חרונו ושותק. ואחרי שזה לש׳ נופל באדם שאינו רגזן נופל גם באותו שהוא כועס מהרה לקרותו גבה רוח.

ט **אל תבהל ברוחך לכעוס.** וכוף את יצרך שלא תכעוס. שהרי כעס אצל כסילים שהם רגזנים.

י **אל תאמר מה היה.** אל תאמר מה הם המעשים הנעשים עכשיו בעולם. שלא תתמה ולא תשאל עליהם לומ׳ שהימים הראשונים היו טובים ומשובחים במעשיהם יותר מאלה הימים. שהרי לא מחמת חכמה שבך שאלת

---

8 Ms. הסכמה, cf. Jellinek.

9 Preceded by a cancelled word.

10 Preceded by a cancelled *Waw*.

11 Ex. 5:16. MT — עמך וחטאת. Cf. Salters, Variant Readings, p. 87 and Ben-Hayyim.

12 Ms. סכמה, cf. Jellinek.

13 Prov. 2:6.

14 Ms. השמיע, cf Jellinek.

15 An empty space in the Ms. indicating probably that the scribe did not understand the word in his *Vorlage* and planned to come back to it.

folly; for you ought to understand of your own accord, from your own observation, that every day the world follows its regular course.

11 **Wisdom is good with an inheritance:** the wisdom of a man is of great value together with an inheritance and property left him by his father, because these will not last in his possession unless he has the wisdom to look after them.

an advantage to those who see the sun: wisdom is better than money to those who see the sun, that is, those who lead their lives in the world, for their wisdom supports and keeps them.

12 **For the protection of wisdom is like the protection of money:** a parallel expression to "Wisdom is good with an inheritance" (7:11), for where there is wisdom there is with it money and other riches.

and the advantage of knowledge: a parallel expression to "an advantage to those who see the sun" (7:11). The advantage of knowledge is that wisdom gives life to the one who possesses it. For by means of his wisdom he leads his life and makes a living in the world, and it saves him from evil deeds.

13 **Consider the work of God:** apply your mind to see and understand the works of the Holy One, so that the fear of him will be upon your face, that you may not sin; therefore he will save you from all evil. For who is he who has the power to straighten that which the Holy One has made crooked? Therefore men should fear him for none can deliver from his hand.

14 **In the day of prosperity be joyful:** at a time of prosperity, when the Holy One has sent you his prosperous blessing, you should receive it with joy and gladness.

and in the day of adversity consider: and when the Holy One sends you a time of misfortune bringing calamity upon you, consider, and bear your calamity. Be still before him and wait patiently for him, and you shall have pardon.

על דבר זה כי אם ברוב כסילותך. לפי שיש לך להבין מעצמך מתוך ראות
עיניך שבכל יום יום ויום העולם מתנהג[16] והולך.

יא **טובה חכמה עם נחלה.** חשובה וטובה חכמתו של אדם. עם נחלה
ונכסים שנשתיירו לו מאבין שלא יתקיימו בידו אם אין לו חכמה כדי לשמור
נכסיו.

ויותר לרואי השמש. וטובה החכמה יותר מן הממון לרואי השמש
ההולכים ומתנהגים בעולם. שחכמתן מסייעתן[17] ועומדת להן.

יב **כי בצל החכמה בצל הכסף.** לש׳ כפול על טובה חכמה עם נחלה.
שהרי במקום שיש שם חכמה יש שם עמה כסף ושאר עושר.

ויתרון דעת. כפול על ויותר לרואי השמש. יתרון של דעת הוא שהחכמה
נותנת חיים לבעליה. שעל ידי חכמתו הוא מתנהג ומתפרנס בעולם ומצילתו
ממעשים רעים.

יג **ראה את מעשה האלהים** תן לבך לראות ולהבין במעשיו של הק׳
בעבור תהיה יראתו על פניך לבלתי תחטא. ועל כן יצילך מכל רע. כי מי הוא
אשר בידו יכולת לתקן את המעוות אשר עיוותו הק׳. ועל כן יש לבני האדם
להתיירא מפניו. כי אין מידו מציל.

יד **ביום טובה היה בטוב.**[18] ביום של טובה ששלח לך[19] הק׳ את ברכתו
הטובה תקבלנה בשמחה ובטוב לבב.

וביום רעה ראה. וכאשר ישלח לך[19] הק׳ יום של רעה ליתן לך פורענות
ראה וסבול פורענותך. דום לפניו והתחולל לו ותהיה לך כפרה.

---

16 Ms. מתנה.
17 Ms. וסייעתן, cf. Jellinek.
18 Ms. — טוב, cf. the Introduction, p. 58, n. 163.
19 Ms. לו, cf. Jellinek. Although the change occurs twice and in the same phrase, it still
   seems to be just a scribal error.

the one as well as the other: also, the prosperity which the Holy One has given you is the payment corresponding to the good deed which you have performed; and the misfortune which he sent you in your time of adversity is the payment corresponding to a misdeed which you have committed. The Holy One does all these things in order that man may not find out anything concerning the Holy One except righteousness and justice; for he grants him prosperity for observing his commandments, and misfortune for sins which he has committed.

15 **In my vain life I have seen everything:** I have set my mind to consider several matters in the affairs of the world during my vain life. For you may have a righteous man in the world who is too righteous, and he perishes because of his great righteousness; for example, a certain righteous man who is killed because of a minor commandment, for he does not want to expound with regard to himself "he shall live by them but not die by them[47]". And you may have a wicked man in the world who transgresses a minor commandment so that he does not get killed; and he expounds with regard to himself "he shall live by them but not die by them[47]", and lives a long life because of his evil, because of a minor transgression which he commits.

and there is a wicked man: this wicked man is not really wicked but righteous; however, on account of a minor transgression which he commits he is called wicked.

16-18 **Be not righteous overmuch:** concerning these things which I have seen, I admonish you not to be very righteous, nor over-wise — why should you be destroyed from the world, for you may be killed because of a minor matter? And do not be very wicked by being a fool, used to acting wickedly — why should you die before your time, by acting so wickedly? It is good for you to hold this,

47 BT Yoma 85b etc.

גם את זה לעומת זה. שאף את הטובה אשר נתן לך הק' הנה היא
תשלום שכר לנגד המצוה אשר עשית. ואת הרעה ששלח לך ביום רעתך הנה
היא תשלום שכר לעומת עבירה אשר עשית. וכל המעשים הללו עושה הק'
על אודות שלא ימצא האדם אחריו של הק' מאומה. כי אם צדק ומשפט.
שעל שמירת קיום מצוותיו נותן לו טובה ועל אודות עבירות שעבר נותן לו
רעה.

את הכל ראיתי בימי הבלי. בכמה דברים נתתי לבי לראות בימיי של   טו
הבל בענייני העולם שיש לך צדיק בעולם שהוא צדיק יותר מדיי והוא אובד
ברוב צדקו. כגון צדיק אחד שנהרג על אודות מצוה קלה שאינו רוצה לדרוש
בעצמו וחי בהם לא שימות בהם. ויש לך רשע בעולם שעבר על מצוה קלה
לפי שלא יהרג ודורש לעצמו וחי בהם ולא שימות בהם. ומאריך ימים
ברעתו. בשביל עבירה קלה שהוא עובר.

ויש רשע. רשע זה אינו רשע ממש כי אם צדיק אבל על עבירה קלה זו
שהוא עובר קוראו רשע.

טז-יח אל תהי צדיק הרבה. על אודות מעשים הללו אשר ראיתי אני מוכיחך
שלא תהיה צדיק הרבה ולא תהיה חכם יותר מדיי למה תשומם מן העולם.
שתיהרג על דבר קל. ואל תהי רשע הרבה להיות סכל וכסיל ומלומד להרשיע.
ולמה תמות קודם זמנך אם תרשיע כל כך. וטוב לך שתאחוז בזה בצדק להיות

namely righteousness, that is, be a righteous man, and also from
that, namely from wickedness, do not withdraw, that is, do not lose
hold of it; for that man who is pious does his duty in both. He guards
himself from being over-righteous or too wicked, for all that he does
is for the sake of God.

תשומם: is of the same form as תכונן, as in תבנה ותכונן עיר סיחון
(Num. 21:27).

19 **Wisdom gives strength to the wise:** wisdom is a strong
tower to a wise man, by which to guard his city — as it is said:
"But there was found in it a poor wise man, and he by his wisdom
delivered the city etc." (9:15) — more than ten rulers which are in
the city to guard it.

gives strength to the wise: the verse is not written "wisdom
makes the wise man wise" but it uses a phrase expressing strength,
namely "gives strength to the wise", because it says later "than ten
rulers", for they give strength and power to a city.

more than ten rulers: these ten are not meant to be taken
literally, meaning neither more nor less; it is rather like "than many
rulers", as in "ten women shall bake your bread" (Lev. 26:26),
which is not to be taken literally.

20 **Surely there is not a righteous man on earth:** and now,
having said to you that there is nothing in the world as important as
wisdom, your mind must grasp this, that since there is no wise man
on the earth who does good throughout his life without sinning,
therefore you must watch yourself very carefully lest you reach the
state of sin, learning from the wise man by the principle of "from
minor to major[48]".

there is not a righteous man: it is the same as "there is not a
wise man". The wise man is called a righteous man, as it is said
above: "Be not righteous overmuch and do not make yourself
overwise" (7:16).

48 "Kal Vahomer" — one of the earliest and most common principles of Jewish exegesis,
cf. *EJ*, vol. 8, 1421.

צדיק. וגם מזה מן הרשע אל תנח ולא תסיר ידך ממנו. כי אותו אדם שהוא
ירא שמים יוצא ידי חובתו בכולם. שהוא שומר את עצמו שאינו צדיק הרבה
ואינו רשע יותר מדיי. לפי שכל מעשיו עושה לשם שמים.

תְּשׁוּמֵם. דוגמ׳ תכונַן. כמ׳ תבנה ותכונן עיר סיחון.[20]

יט וְהַחָכְמָה[21] תעוז לחכם. החכמה[22] היא מגדל עוז לחכם לשמור את
עירו. כעניין שנ׳ ומצא בה איש מסכן וחכם ומלט הוא את העיר בחכמתו
וג׳[23] יותר מעשרה שליטים. שהם בעיר לשמור אותה.

תעוז לחכם. לא כתב המקרא החכמה תְּחַכֵּם[24] לחכם כי אם לש׳ עוז תעוז
לחכם לפי שהוא אומר לאחריו מעשרה שליטים שהם נותנים עוז וכוח לעיר.

מעשרה שליטים. עשרה הללו אינן באין לדיקרוק המלה לומ׳ לא פחות
ולא יותר שהרי הוא כמו מהרבה שליטים. כמ׳ ואפו עשר נשים לחמכם[25].
שלא נכתב לדקדק המלה.

כ כי אדם אין צדיק בארץ. ועכשיו אמרתי לך שאין דבר חשוב בעולם
כחכמה. ועל כן זאת לבך להבין שהרי אין אדם חכם בארץ אשר יעשה טוב
בכל ימיו שלא יחטא. ועל כן יש לך לשמור עצמך שמירה גדולה שלא תבוא
לידי חטא. בקל וחומ׳ מן החכם.

אין צדיק. כמ׳ אין חכם את החכם קורא צדיק. כמ׳ שנ׳ למעלה אל תהי
צדיק הרבה ואל תתחכם.[26]

---

20 Num. 21:27.
21 MT — החכמה.
22 Ms. הסמכה, cf. Jellinek.
23 9:15.
24 Ms. חסכם, cf. Jellinek.
25 Lev. 26:26.
26 7:16.

21-22 **to all the things:** with this admonition also I shall warn you on top of the admonitions with which I have warned you: do not bother to answer all the evil things which men say to you.

lest you hear: so that you do not let it be seen that you have heard your slave speak disrespectfully to you; but act like a deaf man, as if you had not heard. For you yourself know that you have often spoken disrespectfully to others and you did not want the person to whom you spoke disrespectfully to answer you back; likewise you should behave like a deaf man when your slave speaks disrespectfully to you.

מקלל: does not mean 'cursing' but 'disrespect', for it is not appropriate to use 'cursing' and 'blessing' in the case of a slave, but rather 'respect' and 'disrespect' as it is said in: "A son honours his father, and a servant his master" (Mal. 1:6). It is of the same root as ואקל בעיניה (Gen. 16:5), ונקלותי עוד (2 Sam. 6:22).

23 **All this I have tested by wisdom:** I have tested by my great wisdom everything regarding this matter. For I had said in my heart that I would become wise in profound wisdom; but it — this profound wisdom — is far from me, for I am unable to understand it or cope with it.

24 **That which is, is far off:** profound (wisdom), which is of the past, as for example the "Merkaba Mysticism" and the "Book of Creation"[49]; it is far from me in that I cannot cope with it.

and deep, very deep: is the quality of this superior wisdom, and who is that man who, by his great wisdom, can find it out?

25 **I turned:** *atornai* in French[50].

I turned: then I turned my mind and my knowledge to understand the affairs of the world, to know it and to search it out. My

49 Cf. Introduction, p. 66.
50 I turned around.

כא-כב גם לכל הדברים. אף במוסר זה אזהירך[27] על המוסרים אשר הזהרתיך שלכל[28] הדברים רעים שידברו אליך בני אדם אל תתן לבך להשיב להם דבר.

אשר לא תשמע. שלא תעשה את עצמך להראות ששמעת את עבדך שהוא מקללך והראה את עצמך כחרש. כאילו לא שמעת. שהרי גם אתה יודע בעצמך אשר רבות פעמים קללתה אחרים ולא היה רצונך שיענוך דבר אותו שקללתה. כמ' כן אתה תתנהג בעצמך כחרש כאשר יקללך עבדך.

מקללך. אינו לש' קללה כי אם לש' זילזול. שלשון קללה וברכה אינו נופל לומ' בעבד. כי אם לש' כיבוד וזילזול. כמ' שנ' בן יכבד אב ועבד אדוניו.[29] והוא מגזירת ואקל בעיניה.[30] ונקלותי עוד.[31]

כג **כל זו[32] ניסיתי בחכמה.** כל אודות דבר זה ניסיתי ברוב חכמתי שהרי אמרתי בלבי שאחכמה בחכמות עמוקות. והיא אותה חכמה עמוקה רחוקה ממני שאיני יכול להבין ולעמוד בה.

כד **רחוק מה שהיה.** עמוקה שהיתה כבר כגון מעשה מרכבה. וספר יצירה רחוקה היא ממני שאיני יכול לעמוד בה.

ועמוק עמוק הוא אותו מעשה של חכמה יתירה זו. ומי הוא אותו שהוא ימצאנו ברוב חכמתו.

כה **סבותי.** אָה טורניי בלע'.

סבותי אני. וגם את לבי ודעתי סבותי להבין בעייני העולם לדעת ולתור

27 Ms. הזהירך.
28 Ms. של כל.
29 Mal. 1:6.
30 Gen. 16:5.
31 II Sam. 6:22.
32 MT — זה.

mind sought to explore the wisdom and the thinking which are in the world, and to know the wickedness of folly and the foolishness of madness — that evil which is more wicked and evil than all the evils in the world.

26   **And I find**[51]: and I have found one thing in the world which is (worse) than death, that is an evil woman whose heart is a trap and net with which to capture men and make them fall into the traps and snares of her nets.

Whose hands are fetters: her hands are a prison with which to imprison men. Whoever pleases the Holy One escapes from her, that is, he does not fall into her hands; but whoever is a sinner is caught by her.

And I find[51]: since he has said above "and to seek wisdom" (7:25), it is fitting to follow it with an expression denoting 'finding', because a matter which is referred to by an expression denoting 'seeking' is also referred to by an expression denoting 'finding'.

snares and nets (מצודים וחרמים): mean seine (מכמורת) and nets (רשתות).

escapes her: one may use an expression denoting 'capture' and 'escape' because he has likened her to traps and snares, as in "They set a trap (משחית); they catch men" (Jer. 5:26); משחית means 'net' as in המצב והמשחית (I Sam. 14:15); (also) "We have escaped as a bird from the snare of the fowlers; the snare is broken and we have escaped!" (Ps. 124:7)

27-28 **Behold, this is what I found:** thus said the soul of Qoheleth to the person whom he was admonishing.

Behold: this thing I have found in the world, while considering one statement after another — while I was examining it, one matter after another, to search and find out the sum total of the wisdom of the world.

51 RSV: found.

ובקש לבי לחקור חכמה וחשבון שהן בעולם ולדעת רשע של סיכלות וכסילות
של הוללות באותה רעה שהיא קשה ורעה מכל רעות שבעולם.

כו **ומוצא**[33] **אני. ואני מצאתי.** דבר אחד בעולם שהוא יותר ממות. **והיא
אשה רעה ולבה מצודים וחרמים** לצוד בני אדם להפילם בפחי מוקשי חרמיה.

ידיה אסוריה[34] **וידיה** בית האיסורין לאסור בהן בני אדם ומי שהוא טוב
לפני הקדוש[35] **נמלט ממנה** שאינו נופל בידיה. **ומי שהוא חוטא נלכד בה.**

ומוצא אני. לפי שאמ׳ למעלה **ובקש** חכמה נופל אחריו. לומ׳ לש׳
מציאה. שבדבר שמוסב בו לשון בקשה מוסב בו לש׳ מציאה.

מצודים וחרמים. לש׳ מכמורת ורשתות.

ימלט ממנה. ולהרבה.[36] לש׳ לכידה ומליטה נופל בה לומ׳ לפי שהמשילה
לפחים ורשתות. כמ׳ **הציבו משחית**[37] **אנשים ילכדו.**[38] **משחית** הוא לש׳
מכמורת. כמ׳ **המצב והמשחית.**[39] **נפשינו כצפור נמלטה מפח יוקש׳ הפח
נשבר ואנחנו נמלטנו.**[40]

כז-כח ראה זה מצאתי כך אמרה נפש קהלת לאותו[41] שהוא מוכיחו.

ראה. דבר זה מצאתי בעולם בעניין מלה אחת אחר[42] מלה אחרת. כשהייתי
מפשפש אותו בזו אחר זו לחקור ולמצוא חשבון עניין חכמת העולם.

33 Ms. —ומוציא״, cf. the Introduction, p. 58, n. 163.

34 MT — אסורים ידיה.

35 The only instance in this commentary where the appelation הקדוש for God is written in full.

36 The word, which is isolated from its context by a dot, is inexplicable; it is either superfluous, or a mistake for an unknown word.

37 The word is written above the line by the same scribe.

38 Jer. 5:26.

39 I Sam. 14:15.

40 Ps. 124:7.

41 Ms. מאותו.

42 Ms. אחת.

A Commentary of R. Samuel

אשׁר עוד[52]: the logic of facts my soul has sought but I have not found; for I have found one man out of a thousand men, who is perfect in his deeds, but I have not found a woman who is perfect and blameless in her actions, among all these, that is, a thousand women.

אמרה קהלת: one should wonder why it is not written אמר קהלת and one should interpret it אמרה נפש קהלת, as ותכל דוד לצאת (2 Sam. 13:39) whose interpretation is ותכל נפש דוד לצאת.

29   **Behold, this alone I found:** this thing only have I found; see and consider it: the Holy One has created man upright and becoming, in that he created him in his likeness and in his image; but they, that is, men, have sought out schemes, many evil machinations, in order to turn away from the commandments of the Holy One, and it is a great evil about man.

חשבונות: means schemes.

---

52 The rendering of the RSV here does not correspond to the Hebrew lemma.

אשר עוד חכמות של מעשים בקשה נפשי ולא מצאתי. שהרי מצאתי אדם
אחד שלם במעשיו מאלף בני אדם ואשה לא מצאתי שלימה ותמימה
במעשיה בכל אלה אלף נשים.

אמרה קהלת. יש לתמוה[43] למה לא נכתב אמר קהלת. ויש לפתור אמרה
נפש קהלת. כמ׳ ותכל דוד לצאת.[44] שפת׳ ותכל נפש דוד לצאת.

כט   **לבד ראה זה מצאתי.** לבד מעשה זה מצאתי וראה ותן לב עליו אשר
עשה וברא הק׳ את האדם ישר ונאה שברא אותו בדמותו ובצלמו. והם בני
אדם בקשו חשבונות מזימות רעות ורבות לסור ממצותיו של הק׳. ורעה רבה
היא על האדם.

חשבונות לש׳[45] מחשבות.

---

43 Ms. לתמיה, cf. Jellinek.
44 II Sam. 13:39. MT — ותכל דוד המלך לצאת; cf. Salters, Variant Readings, p. 88.
45 Preceded by a cancelled letter.

CHAPTER 8

1 **Who is like the wise man:** who is as important in the world
as the wise man, and who knows the explanation of a matter like he
does, for there is nothing as important in the world as wisdom? The
wisdom of a man makes his face light up and makes him glad: and
the stern look of his countenance is changed into a shining face, due
to the great happiness of his wisdom.

2 **I keep the king's command**[53]: I am continually engaged in
observing the commands of the king, that is, the Holy One, Blessed
be He — keeping his commandments.
and because of ... sacred oath[54]: and any matter about
which I swear by the name of the Holy One saying: "By His Name
thus shall I do", I observe and fulfil.

3 **Be not hasty to go out from his presence**[55]: do not hurry
away from the Holy One in order to shun him, but walk before him,
keeping his commandments.
do not delay: and then do not persist in an evil affair when you
keep his commandments; for the Holy One does all that he desires
and he will give you every good thing if you walk in his ways, doing
his commandments.

53 There is an incongruity here between subject and predicate. RSV "keep the king's command" omits the personal pronoun "I".
54 RSV "your sacred oath" is based on a different exegesis.
55 RSV deviates from MT in the division of verses 2-3.

א   **מי כהחכם.** מי הוא אדם חשוב בעולם כהחכם. ומי הוא שיודע פשר של
דבר כמותו שאין לך דבר חשוב בעולם כחכמה. שחכמת אדם מאירה את פניו
ומשמחתו ועוז קרון תואר פניו משתנה בפנים צהובות מרוב שמחת חכמתו.

ב   **אני פי מלך שמור.** תמיד אני עוסק לשמור דברות פי מלך הוא הקב״ה
לשמור מצותיו.

        ועל דברת שבועת אלהים. ועל אותו דבר שאני נשבע בשמו של הק׳
לומ׳ כך אעשה בשבועת שמו הייתי שומר ומקיים.

ג   **אל תבהל מפניו תלך.** לא תהיה בהול מפניו של הק׳ להתרחק מעליו.
אבל לפניו תלך לשמור מצותיו.

        ואל[1] תעמוד. ואז אל תעמוד במעשה עניין רע כאשר תשמור מצותיו כי
כל אשר יחפוץ הק׳ הוא עושה ויעשה לך כל טוב אם תלך בדרכיו לעשות
מצותיו.

4   **For the word of the king is supreme:** in that place where the Holy One has said he is king, there he rules, and demonstrates his power by doing whatever he finds fit.

and who may say to him "What are you doing?": and therefore men should keep his commandments.

שׁלטון: is a noun.

5   **He who obeys a command:** whoever keeps his commandments shall neither experience any evil nor shall any evil happen to him.

the time and the way: the heart of the wise knows the time of judgement which comes to the world; therefore they keep his commandments.

6-7   **For every matter:** for every matter of the Holy One has a time for the execution of justice, for the evil of man is heavy upon him and the Holy One will grant him his deserts. For he does not know what verdict he shall have in the end and who is to tell him of the judgement which will befall him at his end.

For every matter has its time: as it is said: "and a time for every matter under heaven" (3:1).

8   **No man has power over the spirit[56]:** no man has control over his soul on the day of death, to withhold his soul from being handed over to the angel of death, because he has no power or control on the day of his death.

there is no delegation[57]: and he is incapable of sending a delegation of his soldiers to do battle with the angel of death to prevent him taking his soul from him; for the wickedness which he has done will not save him who is given to wickedness.

לכלוא: is like למנוע as ויכלא העם מהביא (Ex. 36:6), לא תכלה רחמיך (Ps. 40:11 (Heb. 12)).

---

56 The rendering of RSV would not be appropriate in the light of the interpretation.
57 RSV "discharge" would not be appropriate in the light of the interpretation.

ד באשר דבר מלך שלטון. באותו מקום אשר דבר הק׳ שם שהוא מלך
שם הוא שולט ומראה את שליטתו לעשות הטוב בעיניו.
ומי יאמר לו מה תעשה. ועל כן יש לבני אדם לשמור מצותיו.
שלטון שם דבר.

ה שומר מצוה. מי שהוא שומר מצותיו לא ידע ולא יגיע² בו דבר רע.
ועת ומשפט. עת פקודת הדין שבא לעולם יודע לב חכם. ועל כן הם
שומרים מצותיו.

ו-ז כי לכל חפץ. שהרי לכל חפצו של הק׳ יש עת לעשות דין ומשפט. כי רעת
האדם רבה על עצמו והק׳ ישלם לו שכרו. שהרי איננו יודע באותו דין אשר
יהיה בו לבסוף מי הוא אשר יגיד לו את משפטו אשר ימצאהו באחריתו.
כי על כל³ חפץ יש עת. כמ׳ שנ׳ ועת לכל חפץ תחת השמים.⁴

ח אין אדם שליט ברוח אין אדם שליט בנשמתו ליום המיתה למנוע
נשמתו למוסרה⁵ למלאך המות. שאין לו ממשלת ושליטה ביום מיתתו.
ואין משלחת. ואין כח בידו לשלוח משלחת חייליו להלחם עם מלאך
המות שלא יקח נשמתו ממנו. שהרי לא ימלט רשע שעשה⁶ את עצמו שהוא
בעליו של רשע.
לכלוא. כמ׳ למנוע. כמ׳ ויכלא העם מהביא.⁷ לא תכלה רחמיך.⁸

2 Ms. יגיעי, cf. Jellinek.
3 MT — כי לכל.
4 3:1.
5 Preceded by a superfluous של; probably a "vertical" dittography. cf. Jellinek.
6 Preceded by a redundant את, probably due to the influence of the verse. cf. Jellinek.
7 Ex. 36:6.
8 Ps. 40:12 (Eng. 40:11) MT — תכלא.

171

9   **All this:** this whole issue have I seen, and paid attention to all that is done. When man deliberately performs evil deeds, at his time of judgement his evil deeds will be his misfortune — retribution for his actions.

ונתון: is the infinitive absolute.

10-13   **Then I saw the wicked:** this is related to the (texts) above, "all this I have tested by wisdom" (7:23), "I turned my mind to know and to search out" (7:25). This is its interpretation according to its literal sense: thus, when I was considering in wisdom, I saw wicked men in the world, deserving of death and burial, who came and went from a holy place, and they were causing devastation and doing many evil things in it; but the end for them is that their name and memory is forgotten in that city in which they so acted.

   This also is vanity: along with the other vanities. For recompense for their evil is not paid to them speedily; for, because the Holy One is longsuffering toward them, men presume to do evil, and they say: 'What does one lose by doing evil? There is no judgement and no judge. For a sinner may do evil for a long time up to a hundred years, and the Holy One is longsuffering toward him. For I do not even know that it will be well with those who fear God, that is the pious, or that it will not be well with the wicked, and that he will not live long, that he will pass away from the world like a passing shadow, because he does not fear God'.

ובכן: means 'thus'.

wicked buried: wicked men are called buried men while still alive, because they deserve death; the same thought is expressed in "And you, O slain,[58] wicked one, prince of Israel" (Ez. 21:25 (Heb. 30)).

הלכו: is a parallel expression to ובאו.

---

58 RSV "unhallowed" would not be appropriate in the light of the interpretation.

ט **את כל זה** כל המעשה הזה ראיתי ונתתי על לבי בכל המעשים באותו עת
שהאדם שולט בעצמו לעשות מעשים רעים עתיד הוא לעת פקודתו שיהיו
מעשיו רעים לו לרעה. כתשלום תגמולי מעשיו.

ונתון לש' פעול.

י-יג **ובכן ראיתי רשעים.** מוסב למעלה על כל זה ניסיתי בחכמה.[9] סבותי אני
ולבי לדעת ולתור.[10] וכן פתר' לפי פשוטו. ובכן שהייתי מחשב בחכמה ראיתי
בעול' רשעים שראויים למיתה וקבירה שהיו באים והולכים ממקום קדוש
וחורבות ורעות רבות היו עושים בו. וסופן נשכח שמם וזכרם באותה עיר
אשר כן עשו.

גם זה הבל. עם שאר הבלים. שלא נעשה ולא נשתלם להם דבר מעשה
שכר רעתם מהרה. שהרי על כן שהק' מאריך להם אפו מלא לב בני האדם
בעצמם לעשות רעה ואומרים מה הפסד יש לו לעשות רעה. לית דין ולית
דיין. שהוא החוטא עושה רע זמן גדול עד מאת שנים והק' מאריך לו אפו.
שהרי אף איני יודע שיהיה טובה ליראי שמים היריאים ממנו. ולרשע לא
יהיה טובה ולא יאריך ימים כצל יעבור מן העול' לפי שאינֹו ירא שמים.

ובכן כמ' ובכך.

רשעים קבורים. רשעים בעדן בחייהם קוראן[11] קבורים. לפי שהן[12]
ראויים למיתה. כעניין שנ' ואתה חלל רשע נשיא ישר'.[13]

הלכו.[14] כפל מלה על ובאו.

---

9 7:23.

10 7:25.

11 The last *Nun* is preceded by a cancelled *Yod*.

12 Preceded by a dotted word, שאין.

13 Ez. 21:30 (Eng. 21:25).

14 MT — יהלכו.

וישתכחו: means 'forgetting'. It is impossible to explain it as meaning 'finding', for this word is not found in Hebrew with the meaning 'finding'; it is Aramaic.

This also is vanity: that which is hidden from men, which men cannot understand clearly and do not know why the Holy One is so longsuffering with them, is called 'vanity' because men wonder and are amazed at it.

פתגם: means 'matter'.

a hundred: the text is elliptic; it is in the construct state and the *Nomen Regens* is missing, as if to say 'a hundred days' or 'a hundred years'. And he does not use the word 'hundred' literally, but rather to express a long time. So also is ושכורת לא מיין (Is. 51:21) where שכורת is in the construct state and the *Nomen Regens* is missing; (it means) 'drunk with some other affliction but not with wine'.

14 **There is a vanity which takes place on earth:** there is a matter at which men wonder and are amazed, and it is current in the world. There are many righteous men in the world who get what is due to the wicked, for they do not prosper; and there are many wicked men in the world who get what is due to the righteous, for they do not experience misfortune, but very great prosperity.
I said that this also is vanity: I wonder and am amazed at this.

15 **And I commend enjoyment:** and I praise rejoicing, for there is nothing good for a man in the world except eating and drinking and rejoicing, to be happy in his lot. This thing shall join him in his toil during the life which the Holy One has given him in the world.
ילונו: means 'joining' as in "my husband will be joined to me". (Gen. 29:34).

16 **When I applied:** when I set my heart to know wisdom and to see the affairs of the world, I saw vanity in it; for day and night he does not experience sleep in his eyes. The whole verse speaks about

וישתכחו. לש׳ שיכחה. ואי אפשר לפרש לש׳ מציאה. שלא מצינו בלש׳
עברי לש׳ מציאה כזה. שהרי לש׳ תרגו׳ הוא.

גם זה הבל אותו דבר שהוא מכוסה מבני אדם שאינן יכולין לעמוד על
הבירור. ואינן יודעים על מה הק׳ מאריך להם אפו כל כך. קורא הבל. לפי
שבני אדם תוהין ומשתוממין על הדבר.

פתגם. דְּבַר.

מֵאַת. מקרא קצר הוא ודבוק הוא על תיבה החסירה לומ׳ מאת ימים או
שנים. ולא אחז בלשונו מאת לדקדק מלתו כי אם לומ׳ זמן גדול. וכן ושכורת
לא מיין.[15] דבוק הוא על תיבה החסירה. שכורת דבר צער אחר. ולא מיין.

יד וְיֵשׁ[16] הבל אשר נעשה על הארץ. יש דבר שבני אדם תוהין
ומשתוממין עליו והוא נוהג בעול׳. שהרי יש כמה וכמה צדיקים בעול׳
שמגיע אליהם כמעשה הרשעים שלא יהיה להם טובה. ויש כמה וכמה
רשעים בעול׳ שמגיע אליהם כמעשה הצדיקים שלא יהיה להם רעה כי אם
טובה גדולה עד מאד.

אמרתי שגם זה הבל. על זאת אני תוהה ומשתומם.

טו וְשִׁבַּח[17] אני את השמחה. ואני משבח את השמחה שאין דבר טוב
לאדם בעול׳. כי אם אכילה ושתייה ושמחה לשמוח בחלקו. ומעשה זה יהיה
מחובר לו בעמלו. בימי חייו שנתן לו הק׳ בעול׳.

ילונו. לש׳ חיבור. כמ׳ ילוה אישי אלי.[18]

טז כאשר נתתי. כשנתתי לבי לידע חכמה ולראות עניין העול׳ ראיתי בו
הבל. שהרי אף ביום ובלילה לא ראה. שינה[19] בעיניו. כל המקרא הזה הולך

---

15 Is. 51:21. MT — ושכרת ולא מיין; cf. Salters, *Variant Readings*, p. 89.
16 MT — יש.
17 MT — ושבחתי.
18 Gen. 29:34.
19 Preceded by a dotted לפי.

the heart as if it were a man with eyes. This is what is said in this verse, "and to see" — it is the heart who sees the affairs. And thus we find in one place 'seeing of the heart' as it is said: "and my heart has seen great wisdom and knowledge[59]" (1:16).

he does not see sleep in his eyes[60]: for his heart did not lie down and did not sleep. We find 'the sleeping of the heart' in "even in the night his heart does not lie down[61]" (2:23), "I slept, but my heart was awake" (Song of Songs 5:12).

17   **then I saw all the work:** I have seen the works of the Holy One, that a man cannot understand or find out the explanation of what is happening in the world, or know the attributes of the Holy One and how he treats his creatures.

However much man may toil: that matter which man toils to seek out and learn shall not be discovered nor be known by men — the attributes and works of the Holy One. Even if wise men determine to know his works, they cannot find out or know how to comprehend his mind.

---

59 In the light of the use of the verb "to see" in Rashbam's comments, the RSV rendering is unsuitable.

60 Again, Rashbam's comments demand a rendering other than that of RSV.

61 The phrasing differs from RSV here to accord with Rashbam's earlier remarks.

ומדבר על הלב כאילו הוא אדם שיש לו עינים.²⁰ וזהו שנ׳ במקרא זה ולראות
שהלב רואה את העניין וכן מצינו במקום אחד ראייה בלב שנ׳ ולבי ראה
הרבה חכמה ודעת.²¹

שינה בעיניו אינינו רואה. שלא שכב לבו. ולא היה ישן. ומצינו לש׳
שינה בלב שנ׳ גם בלילה לא שכב לבו.²² אני ישינה ולבי ער.²³

יז   **וראיתי את כל המעשה.**²⁴ ראיתי מעשיו של הק׳ שאין אדם יכול
לעמוד על הבירור ולמצוא את מעשי העול׳ ולידע מידותיו של הק׳ שהוא
מודד לבריות.

בשל אשר יעמל. באותו דבר שיעמל האדם לבקש ולידע לא ימצאו ולא
ידעו בני האדם את מידותיו ומעשיו של הק׳. ואף אם יאמרו החכמים לידע
מעשיו ולא יוכלו למצוא ולידע לעמוד על דעתו.

---

20   The last *Mem* is preceded by a dotted *Yod*.

21   1:16.

22   2:23.

23   Song of Songs 5:2.

24   MT — מעשה האלהים.

CHAPTER 9

1   **But all this:** for I applied my mind to all this business in order to
clarify and to examine this whole matter, that the righteous and the
wise and their slaves are all under the rule of the Holy One. They
know neither the love nor the hatred of the Holy One, since they are
unable to discern what is loved by the Holy One and what is hated.
ולבור: is derived from בר, just as ולקום is from קם and ולשוב from
שב.

in the hand of: *en la justice* in French[62], as in "from under the
hand of the Egyptians" (Ex. 18:11 (Heb. 10)), "out of the hand
of the Egyptians and out of the hand of Pharaoh" (Ex. 18:10).
גם אהבה וגם שנאה: two occurrences of גם following each
other are not to be taken literally, as in גם בחור גם בתולה (Deut.
32:25), גם לי וגם לך (I Kings, 3:26).

2-3   **Everything before them**[63]: every misfortune is directed and
designated to come upon them, and the same fate befalls them all.

---

62 In the power, cf. Japhet, *Tarbiz* XLIV 1974-5, p. 79, n. 40.
63 Rashbam and RSV agree in taking the final two words of verse 1 with the beginning of
verse 2; cf. the edition *ad loc.*

פרק ט

א   **כי את כל זה.** שהרי כל העניין הזה נתתי ללבי. ולברר כל המעשה הזה
שהרי הצדיקים והחכמים. והעבדים שלהן כולם הם בממשלתו בידו של הק′
ואף אהבתו ואף שנאתו של הק′ אינן יודעים שאינו יכול להבחין. איזה דבר
אהוב לפני הק′ ואיזהו שנאוי.[1]

ולבור.[2] מגזרת בר. כמ′ מן קם ולקום שב ולשוב.

ביד. אנלא יושטיצא בלע′. כמ′ מתחת יד מצרים.[3] מיד מצר′ ומיד פרעה.[3]

גם אהבה וגם[4] שנאה. שני גמין נוהגין לבוא בזה אחר זה בלא דקדוק
מלה. כמ′ גם בחור גם בתולה.[5] גם לי גם לך.[6]

ב-ג   **הכל לפניהם.**[7] כל הרעות נהוגות ומזומנות לבוא עליהם ומקרה אחד
לכולם.

---

1   Ms. שנאיו.

2   Ms. — ולברר, cf. the Introduction, p. 58, n. 163.

3   Ex. 18:10.

4   MT — גם.

5   Deut. 32:25.

6   I Kg. 3:26.

7   The limits of the exegetical units as determined by the exegetical method, deviate from
the Massoretic division into verses, in which הכל לפניהם is part of the first verse and not
the beginning of the second. (Cf. Japhet, *Tarbiz* XLIV p. 78). It seems that the same
deviation is reflected also by the LXX — indicating the possibility of a different version.

179

all alike to all[64]: this is the explanation of 'everything before them'. All misfortunes and calamities come as they do upon all men. And the same fate befalls all these: the righteous and the wicked and the good, the clean and the unclean, he who sacrifices and he who does not sacrifice, the one like the other. The good man and the sinner alike, he who swears falsely like the man who is afraid to swear — all are the same, and one fate befalls them all. This is an evil fact which is in the world — that all are equal regarding their fate. Also, the heart of men is full of evil and wickedness while they live, to do much evil, for they say to themselves: 'What does the evil-doer lose, for all have one fate, the one like the other? The end for everyone is to join the dead, for death applies to them all.' Therefore wicked men hold to their wickedness in that they do not repent from their evil way; and after death they can repent no more. Because of this I have wondered why Justice is so longsuffering in their case and why all have the same fate.

4   **But he who is joined:** for the man who is alive and joined to the living has the assurance that he can repent; while he is alive he is able to repent but after his death he cannot repent. For a living dog is better than a dead lion which has no strength or power after its death.

5   **For the living know that they will die:** therefore they should repent while they are yet alive. But the dead know nothing and can no longer regret and repent; they shall have no relief, reward or deliverance, because of the evil of their deeds, for memory of them is forgotten.

6   **Their love:** with which they loved people, and their hatred with which they hated some people, and their envy with which they envied others, have already perished; for they are dead, and memory

---

64 The RSV rendering depends upon an emendation of the Hebrew text and the lemma is, therefore, inappropriate.

הכל כאשר לכל. פי׳ הוא של הכל לפניהם. כל הרעות והפורעניות באות כמות שהן לכל בני האדם. ומקרה אחד לכולם הללו צדיקים ורשע וטוב וטהור וטמא זובח ואינו זובח כזה כן זה. כטוב כחוטא וכן הנשבע שבועת שקר. כאותו אדם שהוא ירא לישבע שבועה כולם שוין. ומקרה אחד לכולם. וזהו עניין רע שהוא בעולם על אשר כולם שוים במקרה שלהם. ואף לב בני האדם מלא רע וֶרֶשע בחייהם לעשות רעות רבות לפי שאומ׳ בלבב איזה הפסד יש לו לעושה הרעה כי מקרה אחד להם וכזה כן זה. ואחריתו של כל אחד ואחד אל המתים שבכולם מיתה נוהגת בהם ועל כן מחזיקים רשעים ברשעם שלא לשוב מדרכם הרעה. ולאחר מיתה שוב אינן יכולים לשוב בתשובה. ועל זאת נפלאתי מדוע מידת הדין מארכת להם אף כל כך ומדוע מקרה אחד לכולם.

ד כי מי אשר יחובר. כי אותו האדם שהוא חי ומחובר אל החיים. יש לו בטחון לעשות תשובה. שבעודו בחיים יכול לשוב. אבל לאחר מיתתו אינו יכול לשוב. שהרי כלב חי הוא טוב מן האריה המת. שלאחר מיתתו אין בו יכולת וכח.

ה כי החיים יודעים שימותו. ועל כן יש להם לעשות תשובה בעודם בחיים. והמתים אינם יודעים מאומה ושוב אינן יכולין להתחרט ולשוב בתשובה ולא יהיה להם ריוח שכר והצלה ברוע מעשיהם שהרי נשכח זכרם.

ו גם אהבתם שהיו אוהבים הבריות וגם שנאתם שהיו שונאים כמה בני אדם

of them is forgotten, and they will no longer have any share in all that happens in the world.

7-10 **Go, eat your bread with enjoyment:** and with a merry heart, for the Holy One is already pleased with the propriety of your deeds. Always let your clothes be white and clean, behaving with purity and cleanliness. And be zealous to anoint your head for your own pleasure — for the ancients were accustomed to anoint with oil — and enjoy life, being happy in your lot with your wife whom you love, throughout the life which the Holy One has given you in the world. For this thing, about which I alert you for your pleasure, will be your portion for the toil in which you engage in the world. And all that you are able to do by way of good deeds, that do while you are yet alive; for you will have no opportunity for action, thoughts, knowledge or wisdom in the grave to which you are going.
all the days of your vain life: he repeats himself.
in[65] your might: while you are yet alive; this is related to 'in Sheol' which appears later in the verse.

11 **Again I saw:** again, I observed another thing in the world: that the race does not belong to the swift; frequently it is not worth their while running, for although their running is swift, the appointed time, mishap and fate befalls them, as with other people.
nor the battle to the strong: frequently triumph in battle does not help them, for they have the same fate. And again, bread does not always belong to the wise in spite of their wisdom, nor riches always to the intelligent in spite of their great understanding, for sometimes they become poor. And again, favour does not always belong to the skilful; sometimes they are out of favour and are hated by the people. For one fate befalls them all.

65 RSV "with" would not be appropriate in the light of the interpretation.

וגם קנאתם שקינאו באחרים כבר אבדה כי מתו ונשכח זכרונם ולא יהיה להם
עוד חלק בכל אשר נעשה בעולם.

ז-י **לך אכול בשמחה לחמך.** ובלב טוב שכבר רצה הק׳ בכשרון מעשיך.
ובכל עת יהיו בגדיך לבנים וטהורים להתנהג בטהרה ונקיון ותהיה זריז לסוך
ראשך להנאתך כי היו נהוגין הקדמונים בסיכת שמן וראה חיים לשמוח
בחלקך עם אשתך אשר אהבתה אשר כל ימי חייך שנתן לך הק׳ בעו׳. כי דבר זה
שאני מזהירך להנאתך הוא יהיה חלק שלך בעמלך שאתה עמל בעו׳. וכל
אשר תמצא ידך לעשות טובות ומעשים טובים. בעודך בחיים עשה.[8] שהרי
לא יהיה לך עוד לעשות מעשים וחשבון ודעת וחכמה בקבר אשר תלך שם.
כל ימי חיי הבלך. כופל מלתו פעמיים.
בכוחך. בעודך בחיים. ומוסב על בשאול אשר למטה.

יא **שבתי וראה.** חזרתי וראיתי עוד דבר זה בעול׳. שהרי לא לקלים המרוץ.
שאינה שוה להם מרוצתם תדיר. שאע״פ שהם קלים במרוצתם לרוץ עת
ופגע ומקרה יקרה להם. כמ׳ לשאר בני אדם.
ולא לגיבורים המלחמה. שאין נצחון[9] מלחמות עומד להם תדיר. כי
מקרה אחד להם. ואף לא לחכמים לחם בכל עת בשביל חכמתם ואף לא
לנבונים[10] עושר בכל עת ברוב תבונתם שפעמים שהם יורדין לעניות ואף לא
ליודעים חן בכל עת. פעמים שאין להם חן ושנואים הם בעיני הבריות שהרי
מקרה אחד יקרה לכולם.

8 Ms. שעה.
9 Ms. נצחין, cf. note on 4:12.
10 Ms. לנבוני, cf. Jellinek.

12 **For man:** for man also does not know nor recognise his time when he falls like fish which are caught, falling into a wicked net, and like birds fallen and caught in a snare. For just as they fall and are caught, so men are ensnared and stumble at the time of disaster, when their misfortune falls suddenly upon them.

יוקשים: is like יקושים in Jeremiah (5:26), a passive participle.

13 **I have also seen this:** I have observed in the world this wisdom also, and it is a great wonder to me.

14-15 **There was a little city with few men in it:** it is not necessary to say that if it was a weak city with many men in it to guard it, or a strong city, with few men in it to guard it, and a king who was not so notable and with no great army laid siege to it, it would not seem so surprising to me if a poor and wise man should save it by his great wisdom. But, it was both a weak city with few men in it to guard it, and a great and notable king came against it with a large army, and surrounded it with a siege, building against it great strong fortifications; and there was found in it a man who was poor, needy and wise, and by means of his great wisdom he rescued the city from the great king, his many forces and his great fortifications. Therefore I wondered and was amazed that in the end no one remembered the poor man who, by his wisdom, had rescued the city.

16 **But I say:** the wisdom of this man is much better than might, yet the end for him is that his wisdom is despised and his words are not heeded.

17 **The words of the wise:** the words of this poor wise man are spoken[66] quietly, and his wisdom is much better than the shout of a ruling king who governs and rules over his soldiers who are fools. Because they have no wisdom with which to outwit this man who is poor and wise, they are called sons of fools.

---

66 Cf. 10:12.

יב   **כי גם האדם.**[11] שהרי אף האדם לא ידע ולא הכיר שעתו ועתו. כאשר
יפול. כדגים שנאחזים ונופלים במצודה רעה וכציפורים הנפולות והאחוזות
בפח. כי כאשר הם נופלים ונאחזים כן יוקשים ונכשלים בני האדם לעת
רעתם כשתפול רעתם עליהם בפתאום.
יוקשים. כמ' יקושים שבירמיה.[12] לשון עשויים.

יג   **גם זה ראיתי.** אף חכמה זאת ראיתי בעולם ותמיהא גדולה היא אלי.

יד-טו   **עיר קטנה ואנשים בה מעט.** אינו צריך לומ' אם היא עיר חלשה ויש
בה אנשים הרבה לשומרה. או אם היא עיר חזקה ויש בה אנשים מעט
לשומרה. ויהיה צר עליה במצור מלך שאינו כל כך חשוב ואין לו חיל גדול כל
כך. אין תימ' בעיני כל כך אם ימלטנה איש מסכן וחכם ברוב חכמתו כי אף
היא עיר חלשה ויש בה אנשים מעט לשומרה. ובא אליה מלך גדול וחשוב
בחיל גדול וסבב אותה במצור לבנות עליה מצודים גדולים וחזקים ומצא בה
המוצא איש אחד שהוא דל ומסכן וחכם והוא ימלט את העיר ברוב חכמתו
מן המלך הגדול ומרוב חייליותיו וממצודיו הגדולים. ועל כן נפלאתי ותמהתי
אשר לבסוף לא זכר שום אדם את האיש דל אשר מילט את העיר בחכמתו.

טז   **ואמרתי אני** משובחת וטובה חכמה של זה יותר מגבורה וסופו של זה
שחכמתו בזויה ואינן נשמעים דבריו.

יז   **דברי חכמים.** דבריו של מסכן וחכם זה נשמעין בנחת והיא חכמתו[13] של
זה טובה ומשובחת מזעק מלך מושל. שהוא מושל ושליט על בני חילו שהם
כסילים. על שם שאין להם חכמה להערים נגד האיש הזה שהוא מסכן וחכם
קורא אותן בני כסילים.

---

11 .כי גם לא ידע האדם — MT
12 Jer. 5:26.
13 .בחכמתו Ms.

18 – **Wisdom is better:** (the wisdom of) this poor and wise man is
10:1 better than the weapons of those besieging the city.

but one sinner: just as this poor wise man rescues the city by his wisdom, so one sinner destroys much good; he is likened and is compared to flies which are fit for nothing but death, and which pollute scented oil and cause it to stink.

יח-י:א טובה חכמה של מסכן וחכם זה יותר מכלי מלחמה של אילו הצרים על
העיר.

וחוטא אחד. כשם שמסכן חכם זה ממלט את העיר בחכמתו כך חוטא
אחד מאבד טובה הרבה. ודומה ומשול הוא לזבובים שאינן ראויים לכלום[14]
כי אם למיתה. שמבאישים ומביעים שמן מבוסם.

---

14 Preceded by a dotted and cancelled word.

יביע: its interpretation is according to its context, that is, it contaminates and spoils the oil.

יקר: means 'weight'. A little stupidity and folly have more weight by way of evil than wisdom and honour, for that sinner destroys much good by his stupidity and folly.

2   **A wise man's heart inclines him toward the right:** the disposition of the wise man is to go on the right way, and the disposition of the fool is to go on the left way. Just as the right hand is more important than the left hand, so he uses a metaphor and calls the good way 'the right way' and the evil way 'the left way'. Because it is written 'the heart of the wise man is to his right, to his left' and not 'on his right, on his left', it should be interpreted in this sense.

3   **Even . . . on the road:** and even when the fool is on the road he lacks sense; he is stupified and acts foolishly.
     and he says to every one: because of the levity and folly with which he acts, it is as if he were saying to everyone that he is a fool, for men recognise the folly of his actions. Thus the passage is recounting the importance of the wise man and the disgrace of the fool.

יביע. פת׳ לפי עיניינו שמזהים ומקלקל השמן.

יקר. לש׳ כובד. יש רוע וכובד בסכלות וכסילות מעט יותר מחכמה ומכבוד שזה החוטא מאבד הרבה טובה בכסילותו וסיכלותו.

ב **לב חכם לימינו.** דיעתי לב חכם ללכת בדרך ימין ודיעת כסיל ללכת בדרך שמאל. כשם שיד ימין חשובה מיד שמאל כך המשיל וקורא לדרך הטובה דרך ימין ולדרך הרעה דרך שמאל. ועל אשר כתב לב חכם לימינו לשמאלו. ולא כתב מימינו ומשמאלו. צריך לפתור בעניין זה.

ג **וגם בדרך.** ואף כשהסכל בדרך לבו חסר ומשתומם ומשתטה.

ואמר לכל מתוך נבלותו ושטותו שהוא עושה הרי הוא כאומר לכל שהוא סכל וכסיל. לפי שבני אדם מכירים בכסילות מעשיו כך הולך ומספר המקרא חשיבותו של חכם וגנותו של כסיל.

---

4   If the anger of the ruler: the temperament of a ruler, the governor who rules over you — if he should bring false charges against you, do not leave your place and do not flee from there for fear of him. Because the soothing of your tongue — for you will appease him by your conciliatory words which you will use to entreat him — will cause him to remit great sins which you have committed against him, and he shall no more bring false accusations against you.

מרפא: like in ולשון חכמים מרפא (Prov. 12:18).

5-6   There is an evil which I have seen: I have seen a particular evil in the world, which is as a mistake proceeding from the mouth of a ruler, who says to his servants, 'Do so and so, go and hang such and such a person or do him some other injury' — and they go and hang him who neither sinned nor rebelled, for they go astray with the command of the ruler. For the stupid fool is set in many high positions, becoming a rich man, a great and important chief, while the rich sit in a low place, for they are wretched and humble.

7   I have seen slaves: it is an explanation of "folly is set etc." (10:6). Slaves conduct themselves like masters and rulers by riding horses; but princes walk like slaves and do not ride horses; that is, the superior are down and the inferior are up.

8-9   He who digs a pit: he proceeds to warn a man that if he has another craft he should not engage in the following crafts, because he himself might sometimes be hurt through them: he should not be a digger of pits, because there are times when he himself might fall and die. The same thought is expressed by our Rabbis: "When the arrow-maker is killed by his own arrow, he is paid by his own doing; when the stock-maker sits in his own stock he is paid by his own doing." (BT Pesahim 28a) Nor should he be a breaker of walls, lest serpents, which are to be found in the cracks of a wall, bite him. He should neither move nor remove large stones, because he will hurt himself with the effort; nor should he be a hewer of wood because of

ד אם רוח המושל. דעתו של מושל ושליט השולט עליך אשר ישים לך
עלילות דברים: אל תניח מקומך ולא תברח משם מחמת יראתו. שהרי מרפא
לשונך. שתפייסהו בפייוס דבריך אשר תתחנן לפניו יגרומו שהוא יניח
חטאים גדולים. אשר חטאת לו ולא ישים לך עוד עלילות דברים.
מרפא. דוגמ' ולש' חכמים מרפא[2].

ה-ו וישׁ[3] רעה ראיתי. רעה אחת ראיתי בעולם. שהיא כשגגה היוצאת מפי
השליט אשר יאמר לעבדיו עשו כך וכך לכו לתלותו או לעשות לו רעה אחרת
והם ילכו ותלו אשר לא חטא ולא פשע לפי שטעו בדבר השליט שהרי ניתן[4]
הכסיל הסכל במרומים רבים להיות עשיר שר גדול וחשוב והעשירים יושבים
בשפל שהם דלים ושפלים.

ז ראיתי עבדים. פירוש הוא של ניתן הסכל וג'. שהעבדים מתנהגים
כאדונים וקצינים להיות רוכבי סוסים. והשרים הולכים כעבדים בלי רכיבת
סוסים. שהעליונים למטה ותחתונים למעלה.

ח-ט חופר גומץ. הולך ומוכיח את האדם שאם יש לו אומנות אחר שלא יעסוק
באומניות הללו לפי שפעמ' שהוא עצמו נכשל בהן שלא יהא חופר שוחות
שפעמ' שהוא עצמו נופל ומת. כעניין שאמרו רבותי' גירא בגיראיה
משתדי מדויל ידיה משתלים. סדנא בסדניה יתיב. מדויל ידיה משתלים[5]. ולא
יהא פורץ גדירות. שלא ישכוהו נחשים המצויין בסדקי הגדר. ולא יסיע ולא
יזיז[6] אבנים גדולות לפי שהוא נעצב בעצבון. ולא יהא בוקע עצים מחמת

---

2 Prov. 12:18.

3 MT — ישׁ.

4 Ms. נותן, cf. vs. 7, cf. Jellinek.

5 BT Pesachim 28a. In the Talmud the two parts of the saying are attributed to two different sages. Also, there is a variant reading: מקטיל in place of our משתדי.

6 Ms. יזוז, cf. Jellinek.

the severe hardship, and get over-heated with that work. And so the evil-doer shall eat the fruit of his deeds, for he who sows toil shall reap trouble.

גומץ: means 'hole' and 'pit'.

He who quarries stones: like "they quarried out great ... stones" (I Kings 5:17 (Heb. 31)).

יסכן בם: (the verb סכן) means 'heating', like ותהי למלך סוכנת (I Kings 1:4).

10   If the iron is blunt: even if iron swords are blunt and their edge and point have struck (against something) and are impaired, and one does not sharpen or what their blades so that they are not sharpened or whetted, yet strength is increased; for the sword supplies courage and strength to increase power and success in battle. Thus is the merit of weapons even if they are not sharpened. Yet there is more advantage and merit in the skill of wisdom than in these. This verse is parallel to what is said above: "Wisdom is better than weapons of war" (9:18).

הברזל: means 'weapons', as in ונשל הברזל (Deut. 19:5).

קלקל: means 'whetting' and 'shine', as in נחשת קלל (Ez. 1:7; Dan. 10:6).

11   If the serpent bites: if the serpent bites a man, it is because the charmer did not mutter a charm over it that it bites; and there is no advantage in a person who is a charmer, who knows how to charm but does not do so. In this way he admonishes, for the charmer should mutter a charm that the serpent may not bite.

before it is charmed: the expression is appropriate with 'the serpent' as in "serpents, adders which cannot be charmed, and they shall bite etc." (Jer. 8:17).

הטורח שהוא גדול ומתחמם באותה מלאכה חימום גדול. וכן עושה הרעה פרי
מעלליו יאכל. כי זורע עמל יקצור און.

גומץ. לש׳ גומא ושוחה.

מסיע אבנים. דוגמ׳ ויסיעו אבנים גדולות.[7]

יסכן בם. לשון חימום כמ׳ ותהי למלך סוכנת.[8]

י **אם קהה הברזל.** אם קהו חרבות של ברזל ונתקל והורע פיהם וחידודם.
והאדם לא חידד ולא לטש את פניהם. שלא היו מחודדין ומלוטשין ואעפ״כ
חיילים יגבר. שנותן החרב[9] לב גבורה וחוזק להגביר כח ונצחון במלחמה. כך
היא שבחן של כלי זיין שאע״פ שאינן מלוטשין. ועל כל זאת יש יתרון ושבח
בהכשר חכמה יותר מהן. מקרא זה כפול הוא על שנ׳ למעלה טובה חכמה
מכלי קרב.[10]

הברזל. לש׳ כלי זיין. כמ׳[11] ונשל הברזל.[12]

קלקל. לש׳ לטישה וברק. כמ׳ נחשת קלל.[13]

יא **אם ישך הנחש.** אם הנחש נושך את האדם בשביל שהלוחש[14] לא ליחש
עליו לחש הוא נושך. ואין לו[15] יתרון לבעל הלשון שיודע ללחוש ולא ליחש.
כך הוא מוכיח לפי שיש לו ללחוש על הלוחש למען לא ישוך הנחש.

בלא לחש. לש׳ זה נופל על הנחש. כמ׳ נחשים צפעונים אשר אין להם
לחש ונשכו וג׳.[16]

---

7 I Kg. 5:31 (Eng. 5:17).

8 I Kg 1:4.

9 Preceded by a cancelled word לב.

10 9:18.

11 Ms. ׳כת, cf. Jellinek. Nowhere else is a citation introduced by ׳כת.

12 Deut. 19:5.

13 Ez. 1:7; Dan. 10:6.

14 Ms. שם לוחש, cf. Jellinek.

15 Ms. ׳לי, cf. Jellinek.

16 Jer. 8:17.

12   **The words of a wise man's mouth:** the words of a wise man's mouth who speaks with quietness and persuasion, reasonably and properly, bring and grant him favour in the eyes of people.
but the lips of a fool: every utterance[67] of the fool, in that he speaks with haughty pride, shall destroy him from the world, in that he is despised and rejected by people.

13   **The beginning of the words of his mouth:** this is the rule: the beginning of a fool's speech is folly and stupidity, and the end of it is wicked madness.

14   **A fool multiplies words:** a fool multiplies foolish words, but he neither knows nor understands the misfortune that will happen to him at his end. He is also unaware of the trouble which will suddenly befall him from behind while he goes on his way, for who is to tell him? Therefore one should avoid folly.

15   **The toil of a fool[68] wearies him:** the toil of each fool wearies him; for, as a result of his stupidity he is tired and weary while outside the city, so that he does not know how to return to the city.
תיגענו: 'toil' is regarded as feminine, therefore [there is a prefixed] *Taw.*

16   **Woe to you, O land:** woe to you O land, whose king is a boy and a fool, and destroys the world in his stupidity and youth. And your princes, who are dependent upon the king and close to him, eat in the morning. Because of their much eating they destroy the land, in that they do nothing. Therefore one should avoid a boy-king.

67 Literally "lip".
68 Literally "the fools"; there is no correspondence in the Hebrew between the verbal suffix and its antecedent.

יב **דברי פי חכם** דבריו של פי חכם שמדבר בנחת ובפייוסין כהוגן וכשורה הן
נותנין ומעניקין לו חן[17] בעיני הבריות.

ושפתות כסיל. כל שפה ושפה של כסיל שהוא מדבר בגבהות לב גאוותו
תבלע אותו מן העולם. שהוא נבזה ונמאס בעיני הבריות.

יג **תחילת דברי פיהו.** זה הכלל תחילת דבריו של כסיל הוא סכלות
וכסילות. ואחרית דבריו הן הוללות רעה.

יד **והסכל ירבה דברים.** הכסיל מרבה דברים של כסילות. ואינו יודע ומבין
הרעה אשר תבוא ותגיע לו[17] בסופו. וגם הרעה אשר תבוא עליו פתאום
מאחריו כאשר ילך בדרכו אינו יודע כי מי אשר יגיד לו. ועל כן יש להתרחק
מן הכסילות.

טו **עמל הכסילים תייגענו.** עמל של כל כסיל וכסיל תייגע אותו. שמחמת
כסילותו הוא עיף ויגע. כשהוא מחוץ לעיר עד אשר אינו יודע לחזור אל
העיר.

תייגענו. עמל[18] נקרא בלשון נקבה. ועל כן תי״ו.   נמ[19]

טז **אי לך ארץ.** אוי לך ארץ שמלכך[20] נער וכסיל. ומחריב את העול׳
בכסילותו ונערותו. ושרייך שהן סמוכין ותכופין על המלך אוכלין בבקר
וברוב אכילתן מחריבין הארץ שאינן עושין כלום. ועל כן יש להתרחק ממלך
נער.

---

17 The word is written in the margin.
18 Preceded by a cancelled *Mem*.
19 The Ms. has a beginning of a word (נמ or נני) and an empty space, indicating probably
that the scribe intended to come back to it.
20 Ms. שלמכך, cf. Jellinek.

17   **Happy are you, O land:** happiness is yours, O land, whose king is a free man, worthy and wise, because he maintains the world by his wisdom. And your princes, who are close to the king, eat at a time when other people eat. They fight enemies with great vigour in order to maintain the land, and at eating time they go to their homes and eat.

    and not for drunkenness: and they do not indulge in drinking wine and in gluttony; therefore one should stick to a king who is a free man in order that the world may be maintained.

    בְּשָׁתִי: I have not heard why it has not been vocalised בְּשָׁתִי from שָׁתָה, as קְרִי from קָרָה.

18   **Through sloth:** as a result of the houseowner's laziness the ceiling sinks and sags, for he does not want to repair it. The walls of the house are called 'ceiling' because they are the strength of the ceiling of the house.

    and through indolence: as a result of the sloth of idleness a leakage of rain drips from the house.

    יִדְלוֹף: like דלף טורד ביום סגריר (Prov. 27:15).

    יִמַּךְ: is like יִנָּמַךְ.

19   **Bread is made for laughter:** those who engage in frivolity have bread, and drinking wine makes the living happy; and the essence of 'doing' in regard to money is 'buying' as in אשר יענה יי[69] (Jer. 42:4).

    everything: for bread and wine are acquired with money. And therefore one should exert oneself in order to have money.

    יענה: has the meaning of 'doing'.

20   **Even in your thought:** even within your heart do not consider cursing a king; and in your bedrooms, in your place of privacy, do not curse a rich man.

---

69 RSV "whatever the Lord answers". Rashbam's interpretation of the Hebrew root ענה differs from that of RSV.

יז **אשריך ארץ.** אשרי לך ארץ שמלכך בן חורין חשוב וחכם. לפי שהוא
מקיים העולם בחכמתו. ושרייך התכופין על המלך אוכלין בעת אכילת בני
אדם ברוב גבורה שהם נלחמים עם האוייבים כדי לקיים את הארץ ובעת
אכילה באין לבתיהן ואוכלין.

ולא בשתי.[21] ואין עוסקין בשתיית יין ואכילות גסות. ועל כן יש לך לידבק
במלך בן חורין. למען יהיה העול' מקויים.

בשְׁתִֽי. לא שמעתי בו כלום מדוע לא ננקד בשֶׁתֽי מן שָׁתָה. כמ' קֶרי מן קָרֲה.

יח **בעצלתים.** בעצלות של בעל הבית ימך וישפל המקרה. לפי שאינו רוצה
לתקנו. את[22] קירות הבית קורא מְקָרֶה.[23] על שם שהן חזוק תקרת הבית.

ובשפלות ידים. בעצלות שפלות ידיים ידלוף דלף מן הבית מן הגשמים.

ידלוף. כמ' דלף טרד ביום סגריר.[24]

יִמַּך. כמ' יִנְמַּך.

יט **לשחוק עושים לחם.** לאותן שעוסקין בשחוק יש להם לחם. ואת החיים
משמח שתיית היין. והכסף בעשייה הקנייה. ועיקר של מעשה. כמ' אשר
יענה 🖙 [25]

את הכל שהלחם והיין קנוי בכסף. ועל כן יש לטרוח[26] למען יהיה לו כסף.
יענה הוא לש' עשייה.

כ **גם במדעך.** גם בקרב לבך לא תחשב לקלל מלך ובחדרי משכבך במקום
ייחודך לא תקלל עשיר.

---

21 The *Shin* is corrected in the margin.
22 Ms. או.
23 The vocalization deviates from MT, although the interpretation presupposes it.
24 Prov. 27:15.
25 Jer. 42:4.
26 Ms. has a dittography of the word, as לטורח.

for a bird of the air: this statement is not to be taken literally, but this is what he is saying: it is impossible that it should not become well known to everyone, for hidden things are bound to be revealed.

or some winged creature: a parallel expression of "a bird".

כי עוף השמים. דבר זה לא דיקדוק מלה הוא. אבל כך הוא אומ' אי
איפשר שלא יהא גלוי וידוע לכל. שהנסתרות סופן להיות גלויות.

ובעל הכנפים. כפל מלה על עוף.[27]

CHAPTER 11

1 **Cast your bread upon the waters:** do a favour to a man whom you reckon you would never benefit from, for after many days he too will do you a favour.

2-3 **Give a portion to seven:** to several people — to seven or even eight — give a share of what is yours, even when you reckon that you will not benefit from them. For you do not know what misfortune will happen upon the earth, and today or tomorrow you may benefit from them or need them. For just as when the clouds are full of rain they empty themselves and pour out upon the earth, and just as when a tree falls in the south or in the north it will be on the spot where it falls, so it is impossible that you will not benefit from those to whom you give a share of what is yours.
ְיָהוֹא: is יהא הוא.

4 **He who observes the wind:** whoever keeps watch and expects a wind to come up in the world — because sowing is good when the wind is blowing — he will not sow much, for the wind only happens to blow occasionally. Whoever observes and regards the clouds at harvest time will not reap; for it is impossible that he will not see clouds or not be afraid of rain and showers every morning. But he should reap whatever he can reap, and not be idle because of the clouds which he sees in the morning of that day. If

פרק יא

א   **שלח לחמך על פני המים.** לאותו אדם שתהיה סבור שלא תיהנה ממנו
לעול' עשה לו טובה. שהרי לרוב ימים גם הוא יעשה לך טובה.

ב-ג   **תן חלק לשבעה.** לכמה בני אדם לשבעה בני אדם או אפי' לשמונה תן
חלקים משלך. אפי' כשתהיה סבור שלא תיהנה מהם. שהרי אינך יודע איזה
מעשה של רעה יהיה רעה על הארץ. והיום או מחר תיהנה מהם ותצטרך
להם. שכשם שאם ימלאו העבים גשם שהן יריקו וישפכו על הארץ וכשם
שאם יפול עץ בדרום או בצפון מקום שיפול שם יהיה הוא. כך אי איפשר
שלא תיהנה מאותן שתתן להם חלקים משלך.
יְהוֹא יהא הוא.

ד   **שומר רוח** מי שהוא שומר ומצפה שיבוא רוח בעול' לפי שזריעה יפה
בשעת נשיבת רוח לא יזרע הרבה שהרוח לא בא כי אם לפעמים. ומי
שהוא רואה ומסתכל בעבים בשעת הקציר לא יקצור שבכל בוקר ובוקר אי
איפשר שלא יראה העבים ולא יפחד מגשם וממטר. אבל את אשר יוכל
לקצור יקצור ולא יתעצל ולא מפני העבים אשר יראה בבוקר ביום זה. ואם ימנע

201

he refrains from reaping today for fear of rain, perhaps it will not rain today but tomorrow, and so it (may go on) each day. The result is that he remains idle.

5-6   **As you do not know:** for just as you do not know the way of the wind, and just as you do not know the things which are enclosed in a man's belly which is full, so you do not know the things that the Holy One does. Because you cannot discern when it is going to rain, you should not watch for the wind or observe the clouds; but in the morning sow your seed, and in the evening do not withold your work, do not leave it, but do whatever you can to exert yourself and do your work. For you do not know whether this time is good for sowing or that time, or whether both alike are good; therefore you should not be idle.

כעצמים: as in ועוצם עיניו (Is. 33:15); these are the thoughts of man.

7-8   **Light is sweet:** light is good for the eyes, that is, to see the light of the sun which is in the world. For if a man lives many years he should rejoice in all of them, provided he is righteous and remembers in this world the days of the darkness of death, so that he might not be a sinner in this world.
that . . . will be many: the days of darkness and death. If he has sinned during his life, then, at the time of dying, every day he enters upon will be wretched and frustrating for him.

9   **Rejoice, O young man, in your youth:** you should rejoice when you are young, and be happy in your rejoicing in the time of your youth — following the ways of your heart and the sight of your eyes. But you should know that in the end the Holy One will bring you to judgement about all these things.
your youth: *joventes* in French[70].

70 Youth, cf. Salters, *French Glosses*, p. 250.

כיום מלקצור לפי שיתיירא ממטר שמא היום לא ירדו גשמים כי אם למחר.
וכן בכל יום ויום נמצא שהוא בטל ועומד.

ה-ו   **כאשר אינך יודע.** כי כאשר אין אתה יודע איזה דרך הרוח וכאשר אינך
יודע עצמים שבבטן האדם שהיא מליאה כך אינך יודע מעשיו של הק׳ אשר
יעשה. שהרי לא תוכל להבחין מתי ירדו גשמים ולא תהיה שומר רוח ורואה
בעבים. אבל תהיה בבוקר זרע את זרעך ולערב אל תנח מלאכתך ואל תרף[1]
ממנה ועשה כל אשר תוכל לטרוח ולעשות במלאכתך. שהרי אינך יודע אם
זמן זה טוב לזרוע או זה או אם שניהם טובים כאחד. ועל כן אין לך להתעצל.
כעצמים. לשון ועוצם עיניו.[2] והן[3] מחשבותיו של אדם.

ז-ח   **ומתוק האור.** טוב מאור לעינים לראות מאור השמש אשר בעול׳. שהרי
אם יחיה[4] האדם שנים הרבה בכולם יש לו לשמוח ובלבד שיהא צדיק ויזכור
בעולם הזה ימי החושך של מיתה. למען לא יהיה חוטא. בעולם הזה.
כי הרבה יהיו ימי החושך והמיתה. כל הימים שיבוא בהם לעת המיתה
יהיו לו להבל ורעה אם חטא בחייו.

ט   **שמח בחור בילדותיך.** תהיה שמח בעת ילדותיך. ותהיה טוב לב
בשמחתך בימי בחורותיך ללכת בדרכי לבך ובמראה עיניך. ותדע שלבסוף
יביאך הק׳ במשפט על כל אלה
בחורותיך יוֶנֶטִין בלע׳.

---

1   Ms. חרף. cf. Jellinek.
2   Is. 33:15.
3   Ms. וכן. cf. Jellinek.
4   Ms. יהיה. cf. Jellinek.

10   **Remove vexation from your mind:** that you may not be
bad tempered and do evil, for "the imagination of man's heart is evil
from his youth" (Gen. 8:21).

and blackness[71]: a parallel expression to 'youth'; it is called the
time of blackness because of youth's hair which is black.

---

71 RSV "the dawn of life" is unsuitable here. Rashbam takes שחרות from שָׁחַר "to be
black" whereas RSV takes it to be related to שַׁחַר "dawn".

י   **והסר כעס מלבך** שלא תהיה רגזן ולא תעשה רעה. שהרי יצר לב האדם רע מנעוריו.

והשחרות. כפל מלה על הילדות. ונקרא זמן שחרות על שם שערו שהוא שחור.

CHAPTER 12

1   **Remember also:** you should be careful to remember the Creator in order to refrain from sin during your youth, and to repent.

before . . . come: before the time of evil comes, the time of old age, when you will say of your former deeds 'I have no pleasure in them'. Since, because of the great weakness of your old age you do not know the day of your death, you should be zealous to repent before this.

2-5   **before the sun . . . darkened:** before the world becomes dark and gloomy for you — when the luminaries will not shine for you since you will be near the time of your death — you should repent.

and the clouds return: before darkness after darkness happens to you, you should be zealous to return to the Holy One. This text is like "I clothe the heavens with blackness" (Is. 50:3), and it is a metaphor for the world being dark for them in their great distress.

ושבו: means 'return'. That is, when the rain began there were clouds in the world; after this it rained, and then the world brightened up, and now the clouds have returned. This is darkness after darkness. This is when the keepers of the house will tremble and shake — these are the ribs which protect the inside of the body — at the end of his old age when he will be extremely weak.

פרק יב

א **וזכור.** ותהיה זהיר שתזכור הבורא למען תמנע מחטא בימי הילדות לעשות
תשובה.

עד אשר לא יבואו. טרם יבואו ימי הרעה ימי הזיקנה שתאמר במעשיך
הראשונים אין לי בהם חפץ. מחמת שלא תדע יום מיתתך ברוב חלשות של
זקנתך. ועל כן תהיה זריז לשוב בתשובה מקודם לכך.

ב-ה **עד לא¹ תחשך השמש.** טרם יהיה לך העולם חשוך ומאופל שלא יאירו
לך המאורות לפי שתהיה לך קרוב לזמן מיתתך תשוב בתשובה.

ושבו העבים טרם יבוא לך חושך אחר חושך תהיה זריז לשוב להק׳. מקרא
זה דוגמ׳ אלביש שמים קדרות² ודוגמ׳ שהעולם חשוך להם ברוב צרתם.

ושבו לש׳ חזרה. זהו שבתחילת גשם היו עבים בעולם ואחר כך ירדו גשמים
והאיר העול׳. וגם עתה שבו העבים. זהו חושך אחר חושך. והוא ביום שיהיו
חלים וזעים שומרי הבית הן הצלעות המגינות על חלל הגוף. והוא בסוף
זקנתו שיהיה חלש עד מאד.

---

1 MT — עד אשר לא.
2 Is. 50:3.

and . . . are bent: the mighty men will be crooked and shaky; these are the legs by which the body is supported.

and the grinders cease: the teeth will be idle because they will have diminished in strength.

and those that look . . . are dimmed: the eyes have become dim in their place.

and the doors on the street are shut: his external orifices are stopped up.

on the street: the external orifices which are turned outward, which see the street.

when the sound of the grinding is low: when the noise of millstones grinding the food of his belly becomes low; this is the stomach.

and one rises up at the voice of a bird: he is afraid and alarmed by their sound.

and . . . are brought low: the voice of singing men and singing women will seem low to him, as is said about Barzillai the Gileadite in his old age, "Can I still listen to the voice of singing men and singing women?" (2 Sam. 19:35 (Heb. 36)).

also of what is high: he will also be afraid and in dread of something else, which is of little height; and on the road he will be frightened and afraid of it.

the almond tree blossoms: because of his leanness his hip-bone, *hanche* in French[72], will stick out.

the grasshopper drags itself along: his buttocks will be a load and a burden to him.

and desire fails: his desire will cease; for he is going to his eternal home and will die, and the mourners will go about bewailing him. Before all these things happen to him in his old age he should repent.

72 Hip.

והתעותו שיהיו מעוותים ורתתים אנשי החיל הן השוקיים שהגוף נסמך
עליהם.

ובטלו הטחנות. שתהיו השינים³ בטילות שהרי נתמעטו בכחן

וחשכו הרואות. שחשכו העינים במקומן.

וסוגרו דלתים בשוק שנסתתמו נקביו שמבחוץ.

בשוק. נקבים החיצונים הפונים כלפי חוץ הרואים את השוק.

בשפל קול הטחנה. כאשר ישפל קול ריחים הטוחנין מאכל מעיו והוא
המסס.

ויקום לקול⁴ הציפור. שמתיירא ומתבהל⁵ מקולן.

וישחו⁶ קול שרים ושרות⁷ ישפלו בעיניו. כעיני' שנ' בברזילי הגלעדי לעת
זקנתו. שנ' אם אשמע עוד קול שרים ושרות.⁸

גם מגבוה. אף מדבר אחר שהוא גבוה מעט יירא ויפחד ויהיה חת וירא
ממנו בדרך.

ויאנץ⁹ השקד. שיהא בולט ממנו עצם קליבוסת הנקר' בלע'. מחמת
כחישותו.

ויסתבל החגב שיהיו עגבותיו לו לסבל ומשאוי.

ותפר האביונה. ותהיה בטילה תאותו כי הוא הולך לבית עולמו וימות.
וסבבו הסופדים לבכותו. טרם יגיעו עליו כל אלה לעת זקנתו יעשה תשובה

---

3   Ms. בשינים. cf. Jellinek.

4   Ms. לכל, cf. the Introduction, p. 58, n. 162.

5   Ms. מתהבל.

6   Ms. וישאו, cf. the Introduction, p. 58, n. 163.

7   Following this word Ms. has a dittography of seven words: גם מגבוה, אף מדבר אחר
שהוא גבוה whose original place is a couple of lines later. The dittography was
occasioned by a homoioteleuton; what made the scribe return to his text is not clear.

8   II Sam. 19:36 (Eng. 19:35). Ms. ושרים for MT ושרות is no doubt a scribal error.
Another deviation is קול in place of בקול, cf. Salters, Variant Readings, p. 89.

9   The word is found twice in this context; both deviate from MT in the same way. The difference in the location of the *Alef* could be an indication of a variant reading, a consequence of Rashbam's linguistic view, or simply a scribal error.

שיזועו: like ולא קם ולא זע (Est. 5:9).

בארבות: in their places.

ויראו וחתחתים: is like "do not fear (תירא) or be dismayed (תחת) (Deut. 1:21 etc.); 'fear' and 'dismay' are next to one another.

וחתחתים: a 'doubled word' like ירקרק (Lev. 13:49), אדמדם (Lev. 13:42 etc.), פתלתל (Deut. 32:5).

ויאנץ: the *'Aleph'* is not pronounced; the meaning is as in הנצו הרימונים (Song of Songs 6:11 etc.).

האביונה: means 'desire' אביון is from אבה, just as צביון is from צבה; and the (final) *He* denotes the feminine.

6-7   **before . . . is snapped:** before the spine of a man is severed, his head crushed, his belly split open and his body crushed in the grave.

and . . . returns: he who is compared to dust on the earth (will return) to dust, and the spirit will return to the Holy One who has put it in his body. Before all these things he should repent.

ירתק: like ורתוקות כסף (Is. 40:19).

the silver cord: this is the spine.

the golden top[73]: this is the head, for a top and crown are placed on it.

or the pitcher is broken at the fountain: this is a parallel expression to 'the silver cord'; for when the cord snaps, the pitcher breaks on its face because it is tied and hung up by it. Then the wheel, which is attached to the cord, falls, breaks and is crushed.

73 RSV "bowl" would not be appropriate in the light of the interpretation.

שיזועו. כמ׳ ולא קם ולא זע.[10]

בארובות. במקומותם.

ויראו[11] וחתחתים.[12] דוגמ׳ אל תירא ואל תחת.[13] יראה וחיתוי סמוכין זה לזה.

וחתחתים. תיבה כפולה. כמו׳ ירקרק אדמדם. פתלתל.

ויאנץ.[9] אל״ף אינה נקראת. והוא לש׳ הנצו הרימונים.[14]

האביונה.[15] לש׳ תאוה. שיאמר מן אבה אביון. כמ׳ מן צבה ציביון. והי״ באה ללשון נקבה.[16]

ו-ז עד אשר לא ירתק. טרם ינתק חבל[17] שדרתו של אדם ותתרוצץ גולגלתו ותיבקע כריסו ויתרוצץ[18] הגוף בקבר.

וישוב. הוא המשול לעפר על הארץ להיות עפר והרוח תשוב אל הק׳ אשר נתנה בגופו. טרם כל אלה ישוב בתשובה.

ירתק. כמ׳ ורתוקות כסף.[19]

חבל הכסף. היא השדרה

גולת הזהב. הוא הראש שנותנין עליה גולה ועטרה.

ותשבר כד על המבוע. כפל לש׳ על חבל הכסף. כי כאשר ניתק חבל ונשבר הכד על פניה לפי שהוא קשור ותלוי בו. והן הגל[20] שבחבל נופל ונשבר ומתרוצץ.

10 Est. 5:9.
11 MT יראו.
12 Ms. והתחתים.
13 Deut. 1:21 *et al.*
14 Song of Songs 6:11; 7:13.
15 Ms. כאביונה.
16 The *Beth* is preceded by a cancelled *Yod*.
17 Ms. מכל.
18 ויתאנץ of the Ms. is unclear. According to the structure of the interpretation it is an explanation of ונרץ. Earlier in the verse the word ותרץ of the same root, is explained by ויתרוצץ. It seems, therefore, that an original ויתרוצץ was wrongly read as ויתאנץ. Cf. also Jellinek.
19 Is. 40:19.
20 Possibly הגלגל; the present text could result from an abbreviation, taken to be a complete word.

8 **Vanity of vanities:** now the book is completed. Those who edited it speak from now on, saying: "'All that goes on in the world is utterly futile', said Qoheleth".

הקהלת: the wise man.

9 **Besides being:** wise in this wisdom, he taught that wisdom orally.

to know[74]: so that the people might know and become wise.

listening[75] and studying: he used his ears and mind to search out the affairs of the world, and wisdom. And he prepared the book of Proverbs.

10 **Qoheleth[76] sought:** to find good, valuable sayings, and to write books — writing words of integrity and truth.

11-14 **The sayings of the wise:** and this is what king Solomon used to say: 'wise men are like the goad which teaches the beast to go in a straight way; so he who listens to the sayings of wise men will not pervert or distort his ways so that they become corrupt.

and like nails firmly fixed: a parallel expression. Like nails driven firmly and inserted into the ends of sticks — these are goads — so are the wise men, who hold assemblies, who guide men by instructing them in a straight course; and all their wise sayings were given by one shepherd, for all were said by Moses, who heard and received them from the mouth of God.

beyond these: my son, over and above what the wise men warn you about, be careful; for there is no end, that is, no ability to write many books in which to write all of wisdom.

---

74 RSV "knowledge" would not be appropriate in the light of the interpretation.

75 RSV "weighing" is based on the Hebrew אזן "to weigh", while Rashbam takes it as denominative of אזן "ear".

76 RSV: the Preacher.

ח   **הבל הבלים.** עכשיו נשלם הספר. ואותן אשר סידרוהו אמרו מיכאן ולהבא. לומ׳ כל דברי העולם הנוהגין בו הבל הבלים אמר קהלת. **הקהלת.** החכם.

ט   **ויותר שהיה** חכם על חכמות הללו. עוד לימד אותה חכמה בעל פה. **לדעת.**[21] כדי שידעו ויחכמו העם.

ואזן וחיקר. נתן אזניו ולבו לחקור עינייני העולם ואת החכמות. ותיקן ספר משלי.

י   **בקש קהלת** למצוא דברים טובים של חפץ. ולכתוב ספרים כתוב דברי יושר ואמת.

יא-יד **דברי חכמים.** וכך היה רגיל שלמה המלך לומ׳ חכמים הן כדרבן הזה. המלמד את הבהמה ללכת בדרך יושר. וכן השומע על דברי חכמ׳ לא יסלף ולא יעקל. ויקלקלו דרכיו.

וכמסמרות[22] **נטועים.** כפל מלה. כמסמרות שהם נטועים ותחובים בראשי המקלות[23] שהן דרבונות. כך הן החכמ׳ בעלי אסופות[24] שמיישרים בני אדם להדריכם במעגל ישר ובל חכמותיהן נתנו מרועה אחד שכולן[25] נאמרו מפי משה. אשר שמעם וקיבלם מפי הגבורה.

ויותר מהמה. ויותר ממה שהחכמים מזהירים אותך בני הזהר. שהרי אין קץ ואין יכולת לעשות ספרים הרבה לכתוב כל החכמות בתוכם.

---

21   MT — דעת.

22   MT — וכמשמרות.

23   Ms. המקרא.

24   The *Alef* is corrected in the margin.

25   Ms. שבכולן. cf. Jellinek.

and much study: a parallel expression. Many words of wisdom are an effort for the body, for men cannot write all the books of wisdom.

The end of the matter: of wisdom is: all has been heard. Included therein is: fear God by keeping his commandments; let all your actions be for the sake of God, for this is the essence of the deeds of every man.

For . . . deed: the Holy One will bring a man to judgement for what he does — all his errors and secrets; whether the man is evil or good, he will bring him to judgement.

the end of the matter etc.: he repeats his rule.

בעלי אסופות: wise men are called 'those who hold assemblies' because men assemble to listen to their words.

הזהר: be careful.

ולהג: its interpretation is according to its context: the words of writers of books. All the letters of לַהַג are root letters (as is the case with) לַעַג, לַהַב, לִמַץ and לָחַשׁ.

Behold the book of Qoheleth is completed.

ולהג הרבה. כפל מלה. ודברים הרבה של חכמה יגיעת בשר הן שאין בני
אדם יכולין לכתוב כל ספרי חכמה.

סוף דבר של חכמה הכל נשמע. בכלל דבר זה את האלהים ירא לשמור
מצותיו שיהיו כל מעשיך לשם שמים כי זה עיקר מעשה של כל האדם.

כי את מעשה.[26] אשר יעשה האדם הק׳ יביאהו במשפט על כל שגגותיו
ונעלמותיו בין שהאדם רע בין שהוא טוב יביאהו לדין.

סוף דבר וג׳ [27] חוזר ושונה כללו.

בעלי אסופות. חכמ׳ נקראים בעלי אסופות. על שם בני אדם המתאספין
לשמוע דבריהם.

הזהר. הוי זהיר.

ולהג. פת׳ לפי ענייננו. דברי כתבי ספרים. לַהַג כולו שורש באותיותיו
לַחַץ לַהַב לַעַג לַחַש...

הרי נשלם ספר קהלת

---

26 MT — כי את כל מעשה.

27 The Massoretic repetition of vs. 13 is taken to be an integral part of the text.

FACSIMILE

דברי קהלת׳ **סופה נקרא**
קהלת על שם
שהיה׳ חכמות מכל בני אדם ומחכם מכל
היות כי כן במקום אחד נקרא׳ לוהל אשר
הקט סיאני חכמות. כב דברי אגור בן יקו
מלך׳ אשר היה מלך בירושלים׳ הכל הבלים
אמר׳ עדין אין יותר רמן תהילת מלה׳ נכסף
לטענו אשר לבולן ולפרט דבר שהם הכל
היקרי זה רוני׳ אין לנו יל ואנלנו׳ עשוין כ
שהיות׳ אל עשיון נהיות׳ כי חנם איזניכך יל
כי חנם איזניכך׳ ששותה תפילה כמוה ו
ומזכיר יות השם וחמות שקטען והוא להוכ
יות וסט׳ ומזכירו סטוך וליטו׳ וחזריכן
ותהיל כב ופרטה׳ וכן עתד וחביר שם
קהלת בתהילת המלה׳ ואנחריכן והתהיי כה
ואנוקרה׳ שתך ורישיות חלון׳ דברי קהלת׳
הכל הבלים׳ אין יותר קהלת כי יאף אותן
שפיור הדברים׳ ממות שהן הכל הבלים
עתו לכן לדרוט ולהטר כשעמיכ העול ומיעה
כוה הטי׳ מה יתרון׳ מ הדברים הילו ל
מוססים לעטה ומטה על אין טוב כאדם טיסי פל
ושתה וג׳ לומ׳ מל ימלו ומעטוי היודם כל הם׳
ויון טוב מעטוה להטוות היות רין ולטוחת
ולשמוח כארצו׳ מה יתרון׳ ירזה טכה
וריוח יש לו לאדם בכל עמלו שהוין עול ל
תחת השמט׳ שהרי סופו עבר׳ וטול מן ז
הטל וטוב לוי היהל׳ מבינין זה ומסמכ
הזלה בשיטוה׳ תחת השמט׳ לפי טאין כ
נמאר וחומתו יחא לוו זה׳ והרי הון סיאו
כתוב תחת השמט׳ דר הולך ודור בין
טכוס ותיי׳ ושובים או העבר׳ והוין
לעולם עומדת׳ וקיימת טוינע חרב
דמקומה׳ וזרח השמט׳ לביקר היון זורח
במקומו במזרח׳ ואעף ערב כרב בא וטוקע
כמערב׳ והולך מל הלילה וחמות טהויו ל
טואן׳ ומהיך עד טואין ומבע לטתגביק
במקומו אשר זרח היא היס׳ וגם לאחד הון
זרח שם והולך ביא מן המזרח ועד
דרום והולך דרום ומערב עד שהוין סובכ
והולך יל העפון עד סומבע במקומו כמורי׳
ופובב׳ כיאטר השמט כעבט טהוין קרב
והולך **כוכבי׳ עד המזרח**
שתך בן׳ לומ׳ לט היׁזן׳ וסיבוב׳ סובב סוב
הולך הרוח׳ מלה כפול על הולך אל דרום
וסובכ לומ׳ שהואן פובב והולך כל הרוחות
שעמלם ועל סכיכמות טב היומ׳ וכן חוזר

ולשמחה· מה פרעתי· על השחוק ועל השמחה·
מה כי אשר רבי לך· שמח· כאשר רבי שלך·
וכן אומרי לי אחיו הוה· אומרי עלי יחא הוה·
ותחת לבי· הייתי תר ודרוש במעשי ללוח
ולמשוך ביין· להתעשר· ולשמוח עצמי בין·
דרוגותין ישמח בלב ינטו· ולבי שהג·
בחכמה· שיוין כה שמח שהיין עריכה·
לעולם· וכן ולאחח בפילות· כמו לטוב·
אבל כי ברוב חכמה של ומעלה הייי חכמה·
ומעקה שיוין בי ידרא עביוין לה· ויזין·
תגלה מה· עד משר איזויה· שאיזי ידרע·
על איזה דבר למות· לוסכבו· איזה טוב·
איזה ענין טוב הזיין· מספר ימי חייהם·
בחייהם· עולחח· ולטון בידיהל· מל שהיה·
לפני· יתר ומל אדם שהין לפנו כירושלם·
קודם טעולחתי· וסגלת מלכים· יו ומדיות
חמיד מלכים· והמרימת ותענרת חוחת
המדימה· עשיתי לי תיקנתי לעורכ מו·
וכן הכבר יותר עשה· וכן ועשיתה אות·
עפירויה· שחה ודעדות· מל שיחה תכמה
ותוכל· והף עגלות עב· ותענוג ולבי· וגב·
גורלתי והוספתי· במעטי למעשות כל· יל·
המעברים· הלאה כרוב קשרי· וכמדי· יין·
חמותי· גם חמה היתה לי· וטעיתק הל·
כמעני· וכן לט עה של פשוה· כי עם ייות·
שלושה דריים· שעתו לו הך עשר וחמה·
וחיים· הן לבתו להל· ועשר וחמרד·
וחכר קורירין זה שוה הבל· וגם זה יתה חיים
וחכר לחטוה· נה· וטשמתי את החיים·
ול ין יועלת· ויר הבלתו מהם טעשיתי·
ל כל דבר תשיבות· אשר רויחי· מ· לבי·
טומה· שהיי· לב היה שוחח· זה בהחוקי·
חלו זה היהול· וכטחי ינע· להעלב· כל·
המעשים· הלה ורדיעותו מולה הבל· יל·
וההו מ· למעלה מה יתרין לאדם כמו עמלו·
וגבי מה הידרם· שהירי מה לו של האידם·
שהויו בן יחר המלך להתחנ לפנו של·
ולכסו על עמטו· יתאושי כבר עשוהו·
ואחי תוכבר גמרו גמדיע· טולאיתך·
שנעוכי הדין שוב זין לו תקנה והבל ה·
הוין זה שוב יחר גור דין לבקש חכמה·
וידעתי יפי· שעתטל לבי· לדבר זה לחכמה
לחר מטחה· הין חכמה בגולה ורטיכה·
לעשלם שיויה עמוקה· לחמה מי· לחמה·

ולירתה חמוה שיוטו יבלין בה· יבל אלו וחבר
לחד בחוטו· יוז תהיה שעשעת התכם חימה·
עמיקה· ויתרדה· חמוה טרשולה· לאר· ופלות·
לחטך· זהו מ· החם יעמו בריטו· ומ· שהטמר·
עמנו· לוהם כיוי· ויינו שבל· והחסיל· החלך·
בחושך· ועמו· גם כבל דעת· מה כן זה טומהם·
טמהם כאחד· גם יבו יקרע· טיומוחת כאחר·
מן הפלים· ויויה רוזה יש לי כחומתי יותר·
מוזמן· טוג זה הבל· ועל כן טרמ· מה יתרון·
ליורם· לחכם עם הסכיל· טהרי ייו זכרון לזון·
וזה ולא לזה· שבבר הכל נשוכח כמיה הבירים·
ויורן יומתז· הספרד גבול האיז זה שימות החכם·
עם הסכיל· מל מקום מל ויין· היין דבר·
המותהיים· כו· ויין היתה לטומה יתך נוספת·
לי מרי הכבן נריית· וטטענו יותהמהיים זת·
החיות טענט· יל הך טהריו יוחר וחטולטד·
טטטל ולהך שטעות· ולפי טיוין יון רליורב
כאזריות יומי· רק הבל הל יתמעמל· ויות
עשרי טיוב עול תחת הטומש· כי תחת
הטומרם· יוחרין· היה יומור על עמלו לפי יל·
טיויע רעוה ותות קולות מירח כמצוהי· יל·
ריט לוי· יוחרין של מוחן· ומי ידרב על כי·
טיכיל יוחרי יוחר יף יהיה חכם ויטלוטו כמו·
עמול· טיהכיים עטר· כידי· סל יהיה ויקל·
עמוי· ועטטרי· מירו ליר יוחרים· גם זה הבל·
טיחם גויון פל· יבט עמלי מירד ונעיצין טעל·
הבל עולחו מ· וטמות יפי· ועל מ· סמתך·
ועטריוטטע לבו על מל עמלו· טהרי יטל לך·
ירם בעלם כחות· טעורח כחכמה ובדעת·
ובמטרון לקטת מימן· ולירם שלו טרחבן·
חך יטעט· גם זה הבל· ועל הבל טרח מו· כ·
הריוטטו· כי מה חווה ליורם· טהרי טיוה·
ריווח הויך· ויט לו ליורם טהטוע טורה כן·
טהרי כל ימיו מכוביכ· וכל מתהג כעסו·
מחוחת שהניו וחטכ· וחהזר לקטת ממון·
גם מל וה כטובני טוכב על מוטכבו לבו יוריע·
טוכב· כי תמיר לב חוטב שלוי יביח· ולירי·
יסתך המומן מירח ווזת מ· למטה והטמע·
לעטיר יוטע מבח מבח מל· יין טוב טיוכטי· יל·
יין רבר טוב במעשי חיורם· יולח טיוטל·
וטתה להיות לעטוח טובה כענון מוזמן·
ומור טרח מ· כי מן הקטו מ· הוי רבר זה·
טיון מ· הכל· יבל מל הדברים הללו מטר·
מיפרת לועלה טול דברי הכלהם· מ· מייטל·

ספרים רבים לעשוב מל המעמות מטוכן
והבל הימה · כמו מלח · ורבים הימה מל
חמדה יבעת עשו בן מיין כב ידבם
יכולין לכתוב כל ספרי חמנה · סוף רבר
מל חכמה הכל נשמע · ככל רברוה יות
האלהים ירא לשומר מעותו שימין כל ל
משטין לטם שורים כי אה עייך מעטה
מל כל האדם · כי יות מעשה · יכטר ישטה
הירם הך יביוזו במשפטו על כל שגנתו
ושלוזוזו בין טוהיורס רע בין שהוין ל
עוב יבייזהו לדיך · סוף רבר · ול · חוזר
ושונה כלו · טעי יסומות חכה קריוים
כעלי יסומות · על טם כב יורם המוזעוספן
לשמות רבריהם הזהר · בני זהיר · להבל
פת ולמ עיעיע · רבי כתבי ספריה לקל
כו · טורט כיוותוזתן לתן לתג לעב לתהו ··

הרי נשלם
ספר קהלת

ABBREVIATIONS USED BY THE MANUSCRIPT

אום' — אומר

אעפ"כ — אף על פי כן

אפי' — אפילו

בלע' — בלעז

בלש' — בלשון

בער', בעול' — בעולם

דוגמ' — דוגמה, דוגמת

דומ' — דומה

החכמ' — החכמים

העול' — העולם

הק' — הקדוש

הקב"ה — הקדוש ברוך הוא

ואעפ"כ — ואף על פי כן

וגו' — וגומר

ודוגמ' — ודוגמה, ודוגמת

והק' — והקדוש

וחומ' — וחומר

וכמ' — וכמו

ולש' — ולשון

ופעמ' — ופעמים

ופת' — ופתרונו

חכמ' — חכמים

יוקש' — יוקשים

ישר' — ישראל

כמ' — כמו

כעיני' — כעינין

כפול' — כפולה

להק' — להקדוש

לומ' — לומר

לעול' — לעולם

לש' — לשון

מחשבות' — מחשבותיו

מצר' — מצרים

נאמ' — נאמר

פי' — פירוש

פעמ' — פעמים

פת', פתר' — פתרונו

רבותי' — רבותינו

שאומ' — שאומרים

שאמ' — שאמר

שאע"פ — שאף על פי

שאפי' — שאפילו

שנ' — שנאמר

שפעמ' — שפעמים

שפת' — שפתרונו

תים' — תימה

תרגו' — תרגום

BIBLIOGRAPHICAL ABBREVIATIONS

Books, Handbooks, Commentaries and Others

Aboth De R. Nathan — Aboth de Rabbi Nathan (*The Fathers according to Rabbi Nathan.*) Translated from the Hebrew by J. Goldin, New York, 1976.

Ahrend, Job — M. Ahrend, *Le Commentaire sur Job de Rabbi Yoseph Qara', avec une étude des le'azim par Moché Catane,* Hildesheim, 1978.

Ahrend, Rashi — M. Ahrend, "The Commentary of R. Joseph Kara on Job and its relationship to Rashi's commentary" *Studies in Bible and Exegesis,* Arie Toeg in Memoriam, Ramat Gan, 1980, pp. 183-206.

Ahrend, Rashbam — M. Ahrend, "A Commentary on Job by Rashbam?" *Alei Sefer 5* (1978) pp. 25-47.

Arugat Habosem — E.E. Urbach, *Sefer Arugat Habosem Auctore R. Abraham ben R. Azriel* I-IV, Jerusalem, 1939–1963.

Avineri — I. Avineri, *Heical Rashi,* Thesaurus Linguae Hebraicae auctore Rashi I-IV, Tel Aviv, 1940-1960. Second, enlarged edition of vol. I, Jerusalem 1979.

Banitt — M. Banitt, "Le français chez Rachi", *Rachi,* pp. 123-138.

Barton — G.A. Barton, *The Book of Ecclesiastes* (ICC), Edinborough, 1908.

Beit-Arié — M. Beit-Arié, *Hebrew Codicology,* Paris 1976.

Ben-Hayyim — Z. Ben-Hayyim, "Rashbam's explanations to vehat'at 'ammekah, Ex. 5:16" *Tarbiz* LXVII 1978, pp. 247-248.

Ben Yehuda — E. Ben-Yehuda, *A Complete Dictionary of Ancient and Modern Hebrew* I-XVI, Jerusalem, 1948-1959.

Berger — M.B. Berger, *The Torah Commentary of Rabbi Samuel ben Meir,* Diss. Harvard University, Cambridge, 1982.

237

Bibliographical Abbreviations

Berliner — A. Berliner, *Raschi, der Kommentar des Salomo B. Isak über dem Pentateuch,* Frankfurt, 1905.

BDB — *A Hebrew and English Lexicon of the Old Testament,* ed. F. Brown, S.R. Driver, C.A. Briggs, Oxford, 1907.

BH — R. Kittel, *Biblia Hebraica³*, Stuttgart, 1929.

BHS — K. Elliger-W. Rudolph, *Biblia Hebraica Stuttgartensia,* Stuttgart, 1966/76.

BT — *Babylonian Talmud.* (Translated into English with notes, glossary and indices under the editorship of I. Epstein, London, 1948.)

Daikuth — A Grammar by R. Samuel ben Meir (Rashbam) and his grammatical commentary on the Pentateuch, ed. L. Stein, *Jahrbuch des Traditionstreuen Rabbinerverbandes im der Slovakei,* Trnava, 1923.

EJ — *Encyclopaedia Judaica* 1-16, Jerusalem, 1971.

Galling — K. Galling, *Prediger Solomo* (HAT), Tübingen, 1940.

Gelles — B.J. Gelles, *Peshat and Derash in the Exegesis of Rashi,* Leiden, 1981.

Gesenius — E. Kautzsch, *Gesenius' Hebrew Grammar²⁸*, translated by A.C. Cowley, Oxford, 1910.

Genesis Rabba — Genesis Rabbah. (Translated into English by H. Freedman in H. Freedman and M. Simon (ed.), *Middrash Rabbah,* London, 1961.)

Ginsberg — H.L. Ginsberg, *Koheleth²*, Tel-Aviv-Jerusalem, 1977.

Ginsburg — C.D. Ginsburg, *Coheleth Commonly Called the Book of Ecclesiastes,* London, 1861 (Second edition Ktav, New York).

Golb — N. Golb, *History and Culture of the Jews of Rouen in the Middle Ages,* Tel-Aviv, 1976.

Goldenberg — E. Goldenberg, "Hebrew Language" *EJ* 16, pp. 1566-1642.

Gordis — R. Gordis, *Koheleth, the Man and his World,* New York, 1951.

Greenberg — M. Greenberg, "The Relationship between the Commentary of Rashi and Rashbam to the Pentateuch", *Festsch. Seeligmann,* Jerusalem 1983, 559-567 (Hebrew).

Gross — H. Gross, *Gallia Judaica, Dictionaire Géographique de la France d'après les Sources Rabbiniques²*, Amsterdam, 1969.

Grossman, *Tarbiz* XLV — A. Grossman, "The Commentary to Ecclesiastes Attributed to R. Samuel ben Meir", *Tarbiz* XLV 1976, pp. 336-340.

Grossman, *Tarbiz* XLVIII — A. Grossman, "The Commentary of R. Samuel B. Meir to Qoheleth Once Again" *Tarbiz* XLVIII, 1979, p. 172.

Hertzberg — H.W. Hertzberg, *Kommentar zum Buch der Prediger* (KAT), Gütersloh, 1963.

Japhet, Tarbiz XLIV — S. Japhet, "The Commentary of R. Samuel ben Meir to Qoheleth", *Tarbiz* XLIV (1974/5), pp. 72-94.

Japhet, Tarbiz XLVII — "The Commentary of R. Samuel ben Meir to Qoheleth", *Tarbiz* XLVII (1978), pp. 243-246.

Jastrow — M. Jastrow, *Dictionary of the Targumim, The Talmud Babli and Yerushalmi and the Midrashic Literature*, I-II, Philadelphia, 1903 (Rept. 1972).

Jellinek — A. Jellinek, *Commentar zu Kohelet und dem Hohen Liede von R. Samuel ben Meir*, Leipzig, 1855.

Kamin — S. Kamin, *Rashi's Exegetical Categorization with Respect to the Distinction between Peshat and Derash* (Diss.), Jerusalem, 1978.

Kugel — J.L. Kugel, *The Idea of Biblical Poetry, Parallelism and its History*, New Haven, 1981.

Kutscher — E.Y. Kutscher, *A History of the Hebrew Language*, Jerusalem-Leiden, 1982.

Kogut — S. Kogut, *The Complex Sentence in "Sefer Hasidim"*, Diss. Jerusalem, 1975.

Lauha — A. Lauha, *Kohelet* (BK), Neukirchen, 1978.

Levi — J. Levi, *Wörterbuch über die Talmudim und Midrashim*, Berlin, 1924.

Lifshitz — A.M. Lifshitz, *Rabbi Shelomo Itzhaki*, Jerusalem, 1966.

Mahberet Menahem — H. Filipowski (ed.), *Mahberet Menahem, The First Hebrew and Chaldaic Lexicon by Menahem ben Saruq*, London, 1854.

Melammed — E.Z. Melammed, *Bible Commentators*, I-II, Jerusalem, 1975.

Mishna — *The Mishna*, translated from the Hebrew by H. Danby, Oxford, 1933.

Nite Naamanim — *Nite Naamanim*, oder Sammlung aus Alten Schaetzbaren Manuscripten, herausg. von S.Z. Heilberg, Breslau, 1847.

Poznanski — S. Poznanski, *Kommentar zu Esechiel und den XII Kleinen Propheten von Eliezer aus Beaugency*, Warsaw, 1913.

Pesikta de Rav Kahana — *Pesikta de Rav Kahana, (R. Kahana's compilation of discourses for Sabbaths and festal days*, translated from Hebrew and Aramaic by W.G. Braude and I.J. Kapstein, Philadelphia, 1975.)

239

Bibliographical Abbreviations

Qoheleth Rabba — *Qoheleth Rabbah.* (Translated into English by A. Cohen in H. Freedman and M. Simon. *Midrash Rabbah* London, 1961.)

Rabin — Ch. Rabin, "La Langue de Rachi", *Rachi*, pp. 103-122.

Rachi — *Rachi, Ouvrage Collectif,* Paris, 1974.

Rankin — O.S. Rankin, *The Book of Ecclesiastes* (IB), New York, 1956.

Rosin — D. Rosin, *R. Samuel B. Meir* (רשב"ם) *als Schrifterklärer,* Breslau, 1880.

Rosin, Pentateuch — *Commentarium Quem in Pentateuchum Composuit Samuel ben Meir,* Vratislaviae, 1881.

Salters, French Glosses — R.B. Salters, "The Mediaeval French Glosses of Rashbam on Qoheleth and Songs of Songs", *Studia Biblica,* 1978, ed. E.A. Livingstone, Sheffield, 1979, pp. 249-252.

Salters, Observations — R.B. Salters, Observations on the Commentary on Qoheleth by R. Samuel ben Meir, *Hermathena, A Dublin University Review,* CXXVII, 1979, pp. 51-62.

Salters, Variant Readings — R.B. Salters, "Possible Variant Readings in a Medieval Hebrew Commentary" *JJS* XXX 1979, pp. 85-90.

Sarfati — G.B. Sarfati, "About the French Glosses of Rashi's Bible Commentary" Lešonenu 37, 1972/3, pp. 43-49.

Scott — R.B.Y. Scott, *Proverbs and Ecclesiastes* (AB), New York, 1965.

Silbermann — A.M. Silbermann, editor, *Pentateuch with Rashi's Commentary Translated into English,* London, 1929.

Simon — U. Simon, "The Religious Significance of the Ever-Renewed 'Literal Meanings'", in U. Simon (ed.), *The Bible and Us,* Tel Aviv, 1979, pp. 133-152.

Simon, Ibn Ezra — U. Simon, "The Exegetic Method of Abraham Ibn Ezra as Revealed in Three Interpretations of a Biblical Passage", *Bar-Ilan,* III, Jerusalem 1965, pp. 92-138.

Tobler-Lommatzsch — A. Tobler-E. Lommatzsch, *Altfranzösisches Wörterbuch,* Wiesbaden, 1925-1974.

Tosefta — *Tosephta,* based on the Erfurt and Vienna codices with parallels and variants by M.S. Zuckermandel with 'Supplement' by S. Liebermann, Jerusalem, 1970.

Urbach — E.E. Urbach, *The Tosaphists: Their History, Writings and Methods*[3], Jerusalem, 1968.

Wildeboer — *Die fünf Megillot* erklärt von K. Budde, A. Bertholet und G. Wildeboer, Freiburg, 1898.

Yalkut Shimeoni — *Yalkut Shim'oni,* Jerusalem, 1967.

Zer-Kavod — M. Zer-Kavod, *Koheleth,* Jerusalem, 1973.

Zimmerli — W. Zimmerli, *Das Buch des Predigers Salomo* (ATD), Göttingen, 1962.

Periodicals

Alei Sefer — *A Journal for the Study of the Hebrew Book,* Ramat-Gan (Hebrew).

Bar Ilan — *Annual of the Bar-Ilan University,* Jerusalem (Hebrew).

Beth Mikra — *Bulletin of the Israel Society for Biblical Research,* Jerusalem (Hebrew).

CBQ — *Catholic Biblical Quarterly,* Washington.

JANES — The *Journal of the Ancient Near Eastern Society* of Columbia University, New York.

JBL — *Journal of Biblical Literature,* Philadelphia.

JJS — *Journal of Jewish Studies,* Oxford.

JSS.— *Journal of Semitic Studies,* Manchester.

Lešonenu — *Quarterly for the study of the Hebrew Language and Cognate Studies,* Jerusalem (Hebrew).

MGWJ — *Monatschrift für Geschichte und Wissenschaft des Judentums.*

MWJ — *Magazin für die Wissenschaft des Judentums,* Berlin.

SVT — *Supplements to Vetus Testamentum,* Leiden.

Tarbiz — *A Quarterly for Jewish Studies,* Jerusalem (Hebrew).

Textus — *Annual of the Hebrew University Bible Project,* Jerusalem (Hebrew and English).

UF — *Ugarit Forschungen,* Neukirchen.

Series

AB — *The Anchor Bible*, New York.

ATD — *Das Alte Testament Deutsch*, Göttingen.

BK — *Biblische Kommentar Altes Testament*, Neukirchen-Vluyn.

HAT — *Handbuch zum Alten Testament*, Tübingen.

IB — *The Interpreter's Bible*, New York.

ICC — *The International Critical Commentary*, Edinburgh.

KAT — *Kommentar zum Alten Testament*, Leipzig.

SELECTED BIBLIOGRAPHY ON RASHBAM

1. EDITIONS

Rosin D., *Commentarium Quem in Pentateuchum Composuit Samuel ben Meir*, Breslau 1881.

Bromberg A. I., *The Commentary of Rashbam on the Pentateuch, edited by D. Rosin 1881*[2], Jerusalem 1969.

Jellinek A., *Commentar zu Kohelet und dem Hohen Liede von R. Samuel ben Meir*, Leipzig 1855.

Heilberg S.Z., *Nite Na'amanim*, pp. 9–11 (Rashbam's commentary on Esther).

Stein L., "A Grammar by R. Samuel ben Meir and his Grammatical Commentary on the Pentateuch", *Jahrbuch des Traditionstreuen Rabbinerverbandes in der Slovakei*, Trnava 1923, pp. 33–59, I–VII.

2. STUDIES

Ahrend M., "A Commentary on Job by Rashbam[2]", *Alei Sefer* 5 (1978), pp. 25–47 (Hebrew).

Ahrend M., *Le Commentaire sur Job de Rabbi Yoseph Qara'*, Hildesheim 1978, pp. 65–76.

Ben-Hayyim Z., "Rashbam's explanation to vehat'at 'ammekah: Ex. 5:16", *Tarbiz* XLVII (1978), pp. 247–248 (Hebrew).

Berger M.B., *The Torah Commentary of Rabbi Samuel ben Meir*, Diss. Harvard University, Cambridge 1982.

Dienemann M., "Beobachtungen zum Raschikommentar zum zehnten Abschnitt von Pesachim", *Festschr. Israel Lewy*, Breslau 1911, pp. 259–269.

Esh S., "Variant Readings in Mediaeval Hebrew Commentaries: R. Samuel ben Meir (Rashbam)", *Textus* 5, 1966, pp. 84–92.

Finkelstein L., *Jewish Self-Government in the Middle Ages*², New York 1964, pp. 40–43.

Friedman S., "The Tosafot of Rashbam to R. Isaac Alfasi (Rif)", *Kobez Al Yad* VIII, Jerusalem 1975, pp. 187–226 (Hebrew).

Geiger A., "Die nordfranzösische Exegetenschule um 12 Jahrhundert", *Nite Na'amanim*, pp. 29–39.

Geiger A., *Parschandatha, Die nordfranzösische Exegetenschule*, Leipzig 1856. German part, pp. 20–24, Hebrew part, pp. 34–35.

Gelles B.J., *Peshat and Derash in the Exegesis of Rashi*, Leiden 1981, pp. 123–127.

Golb N., *History and Culture of the Jews of Rouen in the Middle Ages*, Tel-Aviv 1976, pp. 36–40, 60–66 (Hebrew).

Greenberg M., "Bible, Exegesis", *Encyclopaedia Biblica* 8, Jerusalem 1982, pp. 696–698 (Hebrew).

Greenberg M., "The Relationship between the Commentary of Rashi and Rashbam to the Pentateuch", *Festschr. Seeligmann*, Jerusalem 1983, 559-567 (Hebrew).

Grossman A.–Ta-Shma I., "Samuel ben Meir", *Encyclopaedia Judaica* 14 (1971), pp. 809–812.

Grossman A., "The Commentary to Ecclesiastes Attributed to R. Samuel ben Meir", *Tarbiz* XLV (1976), pp. 336–340 (Hebrew).

Grossman A., "The Commentary of R. Samuel ben Meir to Qoheleth Once Again," *Tarbiz* XLVIII (1979), p. 172 (Hebrew).

Japhet S., "The Commentary of R. Samuel ben Meir to Qoheleth", *Tarbiz* XLIV (1974/5), pp. 72–94 (Hebrew).

Japhet S., "The Commentary of R. Samuel ben Meir to Qoheleth", *Tarbiz* XLVII (1978), pp. 243–246 (Hebrew).

Kanarfogel E., "Trinitarian and Multiplicity Polemics in the Biblical Commentaries of Rashi, Rashbam and Bekhor Shor", *Gesher* 7, New York (1979), pp. 15–37.

Margaliot E., "The Relationship between the Commentary of Rashbam and that of Ibn Ezra to the Pentateuch", *Festsch. Assaf*, Jeruslem 1953, pp. 357–369 (Hebrew).

Melammed E.Z., *Bible Commentators*². Jerusalem 1978, pp. 449–513 (Hebrew).

Mutius H.G. von, "Das Tötungsverbot des Dekalogs bei Samuel ben Meir: Exegese und Antichristliche Polemik", *Judaica* 36 (1980), pp. 99–101.

Porges N., "R. Samuel b. Meir als Exeget und die erste kritische Ausgabe seines Pentateuch-Commentars", *MGWJ* 32 (1883), pp. 161–182, 217–228, 271–285.

Poznanski S., *Kommentar zu Esechiel und den XII Kleinen Propheten von Eliezer aus Beaugency*, Warsaw 1913, pp. XXXIX–L, LXXXVII–LXXXVIII (Hebrew).

Rabinovitz H.R., "Rabbi Samuel son of Meir (Rashbam) as Biblical Exegete", *Beth Mikra* 21 (1976), pp. 462–471 (Hebrew).

Selected Bibliography

Rosin D., *R. Samuel ben Meir (Rashbam) als Schrifterklärer*, Breslau 1880.

Salters R.B., "The Mediaeval French Glosses of Rashbam on Qoheleth and Song of Songs", *Studia Biblica* 1978, Sheffield 1979, pp. 249–252.

Salters R.B., "Observations on the Commentary of Qoheleth by R. Samuel ben Meir", *Hermathena, A Dublin University Review*, CXXVII 1979, pp. 51–62.

Salters R.B., "Possible Variant Readings in a Mediaeval Commentary", *JSS* XXX (1979), pp. 85–90.

Shelomo Zalman of Pozen, *Qeren Shmuel*, Pozen 1727 (Hebrew).

Simon U., "The Exegetical Method of Abraham Ibn Ezra as Revealed in Three Interpretations of a Biblical Passage", *Bar-Ilan* III, Jerusalem 1965, pp. 130–138 (Hebrew).

Smalley B., *The Study of the Bible in the Middle Ages*, Indiana 1970.

Touitou E., "Concerning the Methodology of R. Samuel b. Meir in his Commentary to the Pentateuch", *Tarbiz* XLVIII (1978/9), pp. 248–273 (Hebrew).

Touitou E., "Peshat and Apologetics in the Rashbam's Commentary on the Biblical Stories of Moses", *Tarbiz* LI (1982), pp. 227–238 (Hebrew).

Touitou E., "Rashbam's Exegetical Method Against the Background of his Times", *Festsch. E.Z. Melammed* Ramat-Gan 1982, pp. 48–72 (Hebrew).

Yalon H., *Bulletin of Hebrew Language Studies*, second printing, Jerusalem 1963, Bulletin to 1942, pp. 28–29 (Hebrew).

Urbach E.E., *Sefer Arugat Habosem Auctore R. Abraham b. R. Azriel* IV, Jerusalem 1963, pp. 142–144, 153–154 (Hebrew).

Urbach E.E., *The Tosaphists: Their History, Writings and Methods*, Jerusalem 1980, pp. 45–57 (Hebrew).

INDICES

SOURCES

2. RABBINIC LITERATURE

NAMES AND SUBJECTS

HEBREW SUBJECTS